MAN IN THE MIRROR

MAN IN THE MIRROR

John Howard Griffin
and the story of
Black Like Me

Robert Bonazzi

ORBIS BOOKS

Maryknoll, New York 10545

The Catholic Foreign Mission Society of America (Maryknoll) recruits and trains people for overseas missionary service. Through Orbis Books, Maryknoll aims to foster the international dialogue that is essential to mission. The books published, however, reflect the opinions of their authors and are not meant to represent the official position of the society.

Copyright © 1997 by Robert Bonazzi

Published by Orbis Books, Maryknoll, NY 10545-0308

Manufactured in the United States of America

Library of Congress Cataloging-in-Publication Data

Bonazzi, Robert.
    Man in the mirror : John Howard Griffin and the story of Black like me / Robert Bonazzi,
        p.   cm.
    ISBN 1-57075-118-8 (alk. paper)
    1. Griffin, John Howard, 1920–   Black like me.   2. Griffin, John Howard, 1920–   .   3. Afro-Americans—Southern States—Social conditions.   4. Southern States—Race relations.   5. Texas—Biography.   6. United States—Race relations—Religious aspects.
I. Title.
E185.61.G83B66   1997
975'.00496073—dc21   97–18711
                                                                    CIP

For Decherd Turner

Contents

Acknowledgments

All of my work on John Howard Griffin has evolved from our ongoing dialogue that began thirty years ago during our first face-to-face interview. Since his death in 1980, it has continued with the voice I hear on tapes, in his texts, and in memory. I am most indebted to the voice of Elizabeth Griffin-Bonazzi, endearing muse of memory and guiding spirit for The Estate of John Howard Griffin.

Many loyal friends have joined the conversation and have contributed immensely to our efforts—and no one more than Decherd Turner, insightful reader and enduring enthusiast, to whom Griffin and I entrusted our manuscripts-in-progress.

I wish to thank Cornelia Jessey Sussman, prolific and poetic author of essays about Griffin's spiritual vision, who has been a source of inspiration; she and her late husband, Irving Sussman, have greatly edified my views.

Father August Thompson, who had a profound influence on Griffin's critique of white racism, specifically its effects on black Catholics in the rural South, has illuminated the nuances of black experience each time we have dialogue. I have been privileged also to learn about the Merton-Griffin friendship from Brother Patrick Hart, who was Merton's secretary, Griffin's research guide, and my host during memorable retreats at the Abbey of Gethsemani.

Jonathan Kozol has been astute and generous in his suggestions about my work on Griffin; and Studs Terkel has allowed me to quote from his marvelous interviews with John Howard that aired over WFMT radio in Chicago.

A chorus of friends have enriched the work with their vivid anecdotes, and I wish to acknowledge the following: Father George Curtsinger, Penn Jones, Father Tom McKillop, Bridget and Luiz de Moura Castro, Father James Conner, L. A. Jones, Wilenne and Luis Berber, Brother Martin de Porres, Barbara and E. C. Curtsinger, Mario Ramos, Sally and Ron Tomlinson, John Reeves, Tommie and Frank O'Callaghan, James Laughlin, Linda Kaye, Anthony O. Simon and Elizabeth Davis Holland. I extend warmest appreciation as well to Rosa Ellis-Clark, and to the memory of her late husband, the painter Robert Ellis, and to their late daughter, Erendira.

Two mentors—Wallace Fowlie and the late Mark Van Doren—were kind enough to share their wisdom about literature and life during visits and in correspondence.

Several contemporary friends have offered useful criticism over the years, and I wish to acknowledge their help by naming Daniel L. Robertson, Russell Hardin, Amelia S. Simpson, John Herndon, Stephen Michaud, John Campion, Angela de Hoyos, Moises Sandoval, Bryce Milligan, Robert Daggy, Julio Ortega, Keith Lulewich, Terry Halladay, Kenneth MacLean, Bob Ray Sanders and John Owhonda.

I have been aided directly by the research of Beverly Frank; by the photography of Don Rutledge; by the Spanish translation of *Black Like Me* made by Juan Hernandez-Senter; by translations made from the French by Cecilia Berber; and by the Griffin papers bequeathed to The Estate by the late Sallie Gillespie. Thanks also for materials shared by Professor Bernard Doering, Michael Power and Barry Cohen.

I am grateful to Arnold Dolin, Senior Vice President of Dutton Signet, for directing the thirty-fifth anniversary edition of *Black Like Me*; to his editorial assistant, Lisa Hibler, for diligent work; and to Penguin USA Inc. for permission to quote.

It has been a pleasure working with Robert Ellsberg, Editor-in-Chief of Orbis Books, on this our second collaboration. He has remarkable gifts as an editor, writer and scholar and understands the true spirit of Griffin and fraternal dialogue.

Finally, I want to thank those who have encouraged the various projects of The Estate during these past fifteen years, including the extended Griffin family and my own far-flung clan. I dedicate all my efforts to my loving mother, Dolly, and to the memory of my dear father, Lorenzo Bonazzi.

Preface

From the outset of his lecture tours and network appearances in 1960—a year before the publication of *Black Like Me*—John Howard Griffin made it clear that he was speaking only about his experiential encounters with racism. "I don't stand up here and represent myself as a spokesman for black people," he told audiences, repeating this critical point in many of his writings as well.

"This is a personal book," he wrote in the Preface of *A Time to Be Human*, his 1977 overview and final book on the subject. "I will simply talk about my own experiences with racism; first as a white child growing up in Texas, then as a black man in the South in 1959, and since then as a white man once again in the ghettos of most of our major cities and in many other countries."

In a 1975 interview he explained why he was speaking only for himself. "I have become far less visible as a public figure involved in racial reconciliation. Once a few whites had to speak out for justice and interracial dialogue at a time when whites would not listen to blacks and few blacks would listen to whites. But those days are over and it is absurd for a white man to presume to speak for black people when they have superlative voices of their own." Griffin was in agreement with those black leaders who had suggested that white activists needed to focus on educating their own communities.

Throughout his public career, from 1960 to 1975, he addressed predominantly white audiences anyway, because black people knew the conditions under which they lived more profoundly than Griffin did—and certainly more intimately than the audiences to whom he lectured. He perceived his role as "a bridge to reconcile the tremendous duality of information and viewpoint which whites and blacks have and on which they make judgments—as well as the kind of misinformation whites believe that leads them to make judgments that are ethnic rather than human."

Griffin was such an effective voice for equal justice—and against racism—because of the unique perspective of the *Black Like Me* experience and his direct involvement in the human rights movements and crises of the 1960s and 1970s. But he was effective, also, due to his communicative gifts and his compelling qualities as a man. He functioned as a bridge of dialogue between the races, because he had "access to and experience in both black and white cultures." However, his was "not a vocation that is specifically black and white," but rather, "a vocation for the reconciliation of humanity."

Yet he held no heroic illusions about who he was or what he did, realizing that his vocation was "not the kind of work which produces statistical or measurable results." He did not expect to end racism or see a community of equal justice in his lifetime. In fact, he continued the struggle even though it went against his deepest inclinations. "It isn't my nature to be an activist," he told Studs Terkel in 1978, "but your vocation doesn't necessarily conform to your nature." The public life cut against the grain of his deepest desires for family intimacy, for solitary writing, for spiritual contemplation. But he obeyed a greater will that demanded merciful acts in a merciless world and, "if you get the calls you can't say no." He went when he should have stayed home, when he was too ill or in a period of recovery from various surgeries or when his mobility was reduced to crutches or a wheelchair.

Griffin, always the reluctant activist, had hesitated in 1959, before departing on his six-week journey through the Deep South disguised as a black man. He was not fearless, and his fears had to be overcome. Even as he faced the "stranger in the mirror" that first time in New Orleans, he wondered what to do, how to do it, and where he would find the courage. On several occasions during the trip, he retreated from fear and doubt, from despair and exhaustion—to seek refuge and replenishment in the homes of white friends, in the Trappist monastery, or by withdrawing into the solitude of a shanty room. But, always, he returned to the journey in order to test his ethical convictions, to search for a deeper understanding of the truths and to follow his faith in "the reconciliation of humanity."

Man in the Mirror reflects on Griffin's journeys and traces his steps through war zones and crises, through the segregated landscapes of black reality—and beyond to the flashpoints and crossroads of the civil rights movement North and South. It charts his interior passages also—through a decade of total blindness and eventual sight-recovery, through physical pain and emotional suffering, and through his creative process and religious conversion toward the sublime epiphanies of the spirit.

This first book-length inquiry into Griffin's life and work has been designed with several related purposes in mind. While not a full biography, it does portray the events and concerns that directed him toward that experimental encounter—*Black Like Me*—and what emerged during the next twenty years as a consequence of it. "The Path" and "At the Crossroads" frame the central story, chronologically and thematically, within the arc of his life.

"Reflections in the Mirror" serves as a *companion* text to *Black Like Me*—but, in no sense, does it pretend to be a substitute for the original. (In fact, a fresh rereading would be advisable for those who read it many years ago.) However, this section intends to be more than a mere revisitation of those six weeks in 1959. It reads Griffin's text with a critical eye on its literary, philosophical and biographical elements, as well as establishing its historical context.

"The Aftermath" continues the central story but digs deeper than the published account of his return to Mansfield, revealing an untold story discovered in Griffin's personal correspondence and private *Journal* entries of 1960. These disclosures document the ethical integrity and the religious vision that directed his efforts to write and to lecture about his experience.

"Critical Perspectives" surveys the structure and scope of the book and the response it elicited, interprets Griffin's unique double perspective, and examines the spiritual sub-text as perceived by the few who realized its significance. The "Epilogue" explores Griffin's meditations on the universality of suffering in the realms of physical pain and dying; discrimination and injustice; artistic creation and silent prayer—and the mysterious ferment of empathy, mercy and love that leads the sufferer toward humility, acceptance and redemption.

Black Like Me marked the mid-point of Griffin's adult life (around age forty); the breaking-point in his career—from a willingly solitary novelist to a reluctantly famous author and public activist; and the turning-point along his inner path in search of racial liberation and spiritual enlightenment. *Man in the Mirror* constructs a multi-dimensional dialogue between the white man in disguise (*Black Like Me*) and the ex-black man as radically liberated thinker in the later work (*A Time to Be Human, The Church and the Black Man* and others—all out-of-print); between the evolving Griffin and the prevailing discourse of his time; and, finally, between the reader and the mirror of personal reflection.

"Life is a risk," he said toward the end of his life, and "every time you love it's a risk. What a horror if you don't feel these risks." He took all the risks—not because he was a hero or had a martyr's complex, but because he lived life with passionate intensity and loved life with absolute fascination. That is the essence of his story and the meaning of his message.

—January 1997

THE PATH

Traveler, there is no path.
Paths are made by walking.
—Antonio Machado

I experience newness every day and write of it as the first tasting
of passionate interest. I write in order to seek understanding.
—John Howard Griffin

THE UNANSWERED QUESTION

The most common question asked of Griffin after the *Black Like Me* journey was, in his estimation, also the least relevant question.

Why, they asked, had he done such a thing? Why had an educated white man and well-known novelist abandoned the security of family life to risk becoming an anonymous Negro in the Deep South? Variations of this question were asked constantly and, inevitably, Griffin's motives came under scrutiny.

He remarked that it was a question black people *never* asked him.

Griffin believed that white people had asked the question because they were unwilling to face their own rationalized racism (as he had done). Instead, they tried, beyond mere curiosity, to discredit his motivations in order to deny the truth of his experience.

Rather than attempt to explain his personal reasons for the journey, Griffin offered an "official" explanation. He said he was researching the escalation of black male suicides in the South and, because he believed the only way to discover the real causes was to experience black reality directly, he had to become a Negro.

He documented this "official" explanation in *A Time to Be Human*, his final work on the subject of racism, by providing detailed infor-

1

mation about his premise and its data. He had begun by mailing out a questionnaire—to whites and blacks—in the classic mode of the social sciences. However, the replies he received soon convinced him that this basic "objective" approach was useless. He discovered that while many opinions had been gathered, the data revealed no truths.

The replies he received from whites were usually the same; they did not believe that black people committed suicide. "They are just naturally happy-go-lucky people," opined one white correspondent. "When something troubles a Negro," said another, "he goes out and finds a shady spot under a tree and sleeps it off."

Griffin discovered that two things were obvious in these replies from whites. "First, I could not question the sincerity of these people. We have been brought up to believe these myths about blacks. Second, it was evident that no matter how distinguished a person might be, or how much the vast majority accepted such myths, the myths were untrue. The history of suicides among black people and other minorities in this land is, and has always been, appalling. To suggest that black people, by racial characteristic, never commit suicide is simply to lie in the face of fact and history."

The responses of black people to the questionnaire were entirely different—that is, from the few who replied. He was "astonished" that every questionnaire returned to him contained no answers to the questions. "The few that were returned blank were accompanied by explanatory letters. These said, in essence, 'We don't answer this kind of questionnaire anymore. We have answered them in the past but we will not answer them in the future.' For the first time one used the term I had never heard before, but I found it accurate and illuminating. He said, 'You probably can't help it, but you *think white*.' One black sociologist wrote that, 'We don't believe it's possible for a white man, even one trained in the sciences, to interpret his findings without thinking white and thereby falsifying the truth.' "

In the context of offering his "official" explanation, Griffin would add something similar to the following. "It seemed to me that if I could take on the skin of a black man, live whatever might happen and then share that experience with others, perhaps at the level of shared experience we might come to some understanding that was not possible at the level of pure reason."

In effect, he attempted to communicate human experience at the level of human understanding; *being* human—rather than merely *thinking* white or black.

On less public occasions, he gave a more personal answer. "I think it finally boiled down to the fact that I had three children. I knew without a doubt that my own formation, no matter how benevolent, had filled me with prejudices at deep levels that had probably handicapped me for life. And I did not want my children, or the children of any person (of any color), to grow up in a climate of permissive suppression of fellow human beings if I could do anything to prevent it. In other words, my deepest motive was simply to preserve my children and the children of others from the dehumanizing poison of racism."

In an interview with *Latitudes* magazine, in 1966, Griffin echoed this answer quoted from *A Time to Be Human*, except he added something else entirely. "I tell people simply that I don't want my children to become racists. And that's a good enough answer, even though it is not the real answer."

Why was it not the real answer? "In the first place, it was nobody's damned business what my motives were. It's true that I don't want any child growing up being a nasty little klansman with distorted views of what fellow human beings are. But the very idea of anyone probing the privacy of another man's conscience, it seems to me, is the greatest obscenity we know today. I utterly refuse to judge a man's motives," he emphasized, "because I don't think you can *know* a man's motives. And I think this is a frightful, obscene thing to do, and it is also highly dubious."

The integrity of the act was significant for Griffin. Any attempt to affix a motive to a particular action—to psychoanalyze or judge from a distance—was appalling to him. He believed that the fascinating questions emerged from the examination of cultural formations of prejudice. If there were real answers, they would be discoverable in the learned behavioral patterns of a society, because everyone is conditioned by the same cultural cliches, immersed in the same system of unconscious values that are consciously reinforced. The real question must be why is America a racist society and not why Griffin disguised himself as a black man. *Black Like Me*, clarified by his later work, answers the real question; the questions about his motivation for the experiment are answered, indirectly, by the events and influences that led up to that bold encounter.

Griffin's own past conditioning—American in general but specifically that of the traditional South—taught him the "whole mythology of race." This racist myth of white supremacy was exposed ruthlessly in *Black Like Me* and explored, with an ever-deepening understanding, in his subsequent work—in the books, articles and lectures of the 1960s to mid-1970s and most comprehensively in *A Time to Be Human*, published in 1977.

Griffin knew the essential importance of examining one's own background and conditioning, of understanding one's reactions to new situations and the changing effects of those experiences; but he believed firmly that true knowledge was first a matter of personal experience and second a matter of self-criticism. He did not learn about war or pain, about blindness or paralysis, about racism or black experience by reading about them; yes, he read and he listened to those who had known such realities—but his true knowledge came from living. His understanding of that knowledge came from self-criticism and reflective insight. It could not be fully understood from any other point of view; his was a personal witness beyond the vantage of academic armchairs and psychoanalytic couches, beyond any view of *thinking white.* He felt no necessity to explain his reasons in the search for justice any more than he, as an artist, needed to explain his creative process in the quest for art.

A SOUTHERN CHILDHOOD

Both the "official" answer and Griffin's "personal" answer were "good enough" answers because they were actual parts of the complete or "real" answer. Even if the complete answer cannot be known, Griffin did reveal additional details that will illuminate a fuller portrait.

In his case, we are looking at a self-portrait, for which he painted this background. "My childhood was Southern in the old sense, the terrible sense," he told John Egerton in 1970. "We were not rich but not poor either; we were genteel Southerners, and I was taught the whole mythology of race."

He was born in Dallas, on June 16, 1920, the second of four children. The Dallas of some seventy-five years ago must not be confused with the Texas metropolis of today. While it still continues to be the most conservative large city in the state, at the time of Griffin's birth it was strictly segregationist and racist in the intractable mold of the Deep South. Its neighboring city and traditional rival, Fort Worth, more liberal then and now, advertises itself as the place "where the West begins." However, in 1920, this entire area of North Texas was (and in some aspects yet remains) the place where the South continues.

His father, John (Jack) Griffin, was a wholesale grocer descended from a long line of Georgia Griffins who were mostly of Irish ancestry, but Southern Baptist rather than Catholic. His mother, Lena Mae Young, was a classically trained musician who tutored piano students; her lineage was Pennsylvania Dutch and she was a devout

Episcopalian. Both parents were born in Dallas; and married there, when Jack was twenty-two and Lena was only sixteen. Griffin's brother, Edgar, was the first-born, in 1918; his twin sisters, Jacquelyn and Kathlyn (known as Jackie and Katie), were born in 1922. By all accounts, Howard (who later added "John" as a pen-name), was Lena's favorite child. She had a powerful influence on his early moral and social development.

His mother imbued him with a great love of classical music, trained him in basic pedagogy and tutored him at the keyboard. He was endowed with perfect pitch and a photographic memory; he could play by ear and sight-read, and knew many of the scores from memory. He was gifted enough to entertain dreams of becoming a composer and a concert pianist. Even though these dreams were never realized, the musical masterworks would remain a central fascination throughout life, influencing the forms of his novels.

While he became only a decent pianist and an amateur composer, his gifts as a young musician would be fulfilled eventually in the role of musicologist, with particular emphasis in the area of ancient religious music. He was a "model child" who became an altar boy in the Episcopal Church and an excellent student in the Fort Worth school system (in which all the Griffin children were educated when the family left Dallas).

In junior high school he was impassioned by the sciences as well as by literature, augmenting his studies with readings from *The Harvard Classics*, which were passed on to him, volume by volume, by his maternal grandfather. He never ceased reading or listening to music but, little by little, his pursuit of the sciences became the boy's primary focus. However, he became frustrated by the limited curriculum and pace of public school education; he felt thwarted by the low ceiling placed on scientific experimentation and the fact that he was unable to study Latin and Greek, which were not offered. By his early teens, he began to search elsewhere for knowledge.

When he spotted a newspaper advertisement for a boys' school in France, he wrote the headmaster, pleading that he would do anything to gain admittance—including maintenance work (specifically telling the headmaster he would sweep floors). Six months later—after he had forgotten about it—he received a letter of acceptance from the Lycée Descartes in Tours, France. He was offered a full scholarship. No sweeping would be required but fluency in French would be necessary for all coursework. In addition, his parents had to pay for passage (they could afford only a one-way ticket) and had to provide him with a small monthly allowance (which might not reach him promptly since this was prior to air mail delivery).

"It was a horrendous sacrifice," he said in a 1978 interview, because his parents believed that France was "utterly immoral" and they were suspicious of Catholicism—and "they didn't know which was worse." However, after extensive consultation with some of the boy's teachers, with their Episcopal priest and the family doctor, his parents were convinced to let him try.

The next six years would change Griffin's life profoundly, but while France did reshape him in many senses, his unconscious racism would remain. When he reached Tours, he carried little luggage but a load of provincial baggage. Certainly he was extremely bright, eager and idealistic, but he was poorly educated by European standards, immensely challenged by the rigorous discipline of achieving a "classical education" in a new language, and incredibly naive.

Concerning his background, which fostered a monolithic sense of white supremacy he would have denied as a teenager, Griffin described it in these terms in a 1970 interview. "I had the black mammy, the summers in the country; and the kind, Southern, slave-owner mentality was drilled into me, and veneered over with paternalism. We were taught to be good and kind, and we were given the destructive illusion that Negroes were somehow different." He said, however, that his father had "never implanted any of these ideas in me" on a conscious level and that his parents "were horrified at lynching"—and yet, "in a way, we were practicing slavery every day."

A generation later, black journalist and media personality Bob Ray Sanders, who was born in Fort Worth in 1947, experienced prejudice in that segregated society. He once pointed out, however, that it had been "a gentle racism," which he knew was "a contradiction in terms . . . but that's the only way I can describe it." Sanders's phrase, "a gentle racism," sounds precisely like Griffin's remark that "we were genteel Southerners." Both impressions reveal the insidious reality of benign neglect and paternal prejudice that characterized the attitude of at least two generations of whites in North Texas. What Sanders had experienced in the late 1940s and in the decade of the 1950s—from the black perspective—was only marginally less demeaning than what Griffin had experienced from the white perspective during the 1920s and 1930s. Sanders was, of course, more aware of the later, subtler mode of racism, while Griffin was entirely unaware of the earlier, harsher mode of prejudice that dictated his white background (which he would deny until decades later).

As Griffin's parents were products of their Southern culture so were their children. But the Griffins were not overtly bigoted and, in fact, his maternal grandfather from Pennsylvania was undoubtedly less prejudiced than the relatives on his paternal side. In *A Time to Be*

Human, Griffin wrote of his "first vivid memory" of racism that began "with the word 'nigger,' " when, as a child, he had uttered the slur in speaking about a black customer in his grandfather's grocery store in south Dallas. "I had scarcely spoken when I was jolted by a hard slap across my face and by the anger in my grandfather's voice as he snapped, 'They're people—don't you ever let me hear you call them niggers again.' "

That incident was doubly significant, because he greatly admired his maternal grandfather, Samuel Clements Young, who had introduced the boy to a world of ideas beyond the provincial mind-set. Yet, even though his grandfather had ignited an enthusiasm for serious reading, he had also passed along that subtle paternalism toward black people, which remained unchanged in the boy's unconsciousness.

That slap awakened him to the most basic level of racism that his family had rejected—one who was "genteel" did not condone lynching, did not call black people by those crude epithets. "We were taught to look down on the viciously prejudiced, to view them as 'white trash,' " he wrote in *A Time to Be Human*, but the subtler attitudes continued uncorrected, out of awareness. "Many of us in the South had a formation that built racial prejudice in us and at the same time persuaded us that we were not prejudiced; we had the kind of experiences that turned us into racists without our ever understanding what was happening to us."

Most of those experiences came early. "As small children many of us had the experience of frequent and close contact with black people. We were allowed to play quite freely with black children. We were often reared with the help of a black lady. You did not have to be rich to have black help in those days. Our early years were often surrounded by the love of black people. . . . But when we were still very young, perhaps six or seven, society, in the kind and gentle voices of our parents, grandparents, aunts and uncles, did a terrible thing to us. Society told us that the time had come when we must stop playing with black children. We were made to understand that we had to change, in subtle ways, our attitudes toward the black lady who cared for us. . . . Society explained to us that black people preferred it that way, that it would embarrass them if we did not change our behavior and draw away from them. These explanations, filled with racist myths, led us to conclude that black people were somehow 'different' from us. . . . But this was done so gently that we grew up with the illusion that we continued to love those whom we patronizingly called 'our Negroes.' We saw them as 'other' and 'different' and 'not like us'—and always that implied that they were somehow inferior to us."

A CLASSICAL EDUCATION

In 1935, at age fifteen, Griffin sailed to France. He landed at the port town of Saint Nazaire and boarded a train for Tours. When he found his way to the Lycée Descartes, he was informed that he was several weeks early for the school term. This meant that he would have to live off of his small allowance, which was not enough to rent a room and buy food. He slept in doorways until he found a Catholic church that remained open all night. It was not what he had expected, but he was so thrilled to be in Tours and felt fortunate to have a sanctuary and enough money for food, that he concentrated on learning the city and the language of the streets.

When the boys' school opened, he had learned enough basic survival French to comprehend the necessities of finding his assigned lodging, classrooms and dining hall. He carried a dictionary constantly, studied the language diligently, and never resorted to speaking English. Within a month he knew enough to keep pace in his classes, received support from his teachers and schoolmates in improving his accent and, slowly, as he began to meet some of the African students from the colonies, he "was delighted to have black people in my classes." It was the first time he had experienced an open school setting, and he congratulated himself as being "a person without prejudice."

Griffin's next level of awareness was initiated by another "slap in the face," this a symbolic one received from Jean Hussar, a French Catholic classmate who had become one of his closest friends. They were in a public cafe, enjoying supper off campus, when one of their African classmates sat at a table nearby. Griffin became indignant that the French would allow blacks to eat in such close proximity with whites. Without hesitation, Jean asked: "Why not?" The American student was stunned.

He realized "with a sick feeling" that he had turned sixteen "without ever hearing anyone ask that question." And, "even worse," he was embarrassed that he had never thought to ask it himself. "I had simply accepted the 'customs' of my region, which said that black people could not eat in the same room with us. . . . Why couldn't they? It had never occurred to me to question it. . . . Still, if anyone had suggested that we practiced racism in America, I would have denied it with all my heart." What he might not be able to deny, he managed to rationalize. But at least it was a step toward a conscious liberation of his intellect. He was in France and blacks were not segregated. He could accept that as a custom of this region, but it would not force him to accept such a custom for Texas where "Southern Negroes" were still segregated.

After completing his studies at the lycée in two and one-half years, he graduated. The discipline at the boys' school had been imprinted upon his psyche. He had become fluent in French, as well as Latin and Greek, and he continued to be stimulated by the sciences to the extent that he considered a career in medicine. He held enormous respect for his teachers and obeyed their commands and even their suggestions without question. One of his favorite teachers suggested he keep a journal, and so he did. He also went on reading from the expanded syllabus of literature, adding the European masterpieces and modern French works to his literary vocabulary—greatly eclipsing the limited exposure of British and American classics he knew from school in Texas. Everything had been learned in French, of course, and he exercised his adopted language in the boyhood journal as well. Slowly, he was becoming a Francophile.

He entered the school of medicine at the University of Poitiers in Tours, also with a scholarship. Within two years, he oriented his medical training in the new direction of psychiatry; after pre-med, he became an assistant to the Director of the Asylum of Tours. There, he worked with Dr. Pierre Fromenty, who had been experimenting with the physics of sound and the therapeutic effects of music—in particular Gregorian Chant—upon those patients considered previously to be beyond cure. For the young American-turned-Frenchman by age nineteen, this work became entirely fascinating; and doubly so, because he was also developing his musical gifts. Under the direction of Dr. Fromenty, whom he idolized as a mentor, Griffin was encouraged to pursue both psychiatric medicine and musicology.

Very soon after working at the asylum, he began studying with Father Pierre Froger, a musicologist and organist at the Cathedral of Tours. Together they co-authored a technical study, *Interpretation of the Ornaments of the Music for Keyboard Instruments of the Seventeenth and Eighteenth Centuries*, which was published privately in 1939.

However, both areas of research were halted abruptly by Germany's expansion of military aggression to the border of France. All Americans were ordered to return to the United States, but Griffin refused to leave because "France had helped to form me," and he "could not see deserting my friends there in a time of crisis." He did not leave the asylum and, when Dr. Fromenty was conscripted into the military, he was left in charge of those 120 patients he had been treating.

Within weeks, he joined some of his former classmates (including Jean Hussar) in the underground resistance movement (*Defense*

Passive), utilizing the asylum ambulance to transport children of German, Austrian and French Jews out of Tours. The Jewish children, disguised as mental patients in straitjackets, were passed on to other teams in the countryside and eventually smuggled to the port of Saint Nazaire. From there, coastal teams arranged for their escape to England.

However, with the German penetration into the heart of France, new regulations required safe-conduct papers for everyone, including children, and the papers were checked every few blocks. The young resisters had no means of stealing or forging documents in order to move the children of the Jewish families they were hiding in back-street boarding houses. The risks were increased to the degree that the bold effort was doomed.

Griffin realized then that he was "in the presence of terrible human tragedy." Face to face with evil, he judged "all of our endless conversations about racism as university students" to have been "empty and meaningless." Those experiences of "sitting in rooms with men and women and children, innocent of any crime, pursued only because they were born Jewish, made me realize that we had never understood anything about the true evils of a racist system that solved its problems by murder." His horror at what he witnessed in those rooms of condemned refugees never left his memory and, in 1978, he wrote that he would "be haunted to my death by those scenes."

For him, everything had become clear: "the smallness of those cheap rooms, the brightly flowered wallpaper, the living human beings whose lives no one would be able to save. And I knew then that I could walk into the streets and meet people who considered themselves perfectly decent, who had no knowledge of what was going on inside those rooms and who would go on rationalizing and justifying the very racism that led to the tragedy in those rooms."

However, what was not clear at that point was the connection between the total destruction of the Jews by anti-Semitism and the dehumanization of black people by racial prejudice. "I made no connection between the racism that was murdering the Jews of Europe and the racism that afflicted the minority people of America." And he still rationalized his own complicity with white Americans, even as he criticized the complicity of Frenchmen, "who considered themselves perfectly decent" in their denial. He "heard the Nazis say the same things about Jewish people that I had grown up hearing about black people, but I did not recognize the similarities."

He had recognized evil and tragedy, the "racism" in anti-Semitism, but refused to see the same social mechanisms at work in the suppression of American blacks. The real difference was not in the phenomenon of prejudice—because the universal pattern emerges in vastly diverse contexts—but in Griffin's point of view. The Jewish refugees were "white" in his eyes—not intrinsically different from French Catholics or Southern Protestants; whereas, he saw black people—American and African—as he had been taught to see them ("as not like us"). This was consistent with his respect for and obedience to elders he respected; he admired the Frenchmen who fought against anti-Semitism by joining them in the underground resistance, just as he believed that his parents and relatives were "genteel Southerners" and not racists. In both cases, he believed that he was on the "right" side.

Second, the Nazi evil was obvious, massive, extreme and, in his view, not the same as the social segregation of Negroes in the South. He had been forcibly made aware of anti-Semitism by the brutality of the Nazis and the total resistance of the Frenchmen he admired; it was conscious, clear and stark in its contrast. But the opposite was true of his experience in Texas, because he never questioned the segregated system and never heard those around him question it; it was unconscious, obscure, denied.

If he had perceived any connection between anti-Semitism and white racism, he would have associated the Nazis with the Ku Klux Klan, the Frenchmen who denied the anti-Semitic atrocities with most Southerners (and perhaps even some of the less violent "white trash"); but the genteel Southerners, the "good whites" as they were often called, would have been associated with the French resisters and freedom fighters. But, in fact, he and his family and all genteel Southerners were not like the French resisters but like those other Frenchmen in denial. In terms of white racism in America, the real resisters and freedom fighters were nowhere to be found in his cultural background.

Griffin would not become one of them until after the *Black Like Me* experiment, which taught him that black people were not intrinsically different; and he would also learn to recognize that his view of anti-Semitism was as right as his earlier view of white racism was wrong and that both forms of racial oppression were the same. "In Nazi Germany," he wrote in 1962, "this fear of destroying purity through mongrelization was based on the false premise that the Jew was inferior to the Gentile. In the South we segregate the Negro from the white to prevent mongrelization. The core of the matter is the same in both cases since both 'solutions' proceed from the same false premise of racial superiority. And yet, those who called Hitler's logic that of a madman, permit themselves to embrace a logical fallacy that is identical in essence."

But more than twenty years earlier he had been unable, either intellectually or emotionally, to understand or accept such clarity. His final attempt at rescuing an Austrian family out of Tours led to his discovery by the Gestapo. His effort to smuggle a Supreme Court Justice and his wife and children to safety was marked by relief, intrigue and horror. The network succeeded in moving the two young children to England, but the attempt to save the judge and his wife failed, because Griffin had confided in a French politician, whom he was led to believe could secure the essential paperwork for the Viennese couple. The politician was later revealed to be an informer, but not before he was able to alert the Gestapo of the plan. The judge and his wife, as well as Griffin and his liaison partner, were all placed on the Nazi death list.

The leaders of the *Defense Passive* in Paris telegraphed news of the betrayal to Griffin's superiors in Tours. He and Hussar were ordered to leave immediately and the Austrian refugees were moved deeper underground. After several months, the Jewish couple was captured by the Gestapo and shipped to a concentration camp. Griffin and Hussar fled to different port towns and were evacuated to England. The Frenchman returned eventually to his homeland, joined the Free French Army and was later killed in a firefight with the Germans. The American made his way from England to Ireland, where he waited for passage back to the United States.

A STRANGER IN STRANGE LANDS

Griffin reached Dallas, by way of New York, in early 1941. The naive teenager, who had departed six years earlier, returned home as an educated and experienced young man. He was delighted to see his parents and sisters again and, of course, they were relieved to have him back alive and unharmed, especially since the war had prevented any communication between them for more than a year.

He felt a strange dislocation in Texas and, while the war ravaged Europe, he could concentrate on nothing else. Besides his deep concern for French friends and a yearning to be in his adopted country, he was restless, purposeless. These feelings, coupled with a strong sense of patriotism, directed him to enlist in the Army Air Force that spring. His personal plan was to continue the study of psychiatric medicine and musicology, so he filled his duffel bags with medical books and music scores, as well as some of the tattered, inexpensive editions of the literature he had read.

After boot camp at one stateside base and training as a radio operator at another, he was shipped to the Asiatic-Pacific theater in 1942. He was stationed on the base at Guadalcanal for the next two years, serving as a radio operator and also airing classical music for the troops as a disc jockey at the radio station. In late 1943, he volunteered for an unusual and secret assignment.

Griffin was chosen from among several volunteers because his superiors were impressed with his linguistic skills. The assignment sent him to a remote island in the Solomon chain with orders to learn everything possible about the indigenous culture. This meant living as the natives lived, partaking of the rituals and customs, eating their food and residing in a grass hut. He was fascinated by the opportunity and immersed himself in the daily rhythms of village existence. He made an in-depth study of the culture, compiled a glossary of the oral Floridian dialect, which he translated into English, and gathered strategic information about every square foot of the island coastlines and jungles. Also, he was instructed to make certain that the islanders would remain U.S. allies against the Japanese.

He was introduced to Vutha, Grand Chief of the Solomons, who was legendary among his people for having united the various combative enclaves (some of which had been head-hunters) into one peaceful tribe. It was only through Vutha that Griffin's work could be facilitated; the chief was cooperative, immensely knowledgeable about all that the young soldier needed to know, and no stranger to war with the Japanese. In fact, the islanders hated the Japanese, who had been brutal enemies for some time; and Vutha assured Griffin that their loyalty to the U.S. cause was unquestioned. The two men became friends and trusted each other. Griffin learned from the chief and many of the islanders, gleaning from them not only crucial information for the military effort but a depth of insight that would shatter his preconceived notions.

Initially, he had viewed the natives exactly as he had Southern blacks and the African students he had met in France. "I considered, with great affection, my subjects to be 'primitives,' 'unevolved people,' 'aboriginals.'" He did not question his long-held belief that "theirs was an 'inferior' and mine a 'superior' culture." In fact, he considered the black islanders to be even less evolved than the more modern-oriented sharecroppers and domestics of the Deep South, and certainly less intelligent than the educated students from the colonies.

"They were *Other*," he wrote in the 1966 essay "The Intrinsic *Other*," and their *otherness* was different in the extreme. "After many months on the island, however, whenever I went from one village to the other through the jungles, I still had to have a five-year-old lad guide me. I could not find a trail. If I were lost, I would not have known how to survive, what to eat in the jungles."

What had been understood immediately by the natives soon dawned on Griffin. "It became obvious to me that within the context of that culture, I was clearly the inferior—an adult man who could not have survived without the guidance of a child. And from the point of view of the local inhabitants—a valid point of view—I was *Other*, inferior, and they were superior." It was an intellectual point that he could not deny, but he did manage to rationalize it by limiting their superiority "within the context of that culture." They had grown up in the jungle and he had not. It was as simple as that. He recognized the fact from direct experience, but could not accept its implication at the emotional level, still clinging to the delusional attitude of white supremacy. He might have become the *Other* during that year, but his sense of *otherness* was merely a matter of displacement. They were still the *Other* intrinsically because they were black.

From many conversations with Vutha, who described the violent existence on the islands before the current reign of peace, Griffin collected impressions for his second novel, *Nuni*, published in 1956. Because the daily mode of life had not been significantly altered from previous centuries, he was able to texture it with details from his own experiences in the village. All of his characters were imaginary but based on the natives he lived with that year. The allegorical novel is set in a place "where there was no sense of time and goal," a primeval jungle on a remote island. Griffin wondered "what would happen to the average American if he were stripped of all paraphernalia and thrust among total primitives?" This is what happens to the central character, Professor Harper, the lone survivor of an airliner that crashes into the ocean. The professor's experiences are similar to Griffin's, except that his isolation and the shock of adjustment are more extreme; and, because the the book was written fifteen years after the war, its narrator is older and wiser than the young soldier had been.

Griffin enjoyed his duty on the island more than any other assignment during his three-year tour in the Pacific. But when a proposed invasion plan was intercepted from enemy intelligence, he was ordered back into uniform. He was reassigned to the landing base on Morotai and resumed his duties as a radio operator. When the invasion was imminent, orders were sent down to select one soldier for a dangerous mission.

According to Griffin, in his account of the mission, he was among those who drew straws and he drew the short one. He was dispatched to the radar tent at the edge of the airstrip. His orders were to destroy the data in the tent by setting it on fire. He was told not to set the gasoline fire unless he saw the enemy or received telephone orders to strike the match.

He had experienced several air raids but never a full-scale invasion. After many hours alone in the radar tent, evening brought storm clouds and fear. He stepped from the tent and, for the first time, began sensing "a foreboding of violence, a certainty of death." Previously, death had been abstract. "Death did not exist for us," he recalled in *Scattered Shadows*, "except as a cold fact to be recognized and quickly dismissed. We had long ceased to mourn the deaths of our companions. In life, a warm and often devoted friendship existed between us. In death, nothing. They were there at table one day, and then we saw them no more and that was all."

By nightfall, he had eaten tinned rations, and he went outside to start the electric generator. "Nothing moved. No light shone anywhere on the horizons." He returned to the tent, switched on lights and the radio, and waited. Suddenly, he heard the sublime music of Beethoven, the Opus 132 string quartet, and listened intently. "I wondered if a man, tempered to his fullest humanity by this mysterious order of sounds, could actually pick up that gun and kill another man. If one of the enemy appeared in the doorway now, and paused long enough to listen to this music, could either he or I commit the tremendous act of killing?"

Nothing appeared at the doorway but the thunderstorm, which had hesitated since evening to break. It rained hard for almost an hour and then slackened to a drizzle. He stepped outside and then heard sirens and horns blaring across the airstrip, signaling an air-raid alert. He returned inside to the radio and turned it off. The phone rang and he lifted the receiver. He was ordered to take cover away from the radar tent. He cradled the receiver, turned out the lights; the sirens and horns went silent and he listened to the slow dripping of rain off the tent. Then he heard the planes in the distance.

He began trotting down a slope toward a trench shelter. The pattern bombing began at the other end of the airstrip, and he saw an incoming bomber as anti-aircraft guns boomed through the searchlights. "A shell shrieked downward and I threw myself to the ground. Covering my head with my hands, I heard my voice boom back from the wet coral against my cheek—'*Mater misericordiae.*' While I cringed against the falling bomb, I felt astonishment that these words had burst into my consciousness." The shell exploded nearby and shrapnel sprayed around him. He ran as fast as possible toward the trench, listening to the patterns of explosions as the bombs hurtled in his direction. Then he felt his body being thrown over the edge into a darkness he would not remember.

Griffin regained consciousness two days later in the base hospital. Suffering from a severe concussion, he remained in a traumatic state for two weeks, slipping in and out of partial awareness and perceiving only shadows. By the third week he began to improve, but could discern his visitors just as voices; their faces were vague outlines and their names were lost. After the fourth week, he realized he could not see but kept this secret, pretending to read the mail he saw as blurring lines and playing the role of the recovering patient. He was desperate not to be held back in the military hospital.

The role seemed to play well until his day of release. One of the doctors knew that Griffin was still in a traumatic state and recommended he remain for further observation and testing. The exhausted soldier broke down, begged to be released and promised he would go straight to a specialist back home. The doctor did not believe him, but let him go.

He was shipped to San Francisco and flown to San Antonio, Texas, where he was mustered out. His separation papers were dated December 15, 1945. He shed his uniform and bought civilian clothes, then took a bus to Fort Worth. He had earned the rank of sergeant, been awarded several medals and commendations, but did not save his stripes or claim the awards, and never filed for service benefits. He had known war on both sides of the world, and could not bear to be reminded of it.

Back home he consulted an eye specialist and was declared legally blind. His remaining eyesight was registered at 20/200; what most could see at two hundred feet with clarity he could see at twenty feet only vaguely. Return visits to the specialist confirmed the diagnosis and an examination by a neurosurgeon determined a bleak prognosis: His eyesight would not improve and he would be totally blind within a year.

BLIND VISION

In the summer of 1946, Griffin sailed for France, hoping to renew his musical studies beyond what he could accomplish on his own. He studied with Nadia Boulanger, the legendary teacher of Aaron

Copland, Walter Piston, and many other composers, at the Music School of the Palace of Fontainebleau. Initially, he dreamed of becoming a composer, and brought along compositions he had written during his stay in the South Seas. However, Madame Boulanger, herself a failed composer, did not feel he would succeed. She convinced him that, like herself, he had "studied music so much that it had destroyed creativity in that area." While he could compose technically refined works, his efforts lacked originality.

He decided, while minimal eyesight remained, to request a retreat at the Abbey of Saint Pierre of Solesmes, the motherhouse of Gregorian Chant. If he could not be a doctor or a composer, perhaps he might become a professional musicologist. He was invited by the guestmaster of the monastery to visit the Benedictine Abbey. He would have his own cell and be allowed to work in the *Paleographie Musicale*, where the original manuscripts were studied by certain of the monks who were eminent musicologists. His "years of dreaming about someday studying in this great citadel of learning were about to be realized," wrote Griffin in *Scattered Shadows*.

During the final months of rapidly diminishing sight, in the brutally cold winter and early spring of 1947, he experienced the most sublime musical moments of his life to that point. At the same time, his last months of eyesight "were agonizing, but also terrifying," he wrote. "My perception became so impaired that a shadow passing between me and the light made me flinch. The total darkness came as a kind of relief." His blindness ended his studies at Solesmes but initiated an unexpected awakening to the realities of the spirit.

"Then and later, religious faith influenced my developing consciousness. The study of music, of the chants, led me to a fascination with monastic systems, and my association with Jacques Maritain and Father Gerald Vann coaxed me out of the agnosticism I had drifted into and led me eventually into the Catholic Church." This was a long process, which Griffin wrote about in both his first novel, *The Devil Rides Outside* (published in 1952), and in his autobiographical work, *Scattered Shadows*. These books are thematically parallel, but in the novel (written during his decade of sightlessness), the American musicologist is not blind and he does not make the conversion to Catholicism.

It was also during his sightless years that "racism became a preoccupation." The complex combination of Griffin's "past experiences, my religious encounter and academic studies came together with the personal experience of blindness, and the evil of racial discrimination was revealed by all of that in such a way that struck me a tremendous blow."

John Howard Griffin (age 18), as a medical student in Tours, France, 1938.

Griffin with Vutha, Chief of the Solomons (to Griffin's left), 1945. As a member of the U.S. Army Air Force in the South Pacific, Griffin lived for a year in a native village, learning the culture of the Solomons, who were U.S. allies against the Japanese.

Sgt. John Howard Griffin, after being mustered out of the Army Air Force in 1946. At this point he was legally blind.

Fishing at the stream that ran behind the barn studio on his parents' farm in 1950.

Promotional photograph of the
blind author of *The Devil Rides
Outside* (1952).

In 1957, several months after the recovery of Griffin's eyesight. He is
laughing in the foreground with his children Susan and Johnny. In
the rear are his wife Elizabeth, his father Jack Griffin, and his mother
Lena Mae Griffin.

Without eyesight, he was forced to perceive human beings simply as human beings. "For the blind man, the whole issue of racism on the basis of inferiority according to color or race is solved axiomatically," wrote Griffin in his *Journal*. "He can only see the heart and intelligence of a man, and nothing in these things indicates in the slightest whether a man is white or black, but only whether he is good or bad, wise or foolish." He came to realize the overwhelming limitations of relying—as most do, and as he had done—exclusively on physical eyesight. "The racists can see but they have no perception. Is not the gift of sight then being abused, since it leads men to judge an object by the accident of its color rather than by its real substance—is a red table any more of a table than a green one?"

He realized also that the sighted projected similar limitations on the sightless and that a blind person was not viewed as a human being but as a *condition*. Griffin's deepest anguish was not the loss of sight but how he was viewed by the sighted—as an object of pity or a helpless child, as handicapped, inferior, *Other*.

He battled against this misperception in three ways. First, he mastered the scales of darkness by developing and refining the use of his remaining senses; he experienced reality not as a picture but as an evocation through hearing, by touching, tasting and smelling what most merely saw (or thought they saw). Second, he pursued and achieved goals beyond the ceiling that the sighted world's *blindness* presumed. Specifically, he learned to raise pure-bred livestock "by feel" during the early years of sightlessness, winning blue ribbons in competitions with the sighted. He learned to maneuver expertly with the aid of a flexible cane—so fluidly that some doubted that he was actually blind. Third, he engaged in a dynamic dialogue on behalf of the blind, including many other returning veterans who were unwilling to be caged by their loss of sight. He became their voice through lectures and writings. His principal text, *Handbook for Darkness*, was a study "especially prepared for those who are in close contact with the blind," and intended for those who were not "visually impaired" but perceptually impaired by their unquestioned social attitudes toward the sightless.

Concerning his efforts in raising livestock, he worked with the American Foundation for the Blind along with people from Oklahoma A&M and Texas A&M. "I wouldn't show the stock myself because I didn't want any points on sympathy, but I took care of my own animals—penned stock—learning to judge by feel, which is a very good way because there are a lot of things which will escape the eye that won't escape the hands. I bred up to champions in hogs and I experimented with caged chickens and birds, thinking that if the government would subsidize blind people in this kind of thing, there wasn't any limit in their earning a livelihood and being their own bosses."

The universities were enthusiastic about his program and offered him concentrated courses in animal husbandry. He discovered that the men who taught him how to judge the qualities in livestock, as well as those ranchers with whom he competed at the stock shows, were open-minded toward his blindness and his ideas for overcoming its limitations. As a group, these men reminded him of the monks at Solesmes, in their honesty, earthiness and humor; they did not pity or patronize him.

His first two years of blindness were taken up with these activities, but once he had made his point—that the blind could do all that was necessary to raise penned livestock and judge the qualities for selective breeding—he moved on to new pursuits. Along with his lectures about blindness (to the sighted), he gave a series of lectures on the history of music at local universities and public libraries. Most often he lectured on Gregorian Chant and the monastic tradition which produced it, but he also gave informal talks about classical music from Bach to the French moderns. These early public appearances helped him to overcome his reticence to public speaking and his self-consciousness about blindness, as well as organizing his materials in a way that made his presentations informative, insightful and entertaining.

In 1949, Griffin received an unexpected visitor, whose casual advice redirected the course of his life. After a conversation with New York theater critic John Mason Brown, who told him he sounded like a writer and his stories of France and the South Seas were worth writing about, Griffin decided to attempt a novel. Within a week he learned to use a typewriter and seven weeks later he finished a first draft of *The Devil Rides Outside*. The book was composed by an unusual method. First, he based its form on Beethoven's Opus 131 string quartet, because he knew musical forms much more intimately than literary forms. Second, because he felt more comfortable speaking French, he told the story into a wire-recorder each night; then, each following day, Griffin translated the French into English (in his mind), while simultaneously typing the six hundred page manuscript.

In 1951, Griffin converted to Catholicism, remarking that reliving the monastic experience of Solesmes while working on the novel had "written him into the Church." After several revisions, the novel was published in 1952 as the first title issued by Smiths, Inc., of Fort Worth. There was a huge groundswell of state-wide interest, articles about the "blind war hero turned novelist," and eventual national publicity. The cloth edition received excellent reviews in New York and the book went through three large printings before being sold to Pocket Books. It was listed for seven months on *Time's* recommended books of the year, along with novels by Hemingway, Steinbeck, and Ralph Ellison's first novel, *Invisible Man.* In 1953, the novel was published in England by Collins and translated into French and Dutch. The combined sales of *The Devil Rides Outside* in all editions approached 400,000 copies, with more than half this total coming from the paperback sales of the Pocket Books edition published in 1954.

Without question, the "success" of Griffin's first novel greatly altered his life during the 1950s and gave him a "career" he had not anticipated. His royalties did provide enough income during 1953 and 1954, allowing him to feel self-supporting and less dependent on his parents; and it gave him the confidence he needed to continue writing and to propose marriage to his mother's prize music student, Elizabeth Ann Holland. She was the sixteen-year-old daughter of his close friend and business manager, Clyde Parker Holland, himself a Catholic convert. The couple wed in 1953, when he had enough money to remodel a sturdy stucco chicken coop on the Holland farm into a charming cottage. The building and the twenty-one acres around it were given to the couple as a wedding gift by Elizabeth's parents. But the remodeling was expensive—a fireplace and plumbing were added, along with a woodbeam ceiling and a tile floor—and this greatly depleted the couple's savings.

Throughout his adult life, Griffin would be tormented by financial difficulties, primarily because ill health drained his energies and medical costs consumed the couple's resources. The underlying cause of his constant physical problems was a diabetic condition—undetected until 1953 and discovered while undergoing tests during treatment for a broken shoulder. The discovery provided explanations for black-outs and rages he had experienced and, as long as he inoculated himself with proper doses of insulin, the diabetes could be kept under control.

In 1954, Elizabeth gave birth to the first of their four children; she was in labor for sixty-four hours before Susan was born and remained in the hospital for twelve days. Griffin was overjoyed to be a father and greatly relieved that the ordeal resulted in a healthy daughter. The next year, John Jr. was born, but this time the baby was delivered by Caesarean section and Elizabeth's stay in the hospital was nine days. Neither birth was easy and both were expensive; but rather than have the couple go deeper in debt, Clyde Holland paid the bills.

During these years—between finishing the first novel and beginning the second—Griffin wrote short stories but had little success publishing them. However, there was interest in his second novel, and he struck a deal with Houghton Mifflin of Boston to publish *Nuni*. In 1955, as he was attempting to complete *Nuni*, he began to lose sensation in his legs and soon after was paralyzed. He spent most of that year in a wheelchair, but continued writing. The doctors finally diagnosed the cause of his paralysis—it was spinal malaria, which he had contracted in the South Seas, the setting of the novel he was writing. The particular strain of the disease which infected him had an unusually lengthy period of incubation—up to twelve years—and the only known cure was the ingestion of minute doses of strychnine. Griffin, then, was sightless, paralyzed, diabetic, and taking poison to destroy a parasite!

If his first novel had been a bridge to religious conversion, his second had mapped a path through both a painful physical ordeal and a spiritual crisis. When *Nuni* was completed he sensed a spiritual healing and a physical restoration; the book was done and the paralysis was gone; he was whole again. By the end of 1955 he put away the wheelchair, took hold of his cane and ventured back into the world to face a different kind of crisis, which was not personal but social.

He became involved in the school desegregation battle of 1956, which had been fermenting in Mansfield since the 1954 Supreme Court decision. When efforts to enroll black children in the city's white school system were rejected, a lawsuit was filed by black citizens against the Mansfield Independent School District (MISD). In November of 1955, the suit was tried before the Federal District Court in Fort Worth, which ruled it "premature." But after an appeal before the Fifth Circuit Court, the lower ruling was reversed, and MISD was ordered by the court to admit students, without regard to race, to Mansfield's only high school in August 1956.

Prior to the days of enrollment, there were cross-burnings in the Negro section west of town on the nights of August 22 and 23. The president of the Mansfield chapter of the NAACP and community resident for fifty years reported receiving several threats "to get out of town." On August 28, the effigy of a black man was strung up on Main Street in downtown Mansfield; one of the signs attached to the dummy read, "This Negro tried to go to a white School." (These were the precise tactics that the white citizens would use against Griffin, in 1960, in response to news of his *Black Like Me* experiment.)

"During this time," wrote Griffin, who was researching the situation on his own, "no Negroes appeared on the scene and no word has been heard from them. They are keeping at home and quiet." About the white citizens, he wrote that "a small group of fanatics more or less control the town and have the backing of the majority of whites who do not approve of them, but approve of their championing of their mutual cause." The "cause" in this case was not the cause of equal rights, of course, but that of segregation. Griffin used some of these experiences in a short story he later wrote about the lynching of a black man in a small town—a nightmarish story about a real lynching and not merely an effigy hanging, told from the point of view of the white murderers—entitled "The Cause" (it was not published until he included it among his short stories in *The John Howard Griffin Reader*, in 1968).

When it was learned that Griffin was preparing an article, he was warned by members of the White Citizens' Council "to stay out of it." At the same time he was contacted by Theodore Freedman, who recruited him to co-author one of the five field reports being produced by the Anti-Defamation League of B'nai B'rith. "I agree to do the research locally, since we do not think the people would cooperate with outsiders." He began doing interviews, letting it be known that the findings would be objective and that the report would be published nationally.

On August 30, the MISD opened for registration at the high school. A crowd of four hundred people gathered on the school grounds in protest of the court order to desegregate. No black people appeared that first day. According to Griffin's report, several white "interviewees indicated that the 'brutal element' began to take over the proceedings—the element that favored 'anything' to keep the Negroes in their place, to protect white children from 'mongrelization' and to drive the NAACP out of town. A number of persons in the mob carried signs—'Nigger stay out, this is a white school' and 'A dead nigger is the best nigger'—and the effigy of a Negro was found hanging from the school building. The local constable went to the school and, seeing the size of the mob, placed a call to the county sheriff, requesting assistance. The sheriff arrived on the scene and advised the milling crowd that he was there to preserve law and order."

On the following day, August 31, a crowd of more than five hundred gathered at the high school, including media from Dallas and Fort Worth. This was the day when it was anticipated that the three black students would attempt to register. Once again, no black people appeared. "The members of the mob voice open threats," reported Griffin, and "it was stated that the organizers of the protest had done a good job and taken over completely." Many of the white men carried handguns that day, making no effort to conceal them. Later it was discovered that armed white vigilantes had set up roadblocks at either end of town, turning away all blacks and any whites suspected of favoring desegregation. None of these white men were arrested or even confronted by local police officers. On the third and final day of registration, September 1, less than 250 whites appeared on the scene, but the black students had remained home.

The school was closed over the Labor Day weekend. Governor Allan Shivers dispatched Texas Rangers to Mansfield with a document that granted the MISD full authority to transfer any student out of the district whose presence might incite a riot. On the following Monday, September 4, the three black students who had been scheduled to register—but had not because their parents feared the mobs—were transferred to a segregated high school in Fort Worth. The crisis was over, but the problem remained unsolved. The White Citizens' Council declared victory.

Basically, Governor Shivers had merely bypassed every court order to desegregate by having the students removed, because he determined that they (three unarmed black teenagers) "represented a threat to the peace of Mansfield." The Governor of Texas concluded his public statement by saying: "If this course is not satisfactory under the circumstances to the federal government, I respectfully suggest that the Supreme Court, which is responsible for the order, be given the task of enforcing it."

In a later interview, Governor Shivers made his personal position clear. "I am opposed to the mixing of white and Negro children in our public schools. It won't work—and the thinking people of both races know it won't work." The Mansfield school system remained segregated for nine more years. It was not until 1965, under the protection of the National Guard, that black students registered.

Griffin completed his work on the field report, which was published in late 1956, but he was deeply disturbed by the outcome of events. He recognized that the black citizens of Mansfield had been terrorized out of their right to equal education and that the white majority had been manipulated by the White Citizens' Council into pressuring the local school board and law enforcement into passing along their legal responsibilities to the governor. The root cause of all this activity was white racism—both the overt bigotry of the White Citizens' Council and the covert, even somewhat unconscious prejudice of the white majority.

The secondary cause of the dilemma between the races was the utter lack of real communication and understanding. The desegregation crisis had given Griffin his first direct experience with the "race problem" in his own backyard. Even though he was physically blind, he began to perceive what the sighted failed to see; he had heard in those voices, both black and white, a certain tone of truth without being "blinded" by the color of their skin.

What he recognized was not merely the difference between two points of view, but the tragic disparity between two separate modes of experience. The communication gap was inevitable, because he had heard not a dialogue between the races but a double monologue. In real dialogue, people listen openly and then speak in a single, shared form of expression. That is, they communicate because they speak the same language. In the double monologue of the crisis, no one listened because no one could understand what the other was really saying; each side was speaking in a foreign tongue.

His direct encounters with white racism and miscommunication during his work on the field report made a deep and lasting impression. It was an experience that would lay the groundwork for his future experiment, just as it had clarified the connection between white racism and anti-Semitism that he had failed earlier to understand.

BECOMING THE *OTHER*

On January 9, 1957, as he was walking from his barn studio toward his parents' house, Griffin saw "redness" swirling before his eyes. "Then I thought I saw the back door, cut in portions, dancing at crazy angles. I stood dumbfounded." As he continued to encounter fragments of visible perception, Griffin stumbled toward the house. His parents were not at home, but he opened the unlocked door, went inside and found the telephone. He heard Elizabeth's voice answering his call, but all he could say is, "I think . . ." before he collapsed into weeping.

"What is it? What's happening?" she asked.

"I think I can see."

He could not speak but finally managed to mumble: "Call the doctor. Hurry."

"All right. Oh, Lord—go lie down. I'll have the doctor there in a minute."

"You come too."

"Yes. . . . Yes, I will. Don't move. Don't do anything."

Griffin sat in a chair. "Triangles of color faded and swirled. Weird designs of floor and wall and ceiling fused. It was like being hit a terrible blow on the head. My system could not bear the shock. Numbness filled me. Dimly I thought of all those sightless people who had for so long been my brothers and sisters. Was I actually leaving their world, to which I had become so accustomed? I prayed for the presence of mind never to forget them. . . . Was something happening to me that would never happen to them?"

These were Griffin's first visual and mental impressions as he recorded them in *Scattered Shadows*. Next, he wondered about his family. "Was I really seeing? Would their hopes be built up only to crash when this incredible storm passed?" Then a thought struck him and "almost twisted my brain: Was ever a man in a stranger position? My own wife and children—people who were my life—and yet if I saw them in the street, I would not even know them!"

At that point the doctor arrived. Griffin could see him only as "a splotch of blue in the corner." Keeping his eyelids open was exhausting and his eyes ached from the effort to focus. "But there was no focus—only lights and colors in constant movement." Then he heard the doctor ask if he was really seeing, and to tell him the color of his suit. "Blue, I think." The doctor was astonished and overjoyed and he said: "I want you to be aware of everything. This is an experience few can ever have." At the moment, Griffin was not enjoying it, even though he tended to seek unique experiences; instead, he asked the doctor for a sedative. "You've got to give me something. I can't stand it." The doctor gave him an injection of Demerol. Griffin withdrew, not wanting awareness. "I wanted to sleep, to leave this terrifying shock."

His parents were the first to arrive. He was able to tell his mother that she wore a green dress, but he could not see her face. He retreated into a stupor until he heard the voices of his wife and children. He staggered up from the chair as Susan ran toward him. "I concentrated beyond my strength and saw all the radiant wisdom of her face looking up at me. I saw her face and then it blurred." When Elizabeth hugged him he glimpsed only black hair. Then his son tugged at his pantlegs. "I reached down, felt his short-cropped hair, but could not see him. That first clear view of my daughter had been like looking at the sun—blinding me to everything else. That image remained in front of my face during the next dim hours. The effort of seeing her, or perhaps the emotion, shattered me."

He was taken to an eye specialist. The doctor examined him and prescribed a new medication to restore and stimulate blood circulation to the eyes. He was encouraging but gave no definite prognosis; there was no obvious cause for the return of vision, and there could be no assurance that vision would improve, continue to be fragmented and focusless—or disappear once again.

The next day he was fitted with a pair of temporary glasses; the thick lenses forced him to focus, which was still painful, fragmented and frightening for him. He felt safer keeping his eyes closed, comfortable with darkness. The doctor told them that Griffin had to be hidden away somewhere, that he needed extended rest and close attention, especially considering that the incoming phone calls and visitors to the cottage were rapidly creating a circus atmosphere around him. He was still in shock and in no shape to handle any publicity or even visits from friends.

Griffin suggested that he be secluded at the Carmelite monastery at Chalk Hill, south of Dallas. The doctor thought it was an excellent idea and arrangements were made. In the cloister he could be attended to without interruption and media frenzy and be given the chance to rest and recover in seclusion. Over the next few weeks he remained at the monastery, except for visits to the doctor's. A few days later he was fitted with a permanent pair of dark glasses that reduced the glare and, slowly, he began to adjust to the changes and to actually *see* improvement. Later, Griffin recalled that his "recovery of sight was, if anything, more terrifying than the loss of it." But his vision did continue to improve and, within a few months, he recovered normal eyesight with the aid of the glasses and medication.

He gazed upon the world as a series of magnificent paintings, perceiving the intensity in subtle levels of light. "To watch the daylight turn to the obscurity of beginning night, and to feel strange nostalgia for that, and to put off the moment of turning off the lights. And then to see all of this brightness, to see the scene change like a modulation in harmony. Is this what it is like to see? Is this the way other people see? If not, it is surely the way they were meant to."

While Griffin was convalescing at the monastery, he remained out of touch with the news concerning the reviews and sales of *Nuni*, which had been published in late 1956 by Houghton Mifflin. For him, the novel represented the past—blindness, the physical paralysis, his religious struggle and, even in its setting, it represented those earlier years in the South Seas. It had been infinitely more difficult to write than the first novel and, at 310 pages, it had taken several years longer to finish than the mammoth tome that was twice its length.

At the same time, however, he preferred *Nuni* to *The Devil Rides Outside*—because it was the fictional analogue of a personal crisis that had been resolved by a reconversion and abandonment to the spiritual life. He did not view his blindness as a fateful accident or sight-recovery as a medical fluke. Rather, he believed that it had been God's will to plunge him into a Divine Darkness and to deliver him to a mystical light. Griffin did not pretend to understand these mysteries but simply prayed for guidance and followed obediently where faith would lead him.

By early spring he was back at the typewriter, fulfilling requests that he write about the years of sightlessness and his miraculous sight-recovery. He wrote a piece, based on his *Journal* notes at the monastery, about regaining his eyesight—it was published in the Catholic magazine *Jubilee* in late 1957 and then reprinted in *Reader's Digest* and anthologized by Whit Burnett in 1958. Soon after, he completed a series of articles about those years for the International News Service (INS), which was then syndicated in several hundred daily newspapers that summer.

In August, Elizabeth suffered a dangerous fall and was rushed to the hospital. She was seven months pregnant, and the accident induced premature labor, resulting in the birth of their third child, son Gregory, six weeks before the due date. As usual, Elizabeth endured a long stay, and mother and child were kept under close watch. The outcome was joyful, but soon there would be three small children in a crowded cottage.

The critical response to *Nuni* was excellent and most reviewers judged it to be an artistic advance over *The Devil Rides Outside*. Perhaps readers were expecting something like the steamier side of the bestselling first novel, because the Pocket Books edition with its sexy paperback cover had been banned in Detroit. All that was steamy in *Nuni* was the jungle, but it was otherwise an austere novel about the internal adventure of mind and spirit. It did not sell and it was not banned. Sales topped out at eighty-five hundred cloth copies and it was never issued in England or reprinted as a paperback. Its one translation was into German, but the French and Dutch publishers of the first novel did not bring out his second. The book disappeared around the same time that the controversy over the "pornographic nature" of the first novel, banned by several Catholic organizations, was being adjudicated by the Supreme Court of the United States. In a landmark decision, a unanimous one written by Justice Felix Frankfurter, *The Devil Rides Outside* was judged not to be pornographic and the Michigan statutes, which had been tested by Pocket Books, were struck down as unconstitutional.

Thus, 1957 was the year when Griffin's first novel was exonerated and his second was ignored. He began then to rework a very different kind of novel, which he had drafted during the years of blindness. It was a comic satire about censorship, whose central character was a Paris bookseller. The two-hundred page manuscript, a third-person narration (unusual for Griffin), was called *Street of the Seven Angels*. But Houghton Mifflin had no interest in a French comedy and, except for one chapter that had appeared in *New World Writing* back in 1953, the novel never saw publication.

Before Griffin could decide what to write next, he was commissioned by the First National Bank of Midland to write a brief history of the Staked Plain area of Texas. The entire family moved to Midland in the summer of 1958, and Griffin began to gather information about the Comanches, the early white settlers of the region, and the great oil boom in West Texas. He enjoyed the research immensely and was paid well for the project. After six months in Midland, the family returned to Mansfield in February of 1959. He set about writing the book under a hard deadline.

Land of the High Sky was completed by summer and published that autumn in an edition of ten thousand cloth copies. The book was given to customers as a gift when the First National Bank of Midland opened its doors for business in September. His excellent historical work—his first non-fiction book and the only book he would write about Texas—was not distributed beyond Midland and was not reviewed or even read beyond its regional context.

What next? he wondered. His first novel had gone out of print, *Nuni* had "failed" to even recoup his advance, and Houghton Mifflin had "rejected" his third novel. He decided then to propose a daring project to the publisher of *Sepia*, based on the idea that had "haunted" him for years.

On October 29, Griffin drove to Fort Worth to discuss the project with George Levitan, the owner of Good Publishing Company, who produced several monthly magazines for a primarily black readership. At first, Levitan thought it was "a crazy idea," and tried to talk Griffin out of trying it. The writer argued that the "South's racial situation was a blot on the whole country, and especially reflected against us overseas." The publisher countered that Griffin would "be making yourself a target of the most ignorant rabble in the country," but then, after a pause, he sighed and said: "But you know—it is a great idea. I can see right now you're going through with it."

They agreed that *Sepia* would pay all expenses in exchange for articles. Then Levitan suggested that Griffin discuss it with Adelle Jackson before making final plans. He met with Mrs. Jackson, a black woman who had begun as a secretary and had advanced swiftly to become *Sepia*'s editorial director. She tried to dissuade Griffin also, because she believed it would be dangerous if not impossible. After further discussion, he finally convinced her; she invited him to return for lunch the next day so that they could meet with representatives of the Federal Bureau of Investigation.

That evening he told his wife about the project. "After she recovered from her astonishment, she unhesitatingly agreed." This would mean that Elizabeth must take care of the homefront in his absence. But his young wife, then only twenty-four, had already become a veteran of astonishing circumstances. She had given birth to three children before she was old enough to vote, nursed her blind husband through diabetic comas and spinal malaria and kept the family together through stressful financial times. The upcoming experiment, while not average in character, was accepted by Elizabeth as just another extraordinary but *normal* event in their life together.

Griffin returned to Fort Worth the next day for a meeting with Adelle Jackson and three FBI agents from the Dallas bureau. Even though his project would be beyond their jurisdiction, the agents were given a detailed report. Then Griffin asked them if they thought he would be treated as the same man, no matter what his skin color. "You're not serious," replied one of the agents. "They're not going to ask you questions. As soon as they see you, you'll be a Negro and that's all they'll ever want to know about you."

On October 31, Griffin ruminated about the upcoming project in his *Journal*. "This idea, which has so long preoccupied me, is now to be explored. But as the time draws near, many things reveal themselves. The intellectual, scientific fascination remains, but the emotional dread increases to a point of sickness."

His deepest concern was for his family. "What will this do to my parents, my wife and children—not only the unpleasantness that we anticipate from racist neighbors, but in some deeper realm of our experience? We are, after all, white Southerners, living in a land where our lives have been formed by the tainted atmosphere of white superiority. . . . Intellectually we know better and intellectually we have liberated ourselves from these basic concepts. We are on the side of perfect justice. But can one ever root out these mysterious, spontaneous deeper reactions of the viscera? Are we still subverted by the cliches that form our concept of Negroes?"

He explored the question of identity, wondering who he would be once he took on the disguise of a black man. Would his identity change in becoming the *Other*? Yes, he had experienced a sense of *otherness* in feeling inferior to the islanders in the jungle context; but that, too, had been merely an intellectual observation. That experience had not liberated him at the emotional level. However, while he had been blind, he had felt a deeper sense of *otherness*, of being the object of pity to the sighted. And his blindness—especially during his interaction with black people during the Mansfield school desegregation crisis—had forced him to recognize the qualities of individuals, regardless of skin color, because his lack of sight had enabled him to perceive the heart of humanity without blinders, as it were.

But unlike his blindness, this encounter with *otherness* would be a conscious choice and he would be dealing with a widespread and highly controversial issue. And besides, he could see now, he was one of the sighted majority. What he had learned while sightless—that "blind vision" of penetrating intuition—had been replaced by the fascination and domination of eyesight. Would he be able to see with eyes what he had perceived without them?

Griffin did not ask himself this question but, instead, asked: "Why do I find this project so offensive now that I must face the reality of it?" He suspected that the answer to this question had "something to do with identity," and he continued in speculating about this for several more pages in the *Journal*. "Perhaps I feel that the physical change will drag along with it a transformation of identity, even *interior identity*. My family suspects this. It is precisely, I think, their fear that their husband, son and brother, even though theoretically he will change only pigment, will in truth be changed more fundamentally. The eye is more powerful than the intellect in such things. If they should encounter me, they would have to remind themselves that I was *not* a Negro stranger—the *stranger* part is the important one, not the Negro, for we have no thought about a friend's 'Negro-ness.' "

The question of identity is, of course, one of the central themes in *Black Like Me*, which is dramatized by Griffin's encounters with the mirror throughout the book. But here, in passages from his personal *Journal* that are not part of *Black Like Me*, he anticipated the theme of identity and the role of the *stranger* (in the mirror) on the eve of departure for New Orleans.

Later that night he scanned a marked-up copy of Jacques Maritain's *Scholasticism and Politics*, searching for passages that had guided him in the past. "In effect, I am acting his philosophy"—based on the light of St. Thomas Aquinas, who was also Griffin's central theological source—"making it live in action, better than I could act on my own." He realized that the French philosopher's statement that "martyrs to the love of neighbor may first be necessary" had become prophetic for the Catholics of his generation, as students of Thomistic thought for whom Maritain had been their primary interpreter and guide. But "that was the least of it," Griffin wrote, because the "real danger lies in a man's accepting in conscience a task he is ill qualified to undertake." Griffin's conscience was willing but he still had fears; he knew that nothing else mattered except the quest for justice, but he wondered which justice would be served by the task.

"Once again it is necessary to throw off (by an act of will) the great dung-burden of self-fears. But this passage [he means Maritain's statement] now represents a contradiction within me . . . the justice that a man owes a marriage or the justice that he owes his neighbor?" Actually, it was his fear and not Maritain's statement that had raised the question; the "contradiction within" him was a personal doubt which had nothing to do with the concept of justice. Justice, in the ethical view of Maritain's statement, meant absolute justice for all; if there is not justice for all, then there can be no true justice for anyone. His pursuit of justice was a greater responsibility—to both his neighbor and his family—than his immediate duty to his family that Elizabeth was willing and able to manage or any ethical lip-service about martyrdom for one's neighbor that meant nothing if not acted on.

"And in this instance," he speculated, "I feel the conflict between this latter justice and the reality of a suspension of *amoris*; for I will not be loved as myself while I am gone. How can I actually be held in love when even my wife will think of me as a Negro stranger—thus what holds the man in existence will cease for the time that his existence as himself ceases." Again in this case Griffin was projecting his anxieties, intensified by the nearness of departure, upon his loved ones. They were not going to confuse the change in pigment with a fundamental change in his identity, but were concerned only for his safety in undertaking what they considered a dangerous experiment. There would be no suspension of recognition or love in his absence. For Elizabeth, he would not cease to exist and she would not imagine him as anyone other than her husband while he was gone.

Ultimately, Griffin's fear of losing identity had little to do with the reality of his family and everything to do with creative imagination; the metaphors were his, not theirs—and the "Negro stranger" would not be in their thoughts but in his mirror. Meanwhile, he felt the "undercurrent of excitement" but dwelled in the safety of his studio. "I do not allow myself to think of the coming weeks. The full view of life is too much. I pull back and seek these more amiable diversions. But the diversions must be—as a sort of repose from the tension of facing what I am entering. Nothing is more difficult than to face this, than deciding to look squarely at profound convictions and to act upon them, even when doing so goes contrary to all desires."

Finally, he let go his desire for diversion, gathered what he needed from the studio, and concluded the long personal entry. "Yes, it must be done—deciding to abandon ourselves deliberately and completely to that which is so beautiful, justice, and to that which is so terrible, the reprisals, the disesteem of men. We know it, perhaps we have even done it—made the act, said the yes."

He returned home that night to be with his family, to seek the last diversions with his wife and children before departure. The next day, November 1, he made final preparations for his departure. He took a jet out of Dallas and arrived on the night of November 1 in New Orleans. He checked into the Monteleone, a first-class hotel in the

French Quarter, then took a long walk. He recalls, in *Black Like Me*, an earlier decade when, as a unknown young war veteran, he had learned how to adapt to blindness under the tutelage of Miss Sadie Jacobs (whom he does not mention by name in the book). Then, with only his other senses and a flexible cane to guide him, he had been intent on navigating the baroque passageways of the Quarter he never expected to see.

"Strange experience. When I was blind I came here and learned cane-walking. Now, the most intense excitement filled me as I saw the places I visited while blind. I walked miles, trying to locate everything by sight that I once knew by smell and sound." He wandered among the sightseers, "entranced by the narrow streets, the iron-grill balconies, the green plants and vines glimpsed in lighted flagstone courtyards. Every view was magical." No longer the shy, gangly youth, but a well-known author who carried a robust two hundred pounds on his six-feet, two-inch frame. He did not pause as he made his way through the thickly populated din along Royal Street—"past the garish bars where hawkers urged me in to see the 'gorgeous girls' do their hip-shaking."

Finally, he reached Broussard's, one of his favorite restaurants in the Quarter. He was a connoisseur of French cuisine and an excellent chef, and his love of all that was French rekindled whenever he visited New Orleans. On this night he had suppper in the courtyard and viewed the scene "as though I were looking through a fine camera lens." Suddenly, as if the cap had been placed over that camera lens, the view was no longer magical.

"Surrounded by elegant waiters, elegant people and elegant food, I thought of the other parts of town where I would live in the days to come." He wondered: "Was there a place in New Orleans where a Negro could buy *huitres variées*," or dine in such a courtyard? He knew, of course, that there was no such place.

He left the restaurant and made a local call from a phone booth. When he heard a voice, he recognized it as that of an old friend and felt relieved. They spoke of earlier times, but Griffin did not mention his current project. His friend invited him to stay at his home. Griffin accepted the gracious invitation, grateful to have a private place in which to set up his experiment. It was set, then, in a place he knew, as the guest of a friend he trusted.

He was finally about to begin what one writer has called "the pilgrimage *par excellence* of our time."

REFLECTIONS IN THE MIRROR

As the true method of knowledge is experiment, the true faculty of knowing must be the faculty that experiences.

—William Blake

In the realm of the human, when the I-and-Thou relationship is translated into the I-and-it relationship, then the climate is right for every kind of injustice.

—John Howard Griffin

THE EXPERIMENT

He would wait until the final stage of the experiment was completed before checking his disguise in the mirror.

Under the direction of a New Orleans dermatologist, Griffin had taken medication orally and had exposed his entire body to the ultraviolet rays of a sun lamp. For about a week, up to fifteen hours each day, he had stretched out on a couch under the glare of the lamp. His eyes had been protected by cotton pads when he faced the lamp, and he had worn sunglasses when turned away from its rays.

The doctor had prescribed Oxsoralen—a drug used to treat vitiligo, a cutaneous infection most common among but not exclusive to black people, which produces white splotches on the skin. Typically the medication is given over a period of six to twelve weeks. However, Griffin's experiment necessitated an accelerated pace. By taking larger than normal dozes of the drug along with extended exposure under the lamp, the slow darkening process was intensified.

Despite the serious health hazards, the doctor agreed to the acceleration but monitored the experiment with regular blood tests that

37

charted any damage to the liver. None of the blood tests indicated liver damage from the Oxsoralen and, except for lassitude and extreme nausea, Griffin experienced no lasting ill-effects. Unfortunately, even with the increased risk of exposure, the acceleration did not succeed as well as he had hoped. Griffin did acquire a dark undercoating of pigment, however, enough so that it could be touched up effectively with periodic applications of a dark stain.

In addition, Griffin and the dermatologist calculated that he should shave his head and stain the bald pate to achieve a convincing appearance, since he had straight brown hair. This precaution turned out to be as unnecessary as their concern about his green eyes or the sophisticated speech patterns Griffin had cultivated from a classical education! What they had considered strategic attention to detail proved to be no more than evidence of their own unacknowledged paternalism.

Looking back eighteen years later, in *A Time to Be Human*, Griffin realized how false his preconceptions had been. "First I did not think I could possibly pass," he wrote, "because, although I had the skin color, I did not have the kind of bone structure or facial conformation or color of eyes that we think of as 'Negroid.' Yet I did not have to be in the black community, as a black man, for more than an hour to see what I had never before noticed as a white man."

What Griffin had failed to notice—because his perceptions had been blurred by the racist mythology of his Southern background—was reality itself. "I saw black people with every kind of bone structure, every type of facial conformation, and every density of pigment. . . . I saw black people with blue eyes, with green eyes, with gray eyes." In his lectures that grew out of the *Black Like Me* experience, he came to call this deceptive cultural phenomenon *selective inattention*, which was that uncanny ability to perceive what one has been taught to misperceive, while screening out what is actually there. In effect, he had been taught to *think white* rather than to *be human*, to perceive the stereotypes rather than to see another human being.

In a 1969 lecture, published as the monograph *Racial Equality: The Myth and the Reality*, Griffin elaborated on this theme and observed a new dimension of reality. "That first night was one of great revelation," he wrote. "I went out and made my transition after dark. Within thirty minutes I had encountered my first white man. I asked him where would be the nearest place for me to find a room. He didn't know. We whites seldom know this kind of detail about black life. But he handled me with great courtesy, and he indicated that part of town that was set aside for us. I watched him very closely. He didn't show the slightest suspicion about my identity."

He had "passed" as a Negro to the first white man, who had perceived the disguise as real. Then he met two black men and asked the same question. They did not hesitate to suggest several choices of lodging. But to his "complete amazement, neither showed the slightest flicker of suspicion about my identity." Griffin had not expected to "pass" as Negro to black people. This unexpected discovery altered everything.

"I had never anticipated for one moment that I would pass as a black man in the black community. The reasons I thought it would be impossible are explained by the fact that a deeply held prejudice will cause even the senses to accommodate to the image you want to see.... I now wonder what we have been using for sight all these years, particularly those of us who live in the South, claiming to be in constant contact with blacks. I didn't have to be in the black community an hour before the truth struck me. At the age of thirty-nine, I saw for the first time."

Because Griffin had been *thinking white* two problems had been anticipated where no problems existed. His Caucasian consciousness had no more meaning than the driver's license that legally designated him as a member of the white race. Since fellow whites could not read his thoughts or the contents of his wallet, they identified him only by skin color. Their selective inattention reinforced the stereotype that all black people looked alike, blindfolding them to any differentiation of detail.

His second false problem—that he would be detected by black people—was rooted in the same conditioned response. However, for blacks to see variations in the traits of fellow blacks was a normal occurrence. Black people know that the genetic "purity" of most black families has been tainted by white progenitors in their background. The rape of black women by white men is a fact of black history that whites tend to deny or repress. Griffin was forced to consider this fact only when he began to stay in the homes of black families. "The pure African type is a rarity," he wrote. "Black people are deeply aware of this and they discussed quite freely and openly 'where the white blood came from,' which white man had abused whose mother or grandmother or great-grandmother."

While the problem of passing as a Negro to whites and blacks evaporated, a new problem arose, presenting Griffin with an ethical dilemma. "I could not stay in the homes of black people under false pretenses, so I would try to tell my hosts the truth. I would say, 'Before

I can accept your shelter and the food from your table, I have to tell you a truth about myself that may surprise you.' They would look at me expectantly and then I would announce, 'I am not really a black man. I am a white man.' The looks of pain and distress in the eyes of my hosts told me clearly what they were too courteous to say in words. Their looks said: 'Who is this black man who *thinks* he's white?' "

This fascinating fact is not revealed in *Black Like Me* because Griffin assumed such an absurdity might have undercut the seriousness of the book. This aspect had embarrassed him enough, so that he did not confess the omission until he began to lecture on racism, admitting that his naive blunder had been laughable. It is ironic that Griffin, who was determined to be honest about his identity if questioned, was not questioned by whites. (The lurid exception, of course, was to be interrogated by white males about the sexuality of blacks.) However, when he had volunteered the truth of his white identity to black people, they were stunned and disbelieving. Only one individual—a black man named Sterling Williams—appeared to believe that Griffin was a white man in disguise. Yet even Williams harbored some doubts about the writer's true identity, although Griffin was not aware of these reservations.

Williams was the proprietor of a bustling shoeshine stand located on the edge of Jackson Square, where local businessmen and shoppers mingled with tourists at the French Market or relaxed on benches under the tree-lined walks of the nearby park. The sidewalk where Williams catered to his diverse clientele was the unacknowledged zone of social tolerance between the segregated worlds. Looking in the direction away from the market and the park, the eye took in a deteriorated row of abandoned buildings and ragged clusters of derelicts.

Griffin had visited the stand several times as a white man, engaging in friendly conversation with Williams, who took an interest in the unusual cut of his customer's shoes but little interest in what Griffin said (that he was a writer from Texas making a research trip through the Deep South to study living conditions). At that point, however, Griffin had not disclosed the unique nature of his research project. He felt that Williams would make an excellent contact for his entry into the local black community, because the elderly black man was "keenly intelligent, and a good talker." Williams was a veteran of World War I, who had lost a leg from a battle wound. Griffin enjoyed his manner, which "showed none of the obsequiousness of the Southern Negro, but was polite and easy to know."

Williams would become more than a contact in a research project and his shoeshine stand would prove to be more than an objective locus for sociological data-gathering. He would provide resourceful guidance, a place of vital interaction, and a valuable trust beyond Griffin's initial expectations. After the experiment they became close friends, and the writer visited him every time he traveled to New Orleans.

On the morning of November 7, Griffin made a final visit to the doctor's office. The dermatologist established the daily dosage, informing him that it would darken the skin pigment over time. Conversely, if he stopped taking the medicine the color would begin to fade. He noticed that the doctor "showed much doubt and perhaps regret that he had ever cooperated with me in this transformation." Once again, "he gave me many firm warnings and told me to get in touch with him any time of the day or night if I got into trouble." As Griffin left the doctor's office, "he shook my hand and said gravely, 'Now you go into oblivion.' "

It was his last contact with the doctor, whose identity was not made public. However, the unnamed friend who provided the place where preparations were made was Harold Levy. He had met Harold and Gladys Levy in New Orleans in 1949, when he and Robert Casadesus (his old friend and music mentor) were on one of the French pianist's recital tours. At that time, Griffin was still without eyesight, and that visit became providential. The Levys introduced him to Miss Sadie Jacobs, the most innovative teacher of the blind in the country at that time. Sightless from the age of three, she had developed innovative methods that challenged the sightless beyond the limits generally imposed by the sighted world. He was so impressed with Jacobs's attitude and expertise that he stayed on as a guest of the Levys to study with her.

During this trip to New Orleans, however, Griffin did not see Miss Jacobs or Mrs. Levy, and he did not stay in the Levy's lovely home on St. Ann. Instead, he remained secluded in the guest apartment at the back of their property. The stone dwelling had once been the slave quarters of an old plantation, remodeled and modernized during the 1950s. Griffin did not mention his connection to the Levys or the history of the site in the book, but the irony of transforming himself into a black man in the very place where slaves once lived and died was not lost on the author.

Later that afternoon, a cold front reached New Orleans, which made his final treatments under the sun lamp more bearable. Also, he received a visit from Harold Levy, who was checking in on him after an absence of several days. His host was alarmed by Griffin's appearance, wondering what the writer had planned. Griffin let him know that he would be leaving that night, but did not make his plan clear.

He did not want his host involved for fear of reprisals against Levy. Discreet as always, Levy soon departed, asking no more questions.

Griffin had a small supper and drank several cups of coffee. He placed a long-distance call to his wife in Texas, but there was no answer. He began to feel his anxiety mounting and, rather than sit idle in dread of departing, he moved to action.

He began the long tedium of cutting off his hair. Then, using about a half dozen razor blades, he shaved his head. When the pate felt smooth to the touch, he washed away the soap and water with a cloth. He applied coats of dark stain, wiping away the residue after each application.

He accomplished these tasks without checking the mirror. Years earlier he had developed the skill of shaving by feel while sightless. Also, he did not want to see the disguise until it was complete.

He washed off the excess stain with a refreshing shower. Then he dressed in casual clothes and packed two duffel bags. One bag contained clothes and the other was filled with various toilet items, a second pair of shoes, two spiral notebooks, and a batch of ballpoint pens.

Then he went about the apartment, turning off all the lights. He waited a few seconds while his eyes adjusted to the dark.

Entering the bathroom, Griffin stood in the darkness before the mirror. The moment had arrived to witness the end result of his disguise. He hesitated and took a deep breath. With hand poised on the light switch he forced himself to flip it on.

THE MIRROR

In the flood of light against white tile, the face and shoulders of a stranger—a fierce, bald, very dark Negro—glared at me from the glass. He in no way resembled me.

The transformation was total and shocking. I had expected to see myself disguised, but this was something else. I was imprisoned in the flesh of an utter stranger, an unsympathetic one with whom I felt no kinship. All traces of the John Griffin I had been were wiped from existence. Even the senses underwent a change so profound it filled me with distress. I looked into the mirror and saw reflected nothing of the white John Griffin's past. No, the reflections led back to Africa, back to the shanty and the ghetto, back to the fruitless struggles against the mark of blackness. Suddenly, almost with no mental preparation, no advance hint, it became clear and permeated my whole being. My inclination was to fight against it. I had gone too far. I knew now that there is no such thing as a disguised white man, when the black won't rub off. The black man is wholly a Negro, regardless of what he once may have been. I was a newly created Negro who must go out that door and live in a world unfamiliar to me.

The completeness of this transformation appalled me. It was unlike anything I had imagined. I became two men, the observing one and the one who panicked, who felt Negroid even into the depths of his entrails.

I felt the beginnings of great loneliness, not because I was a Negro but because the man I had been, the self I knew, was hidden in the flesh of another. If I returned home to my wife and children they would not know me. They would open the door and stare blankly at me. My children would want to know who is this large, bald Negro. If I walked up to friends, I knew I would see no flicker of recognition in their eyes.

I had tampered with the mystery of existence and I had lost the sense of my own being. This is what devastated me. The Griffin that was had become invisible.

The worst of it was that I could feel no companionship with this new person. I did not like the way he looked. . . . But the thing was done and there was no possibility of turning back.

This seminal passage from *Black Like Me* reads like a "shock of recognition" scene in a modern literary novel. But there is a curious inversion for, in fact, the passage is most notable for its *lack* of recognition. Within that illuminated exposure, Griffin's entire psyche was overwhelmed by a series of nearly simultaneous disruptions. His involuntary reaction to that sudden crisis was massive denial.

On the sensory plane, he seemed to conjure a visual distortion. What his eyes saw, his mind refused to perceive. The dualistic subject-object relation was short-circuited by the unexpected "stranger" glaring back from the glass. But who glared at whom? Was Griffin that dark reflection in the mirror or was he the inner white consciousness that reflected upon it?

This disembodied image stunned his ego into temporary dysfunction. Coherence disintegrated, continuity ceased, identity disappeared. The transformation obscured the outward appearance by which he could be recognized by those who knew him, severing him from all that had been familiar. Even his own name—recalled three times as if to declare individuality—echoed like a litany of disconnection and loss.

Unconsciously, Griffin had projected a primordial shadow figure, causing him to recoil from the truth. The repressed prejudices he had managed for so long to deny or rationalize were exposed with brutal clarity in the "stranger's" glare. The shadow figure was none other than the *Other*—the beast from the jungle of his deepest shame. Without warning, Griffin encountered his own racism face to face.

Perplexed by this starkly new reality, he was incapable of understanding what had happened. For the moment, he dismissed the experience as simply "the shock of first reaction," and that would have to suffice. Instinct demanded action and, since retreat was impossible, going forward was the only option. He knew it was time to leave, yet he hesitated.

"How did one start?" he wondered. "A thousand questions presented themselves. The strangeness of my situation struck me anew—I was a man born old at midnight into a new life. How does such a man act?" Just then the phone rang and Griffin told the caller that his host was not at home. "Again the strangeness, the secret awareness that the person at the other end of the line did not know he talked to a Negro." Then he heard the clock strike midnight, grabbed his duffel bags and stepped outside.

Seeing no one on the street, he walked toward the corner. There he waited under a streetlamp for the trolley. Soon he heard footsteps in the distance and a white man emerged from the shadows. Griffin wondered if the man would speak or question him. The man stared but said nothing. Two men—one white, one black—stood silently on a cold night at a street corner awaiting a trolley. It was as simple as that. Griffin had passed his first test.

Standing there, he felt the sensation of sweat under his clothing. He made the naive observation that the sensation felt no different as a black man than it had as a white man. It was a basic, even childlike discovery, but it gave off a flicker of illumination: Everything was new and, as he had expected, his discoveries would be naive ones.

Through a crude but mysterious alchemy, his scientific experiment had been transformed into a life-study; the seclusion of midnight had changed into a secret human laboratory. Since it was "a new life" into which even this "man born old" entered, the inevitable results would be fresh and fascinating, because the manchild became both the experimentor and the body of experimentation.

When the trolley arrived, Griffin let the white man board first. Even though the New Orleans transit system was no longer segregated at that time, most of the other public facilities remained divided along Jim Crow lines. Griffin took a seat toward the back. When he aroused no suspicion among the black people who were there, he began to feel confident in his disguise. He asked one of the men where he might find a decent hotel. Informed that the Butler on Rampart Street was about as good as any, he got information about how to transfer to the correct bus once he got downtown.

Griffin exited the trolley at the Canal Street stop in the center of the city. Carrying a duffel bag in each hand, he passed the same places of amusement that had solicited his business on earlier evenings when he had been white. This night he was not solicited; the hawkers glanced in his direction but he was not seen. He returned to the drugstore he had patronized nearly every day since his arrival to purchase a pack of Picayunes. One of the clerks with whom he had spoken on earlier occasions did not engage in the usual idle chatter. In fact, she did not recognize him as the white man with whom she had been pleasant, or even regard him at all. Again he was struck by the childlike reaction that everything looked and sounded and smelled the same as before, but now the soda fountain was off-limits.

Later he caught a bus from Canal to South Rampart, where he found the Butler Hotel. He waited at a table in the restaurant while the clerk waited on another customer. Then a large black man entered the restaurant, sat at the counter and turned to him with a wide grin. The ensuing dialogue, which the writer's comic sense might have turned into a farce under less stressful conditions, came across as straight realism. The wit, however, was in the subtle deadpan between the lines. The man grinned and said,

> "Man, you really got your top shaved didn't you?"
> "Yeah, doesn't it look all right?"
> "Man, it's slick. Makes you look real good."
> He said he understood that gals were really going for bald-headed men. "They say it's a sure sign of being high-sexed."
> I let him think I'd shaved my head for that reason. We talked easily. I asked him if this were the best hotel in the area. He said the Sunset Hotel down the street might be a little better. I picked up my bags and walked toward the door.
> "See you around, Slick," he called after me.

Within less than two hours, Griffin had traveled a long psychic road, from feeling that his white identity had been usurped by a black stranger to being that bald black man in the eyes of all he encountered—black and white—including the fellow who called him Slick because baldness was now a new emblem of virility!

Griffin exited without responding to the call and walked a few blocks to the Sunset Hotel. It was located next to a loud bar that was still in full swing. The lobby was quiet, empty, drab. He woke the clerk and paid the rent in advance. He was led up the staircase to the second floor. The clerk informed him that no women were allowed in the rooms and that the toilet was down the hall. One look over the clerk's shoulder into the cramped cubicle almost made Griffin back out, but he realized he would not find a better room at nearly two in the morning.

After the clerk departed, Griffin locked the door, observed that the room was clean and sat on the bed "to the loud twang of springs." The passage continues with a vivid description of precise visual details, the various noises that intrude, and the very air he breathes. The objective elements of the squalid room match his mood. "A deep gloom spread through me, heightened by noise of talk, laughter and juke-box jazz from the bar downstairs," he reports, as the subsequent sensations evoke that gloom, spreading throughout the cubicle as it spreads through him.

"My room was scarcely larger than a double bed. An open transom above the door into the hall provided the only ventilation." There are no windows and he does not mention a mirror. The things themselves are personalized—it becomes *my* room, *my* linoleum floor, *my* light; the room is cramped, the floor is too flimsy to keep out the noises from below, the light is "so feeble" he can barely see and, even the air, which circulates only within the building, is as stale as his gloom. The broken ceiling fan catches the faint light, "casting distorted shadows of the four motionless blades against the wall." The shadowy distortions are the reflections of a metaphorical mirror of his internal despair—useless and without substance. Griffin becomes the room in all its aspects—"boxed in, suffocating"—unconsciously "mingled with that of other rooms," and specifically the room of the *Other Griffin.* This scene at the Sunset Hotel correlates to the earlier scene, but the crisis remains unspoken, unspeakable. His earlier attempt to deny it and this attempt to displace the reality choke him with "an almost desperate sadness."

And worst of all are the aural intrusions that create a chaotic din, an ugly dissonance that jangles his nerves. Griffin longs for the wellsprings of a sublime music—not "juke-box jazz"; or for a supreme silence to harmonize the spirit—not the sounds that "so degrade the spirit." Emotionally overwhelmed and physically exhausted, he feels mocked by "all this evoked" and the powerlessness of his will that "could not shake" it.

When Griffin reflected upon these two scenes—so intimately connected in his unconscious—he merged them into one scene. In the essay "The Intrinsic *Other*," Griffin recounted the experience of encountering the stranger in the mirror as if it had happened in the Sunset Hotel room, rather than in the Levys' guest apartment. The merging of these two interrelated scenes into one combined experience was not a conscious distortion, but the result of their deep association. Apparently he had not been aware of this "revision" of the story, and no one has ever raised a question about the factual discrepancy.

But the experiential authenticity was not vitiated by the lapse and, in fact, the dramatic effect of the unintended "revision" was enhanced. For Griffin, the geographical locations had been confused, but the unifying truth of their psychic dislocation had not. The two events occurred within three hours or less, after all, separated by the brief journey of leaving the Levys and arriving at the Sunset Hotel. The significant connection had been his internalization of the experience and the continuity of his mood of gloom, not the temporal or spatial contexts.

In that 1966 essay, Griffin clarified his reactions to the overall experience even while merging the locales into one psychic space. "Almost the deepest shock I had came the first night that I went out into the New Orleans night as a Negro. I went to a hotel in the ghetto and took the best available room—a tawdry, miserable little cubbyhole. I sat on the bed and glanced at myself in the mirror on the wall. For the first time I was alone as a Negro in the community. That glance brought a sickening shock that I tried not to admit, not to recognize, but I could not avoid it. It was the shock of seeing my face in the mirror and of feeling an involuntary movement of antipathy for that face, because it was pigmented, the face of a Negro."

The surprise of seeing in that reflected image a visual transformation rather than merely a disguise caused the involuntary revulsion for that face and the sense of shame for having reacted so disgracefully. In effect, it had been three shocks in one. "I realized then that although intellectually I had liberated myself from the prejudices which our Southern tradition inculcates in us, these prejudices were so indredged in me that at the emotional level I was in no way liberated. I was filled with despair."

His despair was not merely a matter of the transformation but a sense of utter hopelessness that he "had come all this way, had myself transformed chemically into a black man, *because* of my profound intellectual convictions about racism, only to find that my own prejudices, at the emotional level, were hopelessly ingrained in me." Griffin's ethical commitment to justice was rendered meaningless by the deep revelation of his own racist response to the *Other Griffin*. He was ashamed at his failure to achieve what he *thought* he had achieved—a true liberation from his emotional prejudices. By having failed to achieve this, he felt that he had dishonored his ethics and disgraced his religious faith.

These concerns are hinted at in the action of the book, but its clarifications are necessarily provisional. The intention of *Black Like Me* is to *reveal*, whereas the purpose of "The Intrinsic *Other*" is to analyze and clarify what has been revealed in the book. *Black Like Me* engages the reader in a long process of adaptations, in a slowly developing awareness of new realities—out in the black community and within Griffin's consciousness.

These changes, hinted at in the book, are later compressed into the overview of the essay, which declares that his despair was lifted into a renewal of hope. "However, within five days, that involuntary movement of antipathy was completely dissipated, because I was living in the homes of Negro families and I was experiencing emotionally what intellectually I had long known—that the *Other* was not other at all; that within the context of home and family life we faced exactly the same problems as those faced in all homes of all men: the universal problems of loving, of suffering, of bringing children to the light, of fulfilling human aspirations, of dying."

Griffin concluded the essay by declaring that "the wounds I had carried thirty-nine years of my life were healed within five days through the emotional experience of perceiving that the *Other* is not other at all, that the *Other* is me, that at the profound human levels, all men are united; and that the seeming differences are superficial. The illusion of the *Other*, of these superficial differences, is deeply imbedded through this inculcated stereotype we make of the *Other*, which falsifies man's view of man."

By "superficial differences" Griffin meant everything that characterized extrinsic diversity—gender, age, race, ethnicity and so-called handicaps; he meant religious beliefs, ethical codes, political ideologies and historical traditions—as opposed to the intrinsic human essentials. "I believe that before we can truly dialogue in depth, we must first perceive that there is no *Other*, that *Other* is self, and that the I-and-Thou concept of Martin Buber must finally dissolve itself into the *We* concept. For him, the universals were not white or black or any color, not European or African or Asian, not male or female, not ancient or modern—but *human*.

"It seems to me that this and this alone is the key that can unlock the prison of culture. It is also the key that will neutralize the poisons of the stereotype that allow men to go on benevolently justifying their abuses against other men."

THE MENTOR

The next morning, November 8, Griffin awakened as a black man for the first time. The day would turn out to be the most varied and eventful twenty-four hours of his stay in New Orleans; his entry for this date runs to twenty pages. He began slowly, groggy and disoriented, in dire need of strong coffee. Before noon he dressed and entered the street, immediately aware of a different world. "It was the ghetto. I had seen them before from the high altitude of one who could look down and pity. Now I belonged here and the view was different."

He walked the streets in search of a cafe, taking in impressions at ground zero. "Here it was pennies and clutter and spittle on the curb. Here people walked fast to juggle the dimes, to make a deal, to find cheap liver or a tomato that was overripe. Here was the indefinable stink of despair. Here modesty was a luxury. People struggled for it." Griffin carried his duffel, knowing he would not return to the Sunset Hotel under any circumstances. He was down to his last twenty dollars in cash, yet the bags contained two hundred dollars in traveler's checks. He was wealthy enough at that moment to escape the ghetto but such thoughts were overwhelmed by the harsh sensuality of the streets.

"Here at noon, jazz blared from the juke boxes and dark holes issued forth the cool odors of beer, wine, and flesh into the sunlight. Here hips drew the eye and flirted with the eye and caused the eye to lust or laugh. It was better to look at hips than at the ghetto." Finally he withdrew from the panorama to focus on a little corner restaurant that drew him in with its spicy scent of Creole cooking.

He entered the pleasant place and sat at one of the tables decked with red-checked tablecloths. He ordered breakfast from a young black woman who seemed to be waitress, cook and cashier all in one. She served him a 49¢ breakfast that included eggs, grits, and several cups of coffee; it did not include butter or a napkin, he observed.

A black man at the counter smiled and nodded greetings, then asked Griffin if he was looking for work. Affirming that he was, he inquired about a decent room in the area. The friendly local (nameless in the book) joined Griffin at his table. He suggested the YMCA on Dryades Street and informed him that the Catholic church was near the Y when the newcomer asked. The local accepted a cup of coffee, characterized the area and suggested possible places of employment. Griffin took mental notes and then asked about the location of the nearest restroom. "Well, man, now just what do you want to do—piss or pray?" They chuckled and the waitress let out a high chortle that she quickly silenced.

The man was a wealth of information, pointing out the spots where a black person could find the human essentials and offering survival tips and kind warnings. It was as if the street-wise local knew that Griffin needed to map out enemy territory fast. By quoting the earthy local at length, we hear the voice of a generous and humorous speaker through the writer's sharp ear for dialogue. Griffin appreciated the vital information and the open way in which it was given.

When he had finished breakfast, he walked to the corner bus stop and caught the next carrier into the downtown area. He sat at the back half of the bus with the black passengers, even though the transit system was not segregated. As the bus approached Canal Street, he noticed that many more whites than blacks boarded. Soon the bus was nearly full, but white passengers who did not find an empty seat next to another white stood rather than sit next to a black passenger. When Griffin saw a white woman stand nearby, he began to rise and relinquish his seat.

There was a wave of disapproval from the blacks that forced him to sit back down. This movement caught the woman's attention and, as their eyes met, she scowled at him: "What're you looking at me like *that* for?" Flushed with embarrassment by the lurid implication in her question, he mumbled an apology. This heightened the woman's hostility and stirred even deeper resentment among the black passengers. His innocent act of offering a seat to a lady had been twisted into reinforcing the stereotype that all black men lusted after white women. His apology confirmed rather than denied his social sin to the white gallery. The black passengers frowned at him as if to say: "How can you be so dumb as to fall into that old trap?"

Burned by his blunder, he sat "sphynxlike, pretending unawareness." Soon enough the incident had lost its appeal, even though the woman kept on chattering in an attempt to hold the spotlight. Griffin was relieved to be out of that sudden glare and to withdraw into the shadows. His gaffe was the result of thinking white and, perhaps, even forgetting for an instant that his appearance was now that of a Negro. He had acted out of character for the context and the mistake was a harsh lesson. He learned "a strange thing—that in a jumble of unintelligible talk, the word 'nigger' leaps out with electric clarity." Suddenly this was not simply an observation but a personal experience. He was stung by the epithet because it was aimed at his skin—and at all black people.

In the past Griffin had been ashamed of fellow whites when they had uttered such slurs; formerly it had been enough to feel compassion for the targets of that hatred. But now he began to identify with the victim group, to feel alienated from his own race. At this point he was still relating to whites and blacks as groups, not as individuals. And he viewed his fellow whites as not merely an ignorant group, unaware of the effect of the cultural attitudes they had been taught, but cast them "into a category of brute ignorance." Their racism was not neutral or meaningless—it was compulsive and brutalizing.

He departed the bus at Canal Street and walked to the shoeshine stand, wondering if Sterling Williams would recognize him as the white writer from Texas. When their eyes met, Griffin saw no sign of recognition from Williams. Climbing up into the chair to get a shine, he figured the bootblack would spot his unusual cut of shoes, as he had previously. Again no hint of recognition. They chatted amiably until the job was nearly finished. Then Griffin asked:

"Is there something familiar about these shoes?"
"Yeah—I been shining some for a white man—"
"A fellow named Griffin?"
"Yeah." He straightened up. "Do you know him?"
"I am him."

Williams stared dumbfounded. Griffin reminded him of various subjects they had discussed during earlier visits. Then Williams slapped the writer's leg and shook with boisterous laughter. "Well, I'm truly a son-of-a-bitch . . . how did you ever?" Griffin explained. The bootblack's "heavy head shone with delight at what I had done, and delight that I should confide in him. He promised perfect discretion and enthusiastically began coaching me; but in a guarded voice, glancing always about to make sure no one could overhear."

It was apparent that Williams knew profoundly the local terrain and the social interactions of the races in New Orleans. Because Williams had mastered the survival techniques that worked in that segregated system, Griffin was raptly attentive to the black elder's wisdom. Choosing Williams to be his mentor was a new variation on Griffin's old pattern of becoming a student under an accomplished guide. In the past he had chosen experts in the fields of his pursuit, mentors who were the embodiment of the ideals he cherished. "Most of these people taught me, or showed me by example," he told an interviewer in 1966, "the real meaning of labor, of the total gift of self, as the only possible way to fruition in any field. . . . I learned the value of total isolation in work, of following one's own path, of remaining close to the soul's recognition of reality, taking the chance."

Learning from others had not been an end in itself but an integral part of the overall process. Even when Griffin became a teacher in some realms, he remained the eternal student of his own experience. "All of my mentors have drummed this into me from my adolescence," he said. Their advice had been the same always: "Go it alone, it is the only hope. In the crowd there is nothing but comfort and mediocrity." For Griffin, this basic lesson "became part of my nature."

Now he became an eager apprentice in the Sterling Williams Bootblack School of Survival and Social Discourse. That afternoon served as an object lesson for the model pupil. First, he learned that he was overdressed for the role of bootblack. Second, he was taught the necessity of stocking one's own food and water. Third, it was imperative to locate the nearest "separate facility" in order to relieve oneself. Griffin was sent down the alley to said facility because his mentor had noticed light brown hair glinting in the sunlight against the black skin on the backs of his student's hands.

He grabbed the bag containing a razor and hurried down the alley. Approaching the wrong facility, he was directed to another stretch down the dank corridor to a wooden structure which, to Griffin's amazement, appeared to be as clean as his fastidiousness might have hoped. He shaved the backs of his hands without water, smearing the surface with shave cream. The extra touch in his disguise met with his mentor's approval. It was an unnecessary precaution since no one had yet noticed the flaw and Williams had not seen it as a problem until Griffin revealed himself. The absurdity of the scene flashed in the bootblack's relaxed smile, grinning "the way one would after averting a terrible danger," wrote the student. "His entire attitude of connivance was superbly exaggerated."

These apprenticeship scenes display both serious caution and humorous irreverence. The two men enjoyed the game and each other. It was clear, however, that Griffin was playing the role of straight man. During a brief encounter with an attractive middle-aged widow (who displayed a discreet interest in the well-dressed newcomer) Griffin squirmed in perplexity at the black woman's attentions. After she had departed, Williams kidded him mercilessly.

When there was a break in the flow of business, Griffin asked where he might find a drink of water. Williams gave him a tongue-in-cheek lecture on the subject. Then he "reached behind the shine stand and brought out a gallon lard can with wires looped through holes in each side to make a handle." He noticed one "flake of ash floated on the water's surface." Naturally he did not complain about the primitive container or the ash flake. "I up-ended the bucket and drank." He was happy to have his thirst quenched, and return to work.

Griffin observed that some of the white customers, usually tourists from other parts of the state or from elsewhere in the South, showed no reticence in asking Williams about arranging dates with black women. Courteous and friendly, they treated the bootblack as an equal. However, when Williams made it clear that he was not in the business of satisfying such desires, the smiles disappeared and the men moved on without another word. When he mentioned this pattern, Williams wryly retorted: "Yeah, when they want to sin, they're very democratic." It was one of those flashes of insight that Griffin remembered always in connection with Williams and which he repeated in his lectures and articles.

As the early afternoon business increased, Griffin was struck by Williams's rapid and creative adaptations to the game. The elderly bootblack enjoyed their shared secret and, to the student's surprise, seemed to forget that Griffin was not a real Negro. Williams "lapsed into familiarity" and used the "we" form as he discussed "our situation." Initiated by outward appearance, Griffin's disguise played an uncanny trick on the unconscious minds of both men.

Griffin viewed this interplay with Williams as his "first intimate glimpse" into black consciousness. He immersed himself in the role by drawing on both his northeast Texas background, which was more "Southern" than "Western," and on his sophisticated mimetic skills with various languages and regional accents—to reproduce the tone and phrasing inherent in the local speech patterns.

Their uninhibited sense of "we" became the harmony they shared as the game progressed: the acceptance of Griffin by Williams and the identification with the mentor by his apprentice. It was a temporary "we" against the adversarial "them" (the whites), but it was not the universal *We* postulated by Griffin in his 1966 essay "The Intrinsic *Other*" or in his later books.

By late afternoon they dined on a mixture of coon, turnips and rice. It was well seasoned with thyme, bay leaf and green peppers. Spooning the concoction out of a cut-down milk carton, Griffin ate heartily and thought it was delicious. The next day's menu was scheduled to be a catfish stew over spaghetti. He thought that it sounded like a tasty meal also, even after he had looked into the sack to see dozens of glittering eyes staring back at him.

When the air chilled rapidly and business disappeared, Griffin decided to leave the Quarter and return to the other side of town. Before he set off on foot, his mentor insisted that he take a drink of water because there would be none between the Quarter and the ghetto. He up-ended the bucket and swallowed the last of the warm water.

DIALOGUE AND DISTANCE

Leaving the French Quarter Griffin was overwhelmed by the pungent aroma of roasted coffee and the earthy odors of the market, which recalled the old quarter in Tours, France, during his student days. On the bus his attention shifted from a charming Old World tableau to a bustling cityscape that was typically American Modern.

He departed the bus and walked toward the ghetto. Since Dryades Street was his destination and he knew how to reach it, he tested the responses of white men from whom he asked directions. Each one gave him useful information and all were invariably courteous. Near Dryades, where blacks greatly outnumbered the whites, he spotted a large impressive tower, which turned out to be one of the city's oldest cathedrals, St. John the Baptist.

Inside the massive edifice he felt the grace of silence and a soft illumination through the stained-glass windows. A woman was making the Stations of the Cross and other men and women were kneeling in prayer. He realized they were all Negroes. He sat in a pew, closed his eyes, and imagined his family at supper in their warm, well-lighted home. Then he looked at his dark hands and contemplated the contrasting image of whiteness in the faces of his wife and three children. For him "they seemed so much a part of another life, so separated from me that I felt consumed with loneliness." These lonely distances from family (and self) brought him to the idea of hiding in the church until morning. It would not have been the first time, for as a teenager arriving in Tours he had avoided the coldest nights by sleeping in a church. It was only through a great force of will that he was able to leave this sanctuary and return to the streets.

There were no vacancies at the YMCA, but the desk clerk phoned some of the nearby boarding houses. He was in luck. There was a vacancy next door to the YMCA, and he went over to rent a room from Mrs. Davis. She led him to a freshly cleaned room, which had a window facing the street. The three-dollars-a-day rent afforded him access to a bath and a kitchen down opposite directions of the hall. Mrs. Davis brought him a brighter lamp so that he could see well enough to write in his notebooks. It was such a comfortable place and she was such a kind landlady that he would live there throughout his stay in New Orleans.

He unpacked and returned to the YMCA, which featured an excellent coffee shop. They served strong, chicory-flavored brew and it was the meeting place for the elders of the black community. He met an educated group of men who invited him into their discussion of "the problem" and the forthcoming elections. Griffin noted that his sense of "disorientation diminished for a time" and he felt comfortable in telling them that he was a writer doing research on conditions in the South.

It was clear that by their use of the phrase "the problem" they had not been lured into the common semantic maze of that period known as "The Negro Problem"—a concept appropriated by white social scientists to fit the biased contours of their "studies" (and then reiterated by journalists and politicians). For these black elders of New Orleans, "the problem" was neither black nor white but a human problem. They were not so concerned with what the white power structure should do but what black individuals could do for themselves and their community at the local level. This peaceful yet active role was a refusal to accept the passive role of the victim.

One of the group's current projects was the formation and distribution of a seven-point program aimed at the peaceful desegregation of the New Orleans transit system. While the grip of Jim Crow had not yet been released from other areas—restaurants, drinking fountains and restrooms were still segregated—the bus and trolley systems had been made available to all citizens. The men realized that the manner in which the black community dealt with the experience of desegregation was more important than the political fact. Their seven-point program, patterned after the strategies of Martin Luther King, Jr., stressed the responsibility of Negroes in that new situation to exhibit Christian values in dealing with both whites and blacks.

They asked Griffin for his impressions of New Orleans. Explaining that he had arrived only recently, he expressed surprise at the courtesy of the whites and the atmosphere of reasonableness between the races. The Reverend A. L. Davis, president of the Interdenominational Ministerial Alliance, explained: "Oh, we've made strides. But we've got to do a lot better. Then, too, New Orleans is more enlightened than anyplace else in the state—or in the South." Griffin wondered why he thought this.

"Well, it's far more cosmopolitan for one thing. And it's got a strong Catholic population. A white man can show you courtesies without fearing some neighbor will call him a 'nigger-lover' like they do in other places."

"What do you see as our biggest problem, Mr. Griffin?" asked Mr. Gayle.

"Lack of unity."

"That's it," replied the elderly man who ran the cafe. "Until we as a race can learn to rise together, we'll never get anywhere. That's our trouble. We work against one another instead of together. Now you take dark Negroes like you, Mr. Griffin, and me," he went on. "We're old Uncle Toms to our people, no matter how much education and morals we've got. No, you have to be almost a mulatto, have your hair conked and all slicked out and look like a Valentino. Then the Negro will look up to you. You've got *class*. Isn't that a pitiful hero-type?"

Griffin did not respond to the rhetorical question that brought a pause in the cafe owner's soliloquy. Into that brief silence, Reverend Davis declared that "the white man knows that"—confirming the truth that the Valentino-type was a deficient role model and that whites realized and encouraged its devisive impact on black unity.

Griffin listened to the dialogue without making further comment. He sensed the awakening of racial pride and self-criticism in the personal tone of these elders who represented a transitional generation. They would not live long enough to become black militants, but they would not degenerate into Uncle Tomism either. In their humane, non-violent and responsible way they were enacting solutions at the local level, the very ground where life is lived.

When the gathering began to disperse, Griffin was introduced to J. P. Guillory, who thought that he recognized the author's name. The insurance agent explained that he was an avid reader and wished to know the titles of Griffin's books. When the author named them Guillory's face revealed astonishment. He had just begun reading one of them. Griffin did not know if Guillory thought he was a liar for claiming authorship of a white man's book. Not wanting to confuse the issue further, the author attempted to clarify his assertion without revealing his secret identity. At that point such a disclosure would have been a direct insult to the elders, who had assumed that Griffin was a black man. Uneasy with the guessing game he tried to assure Guillory that he was not a liar. He told him to read a piece in the September issue of *Reader's Digest*, "and you'll know who I really am." For the moment Guillory seemed satisfied and they both departed.

Griffin returned to the rooming house. As he settled in to make notes, Mrs. Davis lit the fire and then brought in a pitcher of fresh drinking water. When he looked up to thank her for the kindness, he glimpsed an image in the wardrobe mirror that startled him. This second mirror reflection caused a brief dislocation but had less impact than the first one. Instead there was only denial. He felt that he was invisible and "observing a scene in which I had no part."

This "scene" from which he had erased himself negates the simple fact that he sees himself in conversation with the landlady. Instead, he chose to perceive two anonymous black people engaged in a brief, inaudible dialogue—as if it were filmed by a remote camera. Unable to accept the *Other* as himself, he retreated to the inward safety of the white man behind the mask.

After Mrs. Davis departed, he withdrew into deeper denial, total exhaustion and sleep. Later he was awakened by the ringing of a telephone that could not be meant for him and struggled out of bed and went to the window. He felt hunger and decided to search for a cafe on South Rampart Street.

As he walked a few blocks from the YMCA he noticed two white youths sprawled on a stoop across a boulevard. The larger one, who was muscular and heavyset, whistled at Griffin. He ignored the taunt, kept walking and did not look back. Soon he spied the young white man angling across the street toward him. With the casualness of a late night stroll, the pursuer matched Griffin's steps without closing the distance between them. "Hey, Baldy," called the man in a soft, almost lascivious tone. The chase was on and Griffin walked faster, not looking back, as the merciless taunts echoed in the empty street.

As if restrained by a long cruel leash that connected him to his stalker, he could not extend the distance that separated them; yet when he slowed down the leash slackened. He knew the leash was imaginary but its control was not. When he picked up the pace his throat felt constricted by panic.

He began to search for other options, realizing that fearful flight could not prevent the inevitable confrontation. He scanned the shop windows for a light, looked into entryways for an open door, but found no escape. Looking ahead to the next block he saw two figures standing on the corner, an elderly white couple waiting for a bus. When he approached they stiffened and Griffin glanced back at his pursuer, who had halted halfway down the block to lean against a wall.

Griffin expressed his concern to the couple. The elderly white man asked who was chasing him. He told them, turned to look behind, pointing in the direction of the stalker. The street was empty. He lingered at the corner, hoping that a bus might arrive, but the tension became too uncomfortable. He had the impression that the couple thought he was hallucinating or drunk, that they considered him to be more a threat than a victim. He moved on down a side street. It was well lighted and more familiar; several black people were on the street and he felt a brief moment of safety. But halfway up that side street he heard the voice again.

The stalker once again shadowed his pace relentlessly, issuing threats and calling names along the way. In that nightmare landscape, Griffin wondered about his family and imagined an absurd scene that might accompany his death. As he walked he pondered the startled expression on the face of a white policeman who would find the identification papers of a Caucasian in the possession of a Negro corpse, perhaps assuming that the papers had been stolen.

When the white bully yelled at him to stop, Griffin let go of his panic and hit on a radically different tactic. Perhaps he could bluff his pursuer. He had been trained in judo in the military, and he might be lucky enough to land the first punch. He darted into a dimly lit alley and issued a deep growl. "You follow me, boy, 'cause I'm just aching to feed a fistful of brass knucks right in that big mouth of yours." He waited and listened for footsteps. He heard himself whisper an involuntary prayer to the patron saint of lost causes: "Blessed St. Jude, send the bastard away." He was surprised by the spontaneous blasphemy of his prayer and, also, by its positive result. After a long time he peeked around the corner and looked down the street. No one was in sight.

Griffin hurried toward the Catholic church on Dryades and sat down on its wide steps. As the bell in the tower tolled loudly over the rooftops of the Quarter, voices resonated in his mind. He heard a litany of epithets and the insulting and even somewhat silly names spewed by the merciless bully. Curiously he had not been called "nigger" or any other racial slur, but Griffin did not analyze that. Instead he wondered if the doctor "could have known how truly he spoke, how total the feeling of oblivion was." When a patrol car cruised by the church and white officers gave him a long stare he moved on before they might circle back. He walked to a cafe and ate a simple meal of beans and rice.

He returned to the rooming house and undressed for bed. The day and night had been nearly interminable. He was exhausted by the overwhelming stress, the constant walking, and the mindbending adjustments he had been forced to endure in the rush of the unexpected. His last thought before sleep was a despairing one.

"The whites seemed far away, out there in their parts of the city. The distance between them and me was far more than the miles that physically separated us. It was an area of unknowing. I wondered if it could really be bridged."

That distance seemed to stretch beyond all efforts at bridge-building. That need for real dialogue seemed lost on the waters. That "area of unknowing" was oblivion.

THE HATE STARE

During the next four days Griffin searched for employment, wearing his best suit and tie, as well as those elegantly cut leather shoes that he had learned to shine like a professional. He applied for jobs as a typist, a bookkeeper and a photographer—vocations for which he was qualified. Although there had been no hateful rejections, the consistently courteous interviews were brief, premeditated exercises. In effect, the interviewers said that there were no openings or, if he made specific reference to a recently advertised job, they informed him that the position had just been filled.

After each day of job-hunting he returned to the shoeshine stand. Usually he took one simple meal with Williams, encountered the same range of customers, observing the invariable pattern of interaction between the races that he had noticed on his first day at the stand. Each day brought back the widow, until Griffin informed the lady in the gentlest manner possible that he was a married man with three children. She did not return after that and, little by little, he withdrew from that scene also.

In *Black Like Me*, Griffin gives very few details about his job-hunting; but *A Time to Be Human* offers a wider view of those experiences. "The best jobs I got were menial—shining shoes, unloading trucks, carrying bags in the bus station. The most I ever earned in one day was $3.95. Since I tried to live on my earnings and since my room usually cost $3.00, little was left for food and transportation. I was reduced to eating beans and rice, or beans and pig tails, or beans and neckbones, but always beans. One day walking down a street I was astonished to hear myself spontaneously mutter, 'Give us this day our daily beans.' "

His first step in each new town was to study the newspaper's help-wanted ads and then to place a call to the prospective employer. He told the truth:

"This is John Griffin. I have just arrived in town and have seen your ad." Then I would list the qualifications that made me feel I could do the job. I did not seek unrealistically ambitious employment. In those days, that would have been a waste of time.

His phone contacts offered a hope that his interviews never fulfilled. "Twice I was hired on the telephone and told to come on to work. But each time I appeared and it was seen that I was pigmented,

I was immediately made to understand that I could not have those jobs. In every other case my qualifications were good enough for an employer to ask me to come in for an interview or fill out an application. There was no question that I qualified for those jobs so long as they thought that they were talking to a white man on the phone. The moment they saw I was black, even though I was the same man, I was turned away."

After two weeks in New Orleans his only job had been at the shoeshine stand. What few dollars he collected in tips were turned over to Williams in exchange for meals. He paid his expenses from the advance he had received from *Sepia*, which had been issued in traveler's checks. Except for taking in an unnamed feature at the local Negro movie house, he had spent most evenings at the YMCA coffee shop or had made notes in his room at the boarding house.

On November 12, Griffin had breakfast at the YMCA coffee shop. He confided in the manager, recounting his failures to gain employment. The elderly gentleman told Griffin that his recent results fit the overall pattern of "economic injustice" and that even educated Negroes could not get beyond the post office, or teaching jobs in dismally run-down segregated schools, or in the pulpit.

"*This is the cream*. What about the others, Mr. Griffin? A man knows no matter how hard he works, he's never going to *quite* manage. . . . Taxes and prices eat up more than he can earn. He can't see how he'll ever have a wife and children. The economic structure doesn't permit it unless he's prepared to live down in poverty and have his wife work too."

"Yes," Griffin agreed, "and then it's these things that cause the whites to say we're not worthy of first-class citizenship." Other elders joined the conversation, sipping coffee as they awaited breakfast. This spirited discussion continues for several pages. They analyze the racist myth of superior white intelligence, examine the current economic realities and outline a necessary "conversion of morals" in the systematically prejudiced system. The honest dialogue of black people in the book permits the reader to hear black voices that would not otherwise be part of the historical record. The survival masks, which blacks assumed so scrupulously in the presence of whites in that place and time, are removed in *Black Like Me*.

Ironically it was the effect of Griffin's own "mask" (as a disguised Negro) that created a unique space in which the real thoughts and feelings are expressed. Without the disguise, which black people did not question, there would not have been real dialogue, because they could not trust any white man. But it is also true that the undisguised Griffin—the human individual of quality, of ethical integrity and dis-

cerning intelligence, of genuine compassion and spiritual vision—
shone through.

After breakfast Griffin left the YMCA and walked to Chartres Street
where he paused in front of Brennan's, one of the elite restaurants of
the city, to take the simple pleasure of studying their menu in the window. For a moment he is lost in the unceasing continuity of his internal identity, the white Griffin who enjoyed the intricacies of cooking
and eating haute cuisine.

In a reverie he writes of "forgetting" himself—meaning that he has
lost the conscious awareness of his disguise—when, in fact, he is
remembering himself, sensing from his internal "white" perspective
the same appetite, appreciation, as well as the same wallet that two
weeks earlier would have allowed him to enter.

Yet everything has changed externally and he cannot step inside.
This would be poignant enough, but even this voyeuristic pleasure of
reading an elegant menu strikes the white onlookers as a grievous
affront. When he looks up to see the disapproving frowns and gri-
maces, he is rudely reminded that he has crossed an invisible "white"
line and must get back in his "place" and not upset the tourists.

"The Negro learns this silent language fluently," he remarks at this
point, but without elaborating on the meaning of the silent language.
In his 1969 study, *The Church and the Black Man*, he discusses this
concept as it related to his experience with racism ten years earlier
in *Black Like Me*, when he was not yet "fluent" in it.

"This problem of an imprisoning and blinding culture expresses
itself in what Dr. Edward T. Hall calls 'the silent language'—a language by which men unknowingly express through attitudes, spring-
ing from learned behavior patterns, truths that contradict their
actual words, and of which they may be wholly unconscious. This
silent language is an intrinsic element in the duality of viewpoint that
persists between black and white Americans. This duality is
grounded in racist mythology so deeply inculcated that men tend to
call it human nature, which it is not at all."

According to the cultural anthropologist Hall, in his 1959 study
called *The Silent Language* (which Griffin had read before his journey but had not comprehended fully until after his experience as a
Negro), it is impossible to understand one's own culture until we
encounter another. Because we are immersed in culture, our attitudes and behavioral patterns reflect our "cultural unconscious"
and we cannot begin to see this consciously until we are made
aware of it by a contrasting culture. *Black Like Me* made whites in
America aware of black experience in a way that black writers of
that era could not, because white ears would not listen to black

voices. In a sense, white readers became caught up in the compelling drama of Griffin's disguise and were forced to identify with his secret identity, thereby eavesdropping upon conversations from a distance.

The book, then, creates a double irony: white readers who would not listen to black voices hearing black voices who would not have spoken in their actual presence. Griffin's disguise became an experimental instrument that mediated an open form of communication between the races. We hear this in the conversations with the black elders (in words on the page) and we are also made aware of the "silent language" in the scene when Griffin contemplates the menu in the restaurant window. Of course, *Black Like Me* does not solve the problem of miscommunication between the races, but it does illuminate a critical blind spot. And Dr. Hall's book, which so influenced Griffin, illuminates a related aspect. "It is essential," Hall writes in his introduction to the 1973 paperback edition of *The Silent Language*, "that we understand how other people read our behavior (not our words, but our behavior)."

Fear is at the core of all hatred, fear of the unknown, fear of those who we think are different; and that fear is projected upon those *Others* as hatred, cruelty, threats and violence by extreme racists or in the form of unconscious disrespect and paternalism by those whites who sincerely believe they are not prejudiced against black people or any minority.

But black people—or anyone who has felt the sting of prejudice— comprehend and parry these irrational thrusts by understanding fluently the "silent language" of well-intentioned whites just as clearly as they know racial epithets, because their lived experience has taught them to hear *how one is meaning* as opposed to *what one is saying*. To black people, "whose lives have forced them to become masterful interpreters of such nuances," wrote Griffin, "this is so degrading that it alienates immediately." Griffin recognized this intellectually before his experiment, but he did not understand it until he had lived it. The incident at the window of Brennan's was like a slap in the face, a wake-up call to the fact that Jim Crow was watching.

Griffin made his daily rounds in search of employment, pursuing several job opportunities to no avail. Everywhere he was greeted with the inhuman smiles of gracious rejection. That afternoon he returned to the shine stand, but when the flow of business slacked off he departed. He did not get far. Feeling weariness from all the walking, he stopped in Jackson Square to rest on a bench.

Out of the corner of his eye, he spied some movement through the bushes. A middle-aged white man approached, ushered by the pleas-

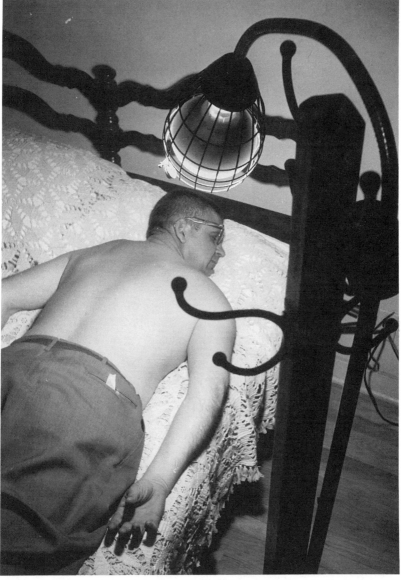

© Don Rutledge

In December 1959 Griffin met up with photographer Don Rutledge in New Orleans to shoot a series of photographs to accompany his *Sepia* stories. By this time his darkened skin had begun to fade and he didn't bother to shave his head. Nevertheless, he had no trouble "passing" as a Negro. Here he demonstrates the sun lamp treatment which contributed to his "disguise."

Griffin found an invaluable guide in Sterling Williams, proprietor of
a shoeshine stand near Jackson Square. He shared his secret with
Williams, who nevertheless remained skeptical that Griffin was
really white.

© Don Rutledge

ant fragrance of pipe tobacco. The unexpected sensation seemed to reassure Griffin and he actually thought to himself that pipe-smoking types were not racists! Then the man spoke to him with discreet courtesy, letting him know that black people were not allowed to sit in the park. Griffin understood the man's words, taking the warning as a favor that would keep him from being insulted by someone else, but he had failed to decipher the real intention behind the words. (Later he was informed by the men at the YMCA that Jackson Square was in fact not segregated.) The man simply did not want him there, but Griffin had not read the white man's behavior.

He left the park, "sick with exhaustion, wondering where a Negro could sit to rest," and walked to the nearest bus stop. To travel anywhere, seated on a bus, made more sense than walking on tired legs. He took the first bus that arrived without any thought about its destination. It took him to Dillard University, where he rested on a bench, admiring the peaceful campus until dark.

On the return trip, he rang the bell as the bus turned a few blocks before reaching Canal Street. The bus halted and he stepped to the open door which, with abruptness, was slammed shut in his face. He politely asked the driver to let him off at the next corner. But the driver ignored him despite several more pressings of the buzzer. The bus cruised past two further stops and halted only when a few white passengers were ready to exit. He followed them to the front of the bus and, when the last one had stepped down to the street, quietly requested to depart. This time the driver, who seemed bored with the cat-and-mouse game, did not slam the door in his face. The cruel exercise outraged Griffin but he held himself in check. He concluded that the driver's reaction had been against skin color and not against him. This did not lessen the indignity; and the fact that it was his first negative experience with a driver for the transit system did not either.

On Griffin's last day in New Orleans, which would end at night in Mississippi, his entry for November 14 covers thirty pages, the longest in the book. It begins with an assessment of his impressions of the Crescent City. "After a week of wearying rejection, the newness had worn off. My first vague, favorable impression that it was not as bad as I had thought it would be came from the courtesies of whites. . . . But this was superficial. All the courtesies in the world do not cover up one vital and massive discourtesy—that the Negro is treated not even as a second-class citizen, but as a tenth-class one."

The overt incidents of racism, like the chase scene and the cat-and-mouse game, were obvious examples that any white person would have seen. But the subtle behavior of whites toward blacks had also begun to clarify his perspective. Every hour of the "day-to-day living is a reminder of his inferior status," to which a black person "does not become calloused," and every "new reminder strikes at the raw spot, deepens the wound."

Some white reviewers of the book argued that Griffin, who was not really a Negro and, therefore, not desensitized to the abuse, had over-reacted. But this criticism revealed more about the reviewers' own rationalized racism than it revealed about Griffin's actual experience. How could they know? The real issue was the behavior of the white majority toward the black minority rather than the intensity of Griffin's reactions. Perhaps as a white man these indignities were more intense at first because they were unexpected. But cruelty always registers in the human psyche and penetrates deeper than the color of one's skin.

On that last morning in New Orleans he headed for the shine stand, observing that the black community seemed particularly "glum and angry." When he saw Williams he did not receive the customary friendly greeting. "You heard?" asked the bootblack, but Griffin did not understand the question. He was told that a Mississippi jury had not indicted in the Parker lynch case.

Mack Parker, a thirty-three-year-old truck driver, had been accused of raping a white woman. Awaiting trial in the Poplarville, Mississippi, jail after having pleaded innocent to the charge, he was dragged from his cell by a dozen men wearing hoods. The jail had been left unguarded, and the mob entered Parker's cell with the key. He was dragged down two flights of stairs and kidnapped. Ten days later his body was found and the coroner ruled it death from gunshot wounds. But prior to being riddled with bullets, Parker had been lynched.

What most crushed the black community was the fact that the FBI had supplied a dossier of evidence that named the murderers, but the 378-page document (including several confessions of guilt) had been ignored by the Pearl River County Grand Jury. The lynching of Mack Parker and the blatant racism of the grand jury's decision not to indict created a national uproar. Both the Justice Department and the Congress pushed for stronger civil rights legislation and enforce-ment. The case eventually went to a federal grand jury, but because there had been no technical violations of kidnapping or civil rights laws, the Mississippi mob was never indicted.

Sterling Williams read an editorial from the pages of *The Louisiana Weekly*, a scathing denouncement of white supremacy and mob rule by the courageous conscience of the black community. He read aloud in an angry voice: "They rant and rave about how the rest of the coun-try's against the Southern white—hell, how could they not be? This is what we can expect from the white man's justice. What hope is there when a white jury won't even *look* at the evidence against a lynch mob?"

Griffin had never seen Williams so enraged. Certainly his reaction was anything but desensitized, proving that even a salty veteran who had endured racism for sixty years could not accept such a massive insult without protest. Appalled by the grave injustice, Griffin decided it was time to leave the relatively safe confines of New Orleans and to travel on to Mississippi. Williams tried to dissuade him, but to no avail.

In order to leave, however, Griffin would need to cash a traveler's check. Since it was past noon on a Saturday and the banks were closed, he took a bus to the dime store on Dryades where he had been a steady customer. But they denied his request to cash a twenty dollar traveler's check, and he had no better luck at other locations. He became angry at "the bad manners they displayed" in rejecting his request, giving him the impression that the checks might have been stolen.

Resigned to remaining in town until the banks opened on Monday, he walked back toward the Quarter. Then he came upon a shop he had not noticed before. It was a book store; in fact, the small gold letters in the window read: "Catholic Book Store." He asked the lady if she would cash a traveler's check. Without hesitation she said of course she would. He was so grateful that he bought paperback titles of St. Thomas Aquinas, Jacques Maritain, and others. He stuffed the books in his jacket and hurried toward the Greyhound station.

Entering the main lobby of the terminal, he scanned the area for black faces and, when he saw only white ones, searched for some indication of a separate waiting room. No actual sign was in place because the Greyhound system was barred from racial segregation under the federal guidelines that controlled interstate commerce.

He approached the white woman at the ticket counter, whose face contorted into a hideous expression. In a belligerent tone she asked what he wanted. With careful politeness he asked about the next bus to Hattiesburg. She glared at him "with such loathing" he realized that he was encountering what blacks had called "the hate stare." It was his first experience with this most toxic example of the silent language. He would have been "amused" if he had not been so startled.

He begged her pardon and asked what he had done to offend her. She said nothing and continued to stare at him with utter contempt. The reason was obvious—his color offended her. He asked for a one-way ticket to Hattiesburg and laid a ten-dollar bill on the counter. She protested that she could not change such a large bill and turned away from the window. He was so bewildered by her venomous attack that he stood in his tracks, as if transfixed. When he did not leave she turned to him and repeated her protest in a shout.

Griffin expressed doubt that his ten-dollar bill exceeded the power of the bus system to make change and then asked to see the manager. Infuriated by his request, she grabbed the money and moved quickly from the open window. When she reappeared she threw the ticket and loose change onto the floor of the terminal. Without moving he gazed at the woman with pity and this reaction caused her to blush involuntarily. He concluded that the enraged woman "undoubtedly considered it a supreme insolence for a Negro to dare feel sorry for her." He broke the silent tension by picking up the ticket and the scattered coins from the floor.

The final sentence of this scene has Griffin wondering how the woman might feel if she knew that her rude behavior was being witnessed by a white man in disguise. His intention was to emphasize the irony of the encounter, which really needs no emphasis. The unintentional effect of this last line, however, reveals the habitual nature of his Caucasian consciousness—he is still *thinking white*.

Since there was an hour to wait until the bus departed, he searched the nearly empty room for a seat. Just then he encountered another hate stare, this time from a white man seated nearby. "Nothing can describe the withering horror of this," he writes, and then he attempts to analyze its effects. "You feel lost, sick at heart before such unmasked hatred, not so much because it threatens you as because it shows humans in such an inhuman light. You see a kind of insanity, something so obscene the very obscenity of it (rather than the threat) terrifies you."

Griffin's use of the second-person viewpoint aims at involving the reader ("you") as directly as possible in the ugly human experience of being hated without reason. His analysis exposes the pathology of white racism buried in the behavioral formation of a supremacist culture. Racism in Jim Crow's segregated society was "a kind of insanity" because it was irrational, reflexive, unaware of itself. It was "obscene" because it debased a black person's individual qualities into a learned set of stereotypes that fit no one. It was "inhuman" because it destroyed the humanity of those who hated just as surely as they dehumanized their victims.

This shock of "unmasked hatred" was "so new" to Griffin that he could not take his "eyes from the man's face," and he "felt like saying: 'What in God's name are you doing to yourself?' " By expressing in the text what he did not ask the man, the question is put to the reader, as if to transcend the kangeroo court of Jim Crow in order to appeal to a higher court of human conscience—one that will not mock God's name with criminal impunity but will demand justice in the light of truth.

There are two reasons why Griffin distinguished between the threat and the terror of the hate stare. First, what was "new" to him was not new to any black person who lived in the segregated South. What was not felt as a threat by a white man (disguised as a Negro) would have been threatening to an actual Negro—even in a public place that was legally desegregated. At that moment he was not identifying with the color of his skin but with the hatred in that white face, for which he felt pity and shame. The hate stare was a far more brutal expression of the silent language than he had detected in his own glaring reflection in the mirror, but they were equally senseless.

The second reason he sensed terror instead of threat—a terror beyond intellect or emotion, beyond black or white—was the recognition that human beings were capable of such merciless cruelty. This was the "withering horror" nothing could describe when one witnessed the "unmasked hatred" that revealed evil incarnate.

The dramatic scene was relieved by the graceful intercession of a porter who, with a touch of Griffin's arm, "in that mute and reassuring way of men who share a moment of crisis," directed him to the "separate but equal" waiting room around the corner. He found the de facto segregated space under the rubric of the "Colored Cafe" and took a seat.

When the bus was announced for various point in Mississippi, the blacks lined up separately behind the whites, conforming to the discriminatory practices without a protest. He boarded the bus and took a seat near the back. He overheard two black men express the bitter irony of the situation. "Well, here we go into Mississippi—the most lied-about state in the union—that's what they claim."

The second man responded. "It's the truth, too. Only it's Mississippi that does all the lying."

MISSISSIPPI JUSTICE

The bus passed through New Orleans, crossed the long bridge over Lake Pontchartrain, and picked up passengers at the edge of the city. Among those boarding was an elegantly dressed, light-skinned Negro, who later identified himself as Christophe. For the next five pages of the book he takes center stage with unpredictable antics and bombastic monologues that create tense encounters with two black men (who happen to be brothers) and with Griffin. Christophe's exchanges with the brothers seem to hint at inevitable physical violence but never go beyond loud name-calling, caustic put-downs, and aggressive bluffing. The two brothers find Christophe's attitude and style outrageous and irritating but not truly threatening. However, all of this has a nerve-wracking effect on Griffin, who wanted to avoid any discussion with "this strange man."

Christophe wore a mustache and a neatly trimmed Vandyke beard. He passed through the white section of the bus with a "fawning, almost tender look" for the whites that turned into a sneering expression when he reached the back of the bus. He took an empty seat near the back and began to hassle the two brothers who sat behind him, denouncing the ignorance of black people in a venomous tone that revealed his own self-hatred. Out spilled polyglot fragments—in German, French, Spanish and Japanese—to punctuate his superiority. One of the brothers reacted and a quarrel reached fever pitch. After a lengthy, posturing exchange their voices subsided.

Then Christophe moved to the vacant seat next to Griffin. He slouched and began to play an imaginary guitar, its mute music accompanied by his mournful singing of the blues. Griffin, attempting to ignore him, felt an elbow in his ribs.

"You don't dig the blues, do you, daddy?"

Griffin made an honest but mechanical reply that he did not know the blues, hoping this would end the conversation. Perplexed by this reticence, Christophe broke into a smile and whispered: "I bet you dig this, daddy." Then he began to chant the Gregorian version of the famous Latin text *Tantum ergo sacramentum, Veneremur cernui* with such perfect diction that Griffin was dumbfounded.

Of all the unexpected encounters on the journey, perhaps this was the most uncanny. How could he have anticipated hearing Gregorian Chant aboard a bus traveling into the teeth of Mississippi? However, sublime experiences had not always happened in the expected circumstances during his life: He had had his first profound encounter with the chants in the insane asylum of Tours. As a medical student in France he had assisted the asylum director in experimenting with the therapeutic effects of this music and its healing qualities had directed him toward a deeper study of musicology. These same qualities seemed capable of transforming Christophe from aggressive bantering to peaceful chanting.

Christophe went on to recite the *Confiteor* with perfect Latin diction and, when he had finished, the back of the bus was immersed in a prolonged silence. He guessed that Christophe had been an altar boy; this guess was affirmed and Christophe told him that he had wanted to become a priest. One of the brothers from across the aisle then warned Griffin not to believe anything he was hearing. Christophe's face "congealed instantly into hatred" and another long exchange exploded the calm. Griffin feared that there would be a fistfight but, as the confrontation reached its apex, Christophe turned quickly to Griffin and winked. Within a moment all the barking had ceased.

Christophe turned back to Griffin and explained that he was not "pure Negro"—that his mother was French and his father was an American Indian. An instant later, he contradicted himself. He said his mother was Portuguese. Then Christophe decided to speculate on Griffin's origins, claiming he never made a mistake in such matters. He examined the author's face and, after a long pause, said, "I have it now."

Griffin feared that he might be exposed as a white man impersonating a Negro. He tried to stop Christophe from making any disclosure. But it was too late.

"Your mother was part Florida Navaho, wasn't she?"

Griffin felt like laughing—initially from relief but then from the absurdity of his Dutch-Irish mother "being anything so exotic as Florida Navaho."

"You're pretty sharp," Griffin said.

"Ha! I never miss." Then Christophe's tone changed to viciousness. "I hate us, Father."

"I'm not a Father."

"Ah, you can't fool Christophe. I know you're a priest even if you are dressed in civilian clothes. Look at these punks, Father. Dumb, ignorant bastards. They don't know the score. I'm getting out of this country."

Just as suddenly as his anger had appeared, it vanished. He leaned toward Griffin and whispered: "I'll tell you the truth, Father. I'm just out of the pen—four years. I'm on my way to see my wife. She's waiting with a new car for me in Slidell. And God . . . what a reunion we're going to have!" Once again a sudden switch—this time from manic joy to pitiful tears. "Sometime, Father, when you say Mass, will you take the white host for Christophe?"

Griffin insisted that he was not a priest but offered to remember him next time he went to Mass. That was "the peace my soul longs for," Christophe told him, but returning to the church after years of absence would be impossible. Griffin assured him that it was not impossible, but Christophe's retort countered the suggestion: "Nah, I've got to shoot up a couple of guys." The swift erratic swings of emotion were too much for Griffin and his expression revealed his shock. Christophe smiled with glee and invited the "Florida-Navaho priest" to join him. Griffin declined.

As the bus slowed at the outskirts of Slidell, Christophe stood to straighten his tie. He stared contemptuously at the brothers across the aisle and then bowed ceremoniously toward Griffin. Everyone in the back of the bus was relieved to see him disappear, but Griffin wondered what Christophe's "life might be were he not torn with the frustrations of his Negro-ness." This fleeting question evaporated into the absence of the mercurial phantom's departure, without further analysis. Griffin-as-author seems to have been satisfied with simply re-creating the tense encounter and to allow the reader to ponder the inherent implications.

These scenes with Christophe represent the "Valentino type" characterized by the elders at the YMCA cafe and, structurally, suggest a counterpoint to the scenes at the bus terminal that precede them. The "Valentino type"—perhaps better named as a "dandy hipster" but nonetheless a "type"—fails to capture the complexity of the character portrayed in the book. This is why Griffin re-created Christophe in the context in which he appeared, as one episodic character in a series of episodes, rather than as a "type" in a case study. However, Christophe's behavior, even though erratic and unpredictable, delineates a consistent set of reactions distinctly different from the range of black characters in the story.

Not only has Christophe been victimized by white racism but he has victimized himself by internalizing the hierarchical prejudice that the lighter the skin the better the person. He feels at once both inferior to whites, whom he hates but also admires, and superior to blacks, whom he hates without admiration. It is important for him that he claim to have "white" lineage—his mother was "French" or "Portuguese" or perhaps he did not know from where or whom he had inherited his "white blood" that resulted in lighter skin and, in his mind, "white intelligence" and superior culture. He is not "pure Negro" and thus better than those "dumb, ignorant bastards" with whom he is forced to sit in the back of the bus.

The close juxtaposition of the terminal and bus scenes points out a thematic connection. The hate stares received by Griffin parallel Christophe's hateful looks toward his fellow blacks. These instances of the silent language are further connected by the tones of voice (if not the actual words) heard from the ticket clerk and the light-skinned dandy. The hatred they express toward black people boomerangs back to aggravate the open wound of their self-hatred. By projecting her own fears of black people and her insecurities about her own superior status, the white woman reveals her inhumane but pitiable nature through her cruel but pitiful behavior.

Christophe's behavior reveals the same contempt for blacks—either because they are darker than he is or because they do not exhibit the intellectual sophistication with which he bludgeons them. But the root of their hatred is the same. It has nothing to do with the black people they feel they must defile but with the white supremacist system that has deformed them (and everyone else in one degree or another). No one is immune because the unconscious cultural toxins damage all—regardless of one's self-awareness or interracial understanding, which can soothe but not heal the wound; or one's lack of awareness or understanding, which can only exacerbate it.

With the departure from the Slidell Greyhound station, the mood of the bus ride shifted radically from a fragmented divisiveness into a communal unity. The enclave of black people cohered into a sisterhood/brotherhood awareness of survival through cooperation. They were now in the bowels of Mississippi, and the bus was commanded by a different driver, a bigoted autocrat devoid of any Crescent City gentility.

Bill Williams, a "stockily built young Negro," boarded the bus at Slidell. He introduced himself to Griffin as he sat in the seat vacated by Christophe. The new conversation flowed smoothly between them and with other black passengers. Since all knew that Griffin was a newcomer to the area, it was not long before he was receiving friendly advice about how to survive in enemy territory, where the only law was the white man's and where "Mississippi Justice" was anything but just.

To add to the strategies he had acquired from Sterling Williams and other black men in New Orleans, he learned some Deep Dixie tactics from Bill Williams (who was not related to Sterling except for his generosity to the traveling Texan). He was warned never to look at a white woman—to look the other way or at the ground—and not even to look at a movie poster if it happened to feature a white woman. If he encountered white boys who bothered him, he was advised to keep moving and never to answer their questions. Since he was well dressed, he was also told to stay clear of alleys because he might get mugged.

When it was nearly dark the bus pulled into a small, nameless town. The driver announced a ten-minute stop and the whites filed off. Williams led the black contingent toward the front but the driver blocked the exit. Williams deftly ducked under the driver's outstretched arm and ambled off to the toilet shed. The furious driver yelled after him. "Hey, boy, where you going? . . . Hey, you, boy, I'm talking to you." Griffin stood on the bottom step, waiting, as the driver turned to him.

"Where do you think you're going?" he asked, his heavy cheeks quivering with each word.

"I'd like to go to the rest room." I smiled and moved to step down.

He tightened his grip on the door facings and shouldered in close to block me. "Does your ticket say for you to get off here?" he asked.

"No sir, but the others—"

"Then you get your ass back in your seat and don't you move til we get to Hattiesburg," he commanded.

"You mean I can't go to the—"

"I mean get your ass back there like I told you. . . ."

"You announced a rest stop. The whites all got off," I said, unable to believe he really meant to deprive us.

He stood on his toes and put his face up close to mine. His nose flared. . . . He spoke slowly, threateningly: "Are you arguing with me?"

At that crucial point, Griffin's protest collapsed under the threat. He sighed in defeat and the group turned back at the driver's command. Some of them grumbled against his unfair actions, and one woman said that blacks were usually let off at that stop. For a few moments they all sat dejectedly in what Griffin described as "the monochrome gloom of dusk." He was appalled at the cruelty of depriving one of something so basic.

Then, in a soft but firm voice, a new form of protest rose from the back of the bus. One man insisted that he would relieve himself on the bus rather than submit to such arrogant torture. Amid an impromtu chorus of whispers, the clearing of throats and soft laughter the man made his protest without being detected by the driver. Another man suggested that they all do it, but the group vetoed the idea. Just then they heard the loud voice of the driver addressing the return of Bill Williams: "Didn't you hear me call you?" Williams replied that he had not and that, no, he was not deaf. When the driver persisted, Williams innocently replied: "I heard you yelling 'Boy,' but that's not my name, so I didn't know you meant me."

Williams returned to the seat next to Griffin. Everyone in the back of the bus smiled at his slyly comic yet serious gesture of courage. "In the immense tug-of-war, such an act of defiance turned him into a hero," Griffin noted.

Heading north the bus plunged deeper into the back country. The obvious communal caring among the black passengers was extended immediately to those who boarded at the small towns and joined them at the back of the bus. Griffin had seen nothing like that in New Orleans. His point of view slowly adjusted from seeing a Negro collective from the outside to identifying with them individually to becoming included as one who "sought comfort from his own."

Griffin's profound sense of inclusion connected at the level of Being, of being spiritually united with fellow human beings. His dissociation from the whites went beyond the physical distance that segregated one group to the back of the bus, beyond the superficial perception of skin color that allowed whites to discriminate against blacks, and even beyond his guilt for rationalizing his own racism. He was alienated from his fellow whites because they were out of touch with their own humanity, just as surely as Christophe had lost touch. That the logic of the segregated system was a massive fallacy, he had no doubt; that Jim Crow's legal ethics were morally wrong, he was certain; that Negroes were individuals of subtle complexity and not stereotypes, he knew from experience.

As the bus neared Poplarville—the sight of the Mack Parker lynching—a wave of "agitation swept through the bus." Bill Williams asked Griffin if he knew of the case and, even though it was a whispered question answered by a nod, several whites looked toward the back of the bus. The once "animated Negro faces turned stony." When they passed through town, Williams pointed out the locations where the tragedy had been played out. There was the jail from where Parker was kidnapped, and there was the courthouse where "Mississippi Justice" was sanctified.

Outside Poplarville the bus moved through the dark countryside on its way to Hattiesburg. They arrived about 8:30 and all the black passengers scurried to the restrooms. Williams gave Griffin the name of a contact in town and sent him off in a cab to that address. The contact inside the Negro quarter referred him to another man just a few blocks away. As Griffin walked down Mobile Street, a car filled with whites sped by. He was assaulted by obscenities and a tangerine that missed. He was assaulted also by "the insane terror" of the black ghetto besieged by whites.

He entered the store of his second contact. This man related a few horror stories and sent him to a drugstore down the block to await yet a third contact. These tense scenes suggest the intrigue of a spy novel. But this was no more fictional than his involvement in the

French Underground had been, or his experiences as a civil rights activist would be during the 1960s.

He drank milk shakes in the drugstore as he waited for the next contact. He thought about the man who had told him the horror stories, reflecting that the man's "bitterness was so great I knew I would be thought a spy for the whites if I divulged my identity." What a curious thought, so curious it almost reads as a misprint or a line wildly out of context. Yet it is clearly indicative of the terror he was then feeling.

Finally a well-dressed man walked in and asked if he were Mr. Griffin. This third contact directed him to a room that, despite being "upstairs in a wooden shanty that had never known paint," was a secure haven. He trudged up the stairs and entered the room. The space was awash in the yellowish light from the street, and he heard a man's voice from the tavern below singing an improvised ballad about Mack Parker.

Without turning on the room light he walked to the bed and sat down to listen to the ballad. When it ended he heard anguished voices from below and then juke-box jazz blasted against his frayed nerves. He walked back across the squeaking floorboards to the closed door. He flipped the wall switch to turn on the ceiling globe.

ESCAPE FROM HELL

The crucial sequence in the barren room of the Hattiesburg shanty marks the turning point in the narrative—a painful breakthrough to a fresh perspective that had been foreshadowed by the evolving perceptions experienced on the long bus ride.

"I switched on the light and looked into a cracked piece of mirror bradded with bent nails to the wall. The bald Negro stared back at me from its mottled sheen. I knew I was in hell. Hell could be no more lonely or hopeless, no more agonizingly estranged from the world of order and harmony."

Like the mirror, he is "cracked" (broken) and his sheen is "mottled" (unclear). This is not just a hellhole of aural dissonance (without harmony) and visual chaos (without order), but an exterior analogue for the interior hell of a man divided against himself.

"I heard my voice as though it belonged to someone else, hollow in the empty room, detached, say: 'Nigger, what you standing there crying for?' I saw tears slick on his cheeks in the yellow light. Then I heard myself say what I have heard them say so many times: 'It's not right. It's just not right.' "

He is detached from self-awareness, hearing the voice of "someone else" uttering the unspeakable epithet, seeing tears as a reflected image but not feeling them as moisture on his skin. Then he hears his own voice saying the words so often said by black people. Their words become his because he lives a painful truth.

At the exhausted edge of breakdown, he breaks through the gloom with his anger. "Then the onrush of revulsion, the momentary flash of blind hatred against the whites who were somehow responsible for all of this, the old bewilderment of wondering, 'Why do they do it? Why do they keep us like this? What are they gaining? What evil has taken them?' " These questions echo his bewilderment at the white man in the bus terminal: "What in God's name are you doing to yourself?" But this time his anger does not allow him to pity the whites. For an instant he can only hate them for their gross injustice and merciless cruelty and for the guilt they make him feel as a fellow white. Then his "revulsion turned to grief that my own people could give the hate stare, could shrivel men's souls, could deprive humans of rights they unhesitatingly accord their livestock."

But it is too much to bear and with the cessation of this outburst he turns away from the mirror, away from self-consciousness toward anything outside himself. The focus shifts as he surveys the room, noticing some discarded objects on the floor.

"A burned-out light globe lay on the plank floor in the corner. Its unfrosted glass held the reflection of the overhead bulb, a speck of brightness. A half-dozen film negatives curled up around it like dead leaves. I picked them up and held them before the light with strange excitement, curious to see the image that some prior occupant of this room had photographed."

He discovers that the negatives are blank. Nonetheless he imagines a possible scenario to account for their existence. He posits a vignette for the prior occupant who returns to his squalid room (this very room) with the hope that he will "warm himself with the view of his wife, his children, his parents, his girl friend—who knows?" Griffin has identified with the man and his hope of seeing images of his loved ones at the basic level of humanity. But the blank negatives, "masterpieces of human ingenuity wasted," bring no warmth; they are the "dead leaves" of a blighted family tree.

Like the prior occupant, who was certainly a black person and likely a man, Griffin is reduced to nothingness. The film that could have been transformed into something *positive* through "human ingenuity" remains *negative*—as "blank" as the "empty" room and the "burned-out light globe"—all "wasted" by the white society that has also discarded black people as useless objects (stereotypes) on the junkheap.

In contemplating these objects Griffin attempts to fill a void with the plenitude of his imagination; by projecting himself into the life of the former "occupant" he attempts to rescue that life and his own from oblivion. Yet it appears that he has failed and thus, "as he must have done," Griffin flings the batch of negatives to the same corner where the discarded light bulb lies.

Suddenly something accidental occurs when one of the negatives strikes the bulb, "causing it to sing its strange filamental music of the spheres, fragile and high-pitched above the outside noises."

But what is the meaning of this "strange" and very brief accidental music? If all these oddities on the surface of the story are translated into a metaphorical reading of the text, a spiritual significance emerges.

The burned-out bulb reflects the light source from above to become illuminated as "a speck of brightness"—it is a "dead globe" yet it radiates life. The filament at its core, that thinly spun thread which once conducted electrical energy, is suddenly transformed into a sensitive tuning fork that "sings" when struck. In the metaphorical structure it represents the spiritual core that connects the globe's body to the celestial sphere. The discarded negative, also a light-sensitive and transformational masterpiece of human ingenuity, produces a postive tone when it makes accidental contact. For an instant together they make a "high-pitched" leap above the "noises" of the world to make a "fragile" connection with the metaphysical beyond. This "strange filamental music of the spheres" signals Griffin's spiritual epiphany with the Divine.

The sudden epiphany was drowned almost immediately by the noises from the street below and once again his fragile harmony was shattered by dissonance. He caught the aroma of barbecue with the intense sensation of a man starving for more than food. But he feared returning to the street. Instead he removed one of his notebooks and stretched his weary body across the bed. He "attempted to write— anything to escape the death dance out there in the Mississippi night." But no words came.

Next he tried writing a letter to his wife, but the distance he felt from true intimacy with her made this impossible. Finally, in an effort to break free of his grief, he turned toward analyzing the implications of cultural prisons. He "began to understand Lionel Trilling's remark that culture—learned behavior patterns so deeply engrained they produce unconscious, involuntary reactions—is a prison. My conditioning as a Negro, and the immense sexual implications with which the racists in our culture bombard us, cut me off, even in my most intimate self, from any connection with my wife."

But was it Griffin's short time as a "Negro" or his lifetime as a Caucasian that had produced such entropy? Yes, he had been warned not to look at a white woman, and he was conscious of the seriousness of the warnings and the severe punishment for not heeding them. However, it was the unconscious conditioning of his Southern upbringing—in particular the sexual taboos he had learned—which imprisoned him.

He stared at the page in his notebook and, except for the preliminary heading and an intimate salutation, the page remained as blank as the negatives. "The visual barrier imposed itself. The observing self saw the Negro, surrounded by the sounds and smells of the ghetto, write 'Darling' to a white woman," he noted. He concluded from this that the "chains of my blackness would not allow me to go on," even as he believed that he "understood and could analyze what was happening."

Certainly Griffin understood the rational response to the irrational taboo; it was not his intellect but his emotions that constrained him. If he perceived his "visual barrier" as a length of black chain, he was blind to the white lock that secured it. After all, the private act of corresponding with his wife from the room in the shanty hardly constituted a danger. Mailing a letter that would have reached her in the concealment of an envelope and that would have been read in the privacy of their home required no risk at all.

He decided to descend into "the mainstream of hell" on Mobile Street to find a place to eat. A few blocks away he saw a dimly lit sandwich shop with a sign over its door that read: NO OBSENETY ALLOWED. He made no comment about the misspelling but the silent tableau that followed illustrated the irony of its message.

"A round-faced woman, her cheeks slicked yellow with sweat, handed me a barbecued beef sandwich," he wrote. "My black hands took it from her black hands. The imprint of her thumb remained in the bread's soft pores. Standing so close, odors of her body rose up to me from her white uniform, a mingling of hickory-smoked flesh, gardenia talcum and sweat." The obscenity was not the language one might hear in such a degraded place but that the place exists at all. The ghetto is the real obscenity. The woman did not speak, but the "expression of her full face cut into me. Her eyes said with unmistakable clarity, 'God . . . isn't it awful?' " He watched her return to the kitchen and, as she lifted the "giant lid of the pit," her face turned ashen from the smoke. This vision looks every bit like the obscene "mainstream of hell."

Griffin retreated to the staircase that led to his room. He sat to eat the hot sandwich. He listened to the night throng of shouts, and the raucous "music consumed in its blatant rhythm all other rhythms, even that of the heartbeat." He considered the reality of the Hattiesburg ghetto in relation to an unnamed scholar's assessment of segregated Americans. "Despite their lowly status," claimed the white scholar, "they are capable of living jubilantly." Griffin disagreed with the scholar and wrote: "The laughter had to be gross or it would turn to sobs, and to sob would be to realize, and to realize would be to despair. So the noise poured forth like a jazzed-up fugue, louder and louder to cover the whisper in every man's soul, 'You are black. You are condemned.' This is what the white man mistook for 'jubilant living.'. . . ." This painfully accurate passage cuts to the immediate emotional reality that whites, including academics, could never know. He "felt disaster" at the human level, knowing that "somewhere in the night's future—the tensions would explode into violence."

In her 1971 monograph on *Black Like Me*, Margaret Mansfield pointed out the eerie accuracy of Griffin's predictions for the 1960s. "From the perspective of a decade which has seen Watts and Jackson State," she wrote, "we see that his words were prophetic." Unfortunately his words were no more prophetic than those of Martin Luther King, Jr. and James Baldwin, but during that era it took Griffin's warnings to make whites listen; not all whites, of course, but those with a sense of justice.

As the trivial and hypocritical lyrics to the Mississippi state song hummed in his memory, he visualized the equally tawdry scenes from books and movies about the Deep South. That magnolia heaven was a bitterly obscene joke to the bottom dwellers of the ghetto. "I could not take this land of home and church," he remarked in a line that was cut from the published book, "where white men drove through the streets shouting their scatologic taunts at men and women alike."

He sat on the bottom step of the stairs that led back up to his shanty room. He was utterly exhausted. It had been the longest and most despairing day of his life. November 14, 1959—the day he had tried to cash a traveler's check, thinking he would never get out of New Orleans. The news of the ruling not to punish the lynchers of Mack Parker and how that injustice rang through the day and night in the words of Sterling Williams and Bill Williams. Passing by the scenes of the crime in Poplarville and the pitiful ballad that rose up from the Hattiesville bar. Would it ever end?

It had been a day of unmitigated horror: the stares at the bus terminal and the rancor of Christophe toward his fellow blacks that twisted into self-hatred; the bus driver's cruelty in denying black passengers a basic human need and the violent obscenities from a car-load of whites on Mobile Street. The day had been followed by a night of stress that had brought him to the breaking-point.

As he sat on the bottom step, he decided on a plan of escape, a way of ending the despair in a positive way, even if it would be only temporary. "I rose stiffly to my feet," he wrote. "Suddenly I knew I could not go back to that room with its mottled mirror, its dead light bulb, and its blank negatives."

He decided to call P. D. East, the only white man in Hattiesburg who might be able to help him. He reached the journalist's wife by phone. She assured him that she would contact her husband and that he would be glad to make a rescue. Griffin waited in front of a brightly lit drug store, realizing it would be safer to hide in a dark corner but determined not to allow fear to chase him from the designated spot. As he waited like an illuminated target for the next wave of night-cruising racists, Griffin did not question his ethics or motives for seeking refuge from the ghetto. He was desperate to escape from hell.

P. D. East was the only person in Hattiesburg he believed he could trust. They had never met but had been introduced through correspondence by their mutual friend, the literary historian Maxwell Geismar. East was the editor/publisher of *The Petal Paper*, a monthly newspaper considered to be communist-inspired because it advocated justice and equality for all citizens. Their meeting would mark the beginning of a lifelong friendship.

East cruised past the watchful Griffin on Mobile Street and parked his station wagon down the block. The tall, lanky editor strode out of the shadows into the light. He shook the hand of the "Negro" and asked if he was ready. They returned to the car and set out for East's home. At first they spoke in "a strangely stilted manner," and Griffin wondered why. Then he realized that he had grown accustomed to expecting contempt from whites and he was being cautious. He felt "embarrassed to ride in the front seat of a car with a white man." Griffin insisted that East not help him if it meant danger or embarrassment for his family, but the editor kept driving in silence.

When they arrived, East's wife was in the shadows. "Well, hello, Uncle Tom," she said. "Once again the terrible truth struck me," Griffin observed. "Here in America, in this day, the simple act of whites receiving a Negro had to be a night thing and its aura of uneasiness had to be countered by gallows humor." But once in their house for a few moments his awkwardness dissipated and he was struck by a sense of warmth, naturalness and trust. He also noticed that their modest home was a palace compared to his recent lodging in the ghetto.

Finally he was safe, and his fears would not invade him for the next two days. Yet an unconscious anxiety was still with him, with all of them, reminding him of "the nagging, focusless terror we felt in Europe when Hitler began his marches." Apparently they discussed this at greater length than the published text indicates. Griffin summed up their feelings in a passage that was cut from the original manuscript. "We felt that fear, and it outraged something in our consciousness," he had written, "for it had its roots in the threats of unjust men. In reality, the Southerner, white or black, was no longer a free subject in a free land; he was a vassal of the pressure groups, the Klans and Councils, the racists. The race issue was merely a covering. The real issue, I knew then, was simply the conflict between just and unjust men."

Griffin stayed on with the Easts the next day and night (November 15) and rode with his host from Hattiesburg back to New Orleans on the morning of November 16. The forty hours he spent in the East home was relaxing in the sense that he was able to let go of his defenses but the time was anything but restful. Before retiring that first night, East had handed him a manuscript to read. It was his autobiography, *The Magnolia Jungle*, which was due to be published in 1960. Griffin began reading it and immediately became caught up in East's life story. He was so fascinated with the mixture of genuine tragedy and wild satire that he did not stop until the book was read. All the while he read and chain-smoked, East slept deeply and snored loudly.

At daybreak Griffin dozed off for less than an hour only to be awakened by his host. That entire day (November 15) was spent discussing the manuscript, that evening East regaled everyone with his incredible but true tales, and that night Griffin sifted through a massive file of materials. The content of the file formed what East called his annals of "assdom"—legal documents and hate letters. Griffin found the evidence of "legalized injustice" to be far more incredible than the hate mail, because the leaders of the white community wielded greater power than the uneducated racists. What struck him most deeply was the premeditated cynicism of the lawmakers.

Again he had been awake most of the night, making notes on the dossier. After only a few hours of sleep he was awakened for his departure to New Orleans. That morning drive seemed an instant compared to the eternal bus trip. They spent some time on the campus of Dillard University, and then East drove Griffin to downtown New Orleans where the two new friends bid each other farewell.

According to the published text and the original manuscript of *Black Like Me*, Griffin purchased a one-way ticket back to Mississippi on a bus bound for Biloxi. These three pages in the book record a few activities within the three hours before departure. However, there is a three-day gap—between the afternoon of November 16 and his arrival at the Biloxi bus station on the night of November 19—which was not covered. The missing days, apparently overlooked by his editor and never mentioned in published reviews, were a purposeful omission on the part of the author.

This time of renewal was spent with an Episcopal priest in a small house on Canal Street. There, resting in seclusion to regain his strength for the next leg of the journey, Griffin did the solitary work of bringing his notebooks up to date. The Reverend Sherwood Clayton, living in semi-retirement in New Orleans, was his host. This longtime family friend from Fort Worth was a gentle, cultured man who spoke French, loved classical music, and was a marvelous cook; just the set of ingredients that Griffin needed at that time. Since this unrecorded time span was not integral to the story and because Griffin chose to protect Father Clayton from possible reprisals, there was no mention of this period in the book.

During those restful days he called his wife and enjoyed hearing her voice and those of their three children. He was upbeat, interested in hearing about what and how they were doing, but saying little (as usual) about any of his experiences. He did not want to worry Elizabeth or his parents, whom he asked her to call. He knew that they would be especially relieved to know that he was safe with Father Clayton. He did share a big laugh with Elizabeth when he told her about the black towels that the Easts had set out for him when he was their guest in Hattiesburg.

VERBAL PORNOGRAPHY

Griffin records only one significant scene during the New Orleans interlude. It occured in the bus station restroom on November 16, the day he was dropped off by P. D. East and purchased a one-way ticket in advance for Biloxi, Mississippi.

He read a typed message that was taped to the wall of the segregated restroom. It was a list of prices a white man was willing to pay for sex with black females: $2 for a nineteen-year-old and more, along an ascending pay scale, for younger ones, with top dollar offered for a girl of fourteen ($7.50); additional sums were offered for various acts of perversion and a $5 fee was posted as a procurement bonus for any black man who provided the merchandise within the pay scale.

Griffin and Rutledge resorted to several strategies to avoid attracting attention. Rutledge would pretend to be a tourist taking casual pictures, and Griffin would find ways of slipping into the frame.

When a young black man entered the restroom, he nodded to Griffin and then, glancing at the notice, "snorted with amusement and derision." Griffin summed up this interracial social dynamic with the following comments: "In these matters, the Negro has seen the backside of the white man too long to be shocked. . . . He cannot understand how the white man can show the most demeaning aspects of his nature and at the same time delude himself into thinking he is inherently superior. To the Negro who sees this element of the white man's nature—and he sees it much more often than any other—the white man's comments about the Negro's alleged 'immorality' ring maddeningly hollow."

The November 19 entry begins with his arrival at the Biloxi bus terminal. Since he arrived late he did not find any black people who might direct him to decent lodging. Instead of searching for a room or languishing in the station, he began to walk. He located an abandoned shed, which had a tin roof but only three walls. He managed to sleep, but because the open area of the shed faced south, he nearly froze from the winter wind that whipped inland from the Gulf of Mexico.

The following morning, November 20, he had breakfast at a Negro diner and headed for the highway, hoping to hitch a ride to Mobile, Alabama. Walking along the shoulder that bordered on the lovely beachfront, he struck a leisurely pace in the warm sunlight and checked historical markers along the route. Many cars passed but did not stop. By midday he stopped to buy milk and a bologna sandwich at a highway store. He carried the food over to the sidewalk along the low sea wall. There he was soon engaged in a conversation with a local black man.

He asked him about the splendid beaches and was informed that they were manmade, intended for whites only, even though the project had been funded by a gasoline tax. The local man expressed his protest of the segregation policy and said that he and other black taxpayers were considering political action to right the injustice.

After the man had departed, Griffin rested for a while and then continued his trek east along the shoulder of the road. Within an hour, he began to tire, but a car pulled up. The white man offered a ride. Griffin learned that the driver was a native of Massachusetts, who had lived in Mississippi for five years. The driver expressed perplexity about his good neighbors who seemed decent in every way except when it came to the issue of race. He said this without any note of condescension. Griffin laughed, told him he understood, and thanked him for his courtesy and kindness. The ride was pleasant but brief, and it would be his only ride during the daylight.

By late afternoon he had walked between ten and fifteen miles by his estimate, and he was near exhaustion. He decided to keep walking in the hope of finding a cafe. Not long after that he spotted a place in the distance. It turned out to be a custard stand, where he was able to sit at a table under shade trees and enjoy a bit of ice cream. The respite was short-lived, however, because a carload of white teenagers arrived and he thought it best to stand away from the tables. He leaned against a tree and noticed an "old unpainted privy" and, when the teenagers had departed, he returned to the window of the custard stand.

Griffin asked about the nearest restroom he could use. The man deliberated and then directed him up the road about a mile to a black settlement. Griffin asked if there might not be something closer, "determined to see if he would offer me the use of the dilapidated out-house, which certainly no human could degrade any more than time and the elements had."

When he asked about using the privy, the man replied, "Nope," in a voice that was softened by his regret for having to refuse but also final in its refusal. That was that. The little verbal dance was done as soon as a black man tried to cross the white man's inculcated line of defense.

Very little is related about the next few hours, except that he moved along the road as it turned inland from the beach to the countryside. How many more miles he trudged we are not told, but it is clear that he received no more rides.

However, once the light of evening had faded into night, everything changed. He began to get rides, perhaps as many as a dozen short lifts, which took on the pattern of a nightmare to the suddenly popular hitchhiker. "All but two picked me up the way they would pick up a pornographic photograph or book," he observed, "except that this was verbal pornography." The hitchhiking sequences—these in Mississippi and others that follow in Alabama—were awkward and tormenting for him personally, but they are described with elegant detachment. Griffin views these episodes from a distant and high moral perspective, but with flashes of humor that keep the discourse from turning sanctimonious. With the subtlety of an accomplished storyteller and the insight of a depth-psychologist (but without the jargon), he weaves a shadowy tapestry. We sense the inherent mystery of night, the dark underside of forbidden fantasies and the ignorant projections of sexual stereotypes.

Several incidents are compressed into a clarifying critique of behavior. Because Griffin appeared black, the white male drivers "assumed they need give no semblance of self-respect or respectability. . . . A man will reveal himself in the dark, which gives an illusion of anonymity, more than he will in bright light. Some were shamelessly open, some shamelessly subtle. All showed morbid curiosity about the sexual life of the Negro, and all had, at base, the same stereotyped image of the Negro as an inexhaustible sex-machine with over-sized genitals and a vast store of experiences, immensely varied. They appeared to think that the Negro has done all those 'special' things they themselves have never dared to do. They carried the conversation into the depths of depravity."

He contrasts this behavioral pattern with conversations he had had with other white men in which "the atmosphere, no matter how coarse, has a verve and an essential joviality that casts out morbidity" and implies mutual respect. These scenes are most notable for their evident *absence* of respect and their utter lack of decency (in the ethical realm rather than merely the sexual). Griffin's response is in no sense a prudish one; he found prudes insufferable. But these men's attitudes were not just tainted by the lewd—they reeked of bestiality. He recoiled from their voyeurism that debased black people (and themselves) with the stench of sub-human obsession.

Had these encounters not been so pathetic they might have been comical. But they are humorless, incessantly so, and the only humor comes from Griffin, who could only hope that "the next would spare me his pantings." When he is not spared, he attempts to dodge their obscene questions, which are "cynical in their lechery." When asked "Did you ever get a white woman?" he responded with his own question:

> "Do you think I'm crazy?" I tacitly denied the racist's contention, for he would not hesitate to use it against the Negroes in his conversations around town: "Why, I had one of them admit to me just last night that he craves white women."
>
> "I didn't ask if you was crazy," he said. "I asked if you ever had one—or ever really wanted one." Then, conniving, sweet-toned, "There's plenty white women would like to have a good buck Negro."

When Griffin changed the subject, the driver called him a liar. Of course, he was lying, but not for the reason the driver suspected. Soon after, the driver was bored with the game and pulled the car onto the shoulder. The hitchhiker was summarily dismissed, "as though he resented my uncooperative attitude, my refusal to give him this strange verbal sexual pleasure."

The next encounter, treated at greater length and in minute detail (six pages in the book), forms the centerpiece of the hitchhiking sequence. This exchange was more of a joust than a mad chase. The white antagonist—"a young man in his twenties who spoke with an educated flair"—posed no physical threat, but his challenge was more cunning. "His questions had the spurious elevation of a scholar seeking information, but the information he sought was entirely sexual and presupposed that in the ghetto the Negro's life was one of marathon sex with many different partners, open to the view of all; in a word, that marital fidelity and sex as love's goal of union with the beloved object were exclusively the white man's property."

The ensuing conversation provides a forum for Griffin to argue against the inculcated prejudices of white society. To some degree, the young antagonist is a "straw man" because his devious motives are laid bare and his "logical" arguments rationalize the facts. While the ostensible discussion concerns black sexuality, the broader implications are directed to the reader: the intelligent, compassionate reader who does not identify with the blatant racism of the white men characterized in the previous episodes of the sequence; the reader who is not consciously racist, but who may hear something in the young man's talk that sounds all too familiar.

The strategy of this particular discourse is to deconstruct the logical fallacies inherent in the young man's point of view and to unmask his real intentions. The antagonist frames his remarks to create the illusion that he seeks only information to clarify his intellectual curiosity when, in reality, he desires only lurid details to satisfy his sexual fantasies. His monologues are littered with the terminology of popular psychology and he pretends to be not only tolerant but admiring of black attitudes toward sexuality (as he sees them). Listen:

"Well, you people don't seem to have the inhibitions we have. We're all basically puritans." Translation: Black people are less inhibited about sex because they have not been civilized by the puritan ethic; therefore, blacks are socially inferior.

"I understand Negroes do a lot more things—different kinds of sex—than we do." Translation: Black people are more adventurous in their sexuality because they are not bothered by promiscuity or perversion; that's why they breed like animals.

"You people regard sex as a *total* experience—and that's how it should be. Anything that makes you feel good is morally all right for you." Translation: Black people experience sex as a totality—thus, they are incapable of knowing the higher realms of human expression. Since anything goes in black sexuality as long as it feels good, then obviously they are immoral.

He refers to Negroes as "you people"—as if to imply that the difference is not a matter of ethnic diversity or extrinsic appearance, but that blacks are intrinsically different from whites in the profound sense that they are a lower species on the evolutionary scale.

"Oh, don't get me wrong," he implores. "I admire your attitude, think it's basically healthier than ours. . . . Negroes don't have much neuroses, do they? I mean you people have a more realistic tradition about sex—you're not so sheltered from it as we are. . . . Isn't that the main difference?"

Griffin disagreed. "We've got the same puritanical background as you. We worry just as much about our children losing their virginity or being perverted. We've got the same miserable little worries and problems over our sexual effectiveness, the same guilts that you have."

The young man was impressed by the hitchhiker's intelligence—not by what he had said, which was not what he wanted to hear, but by the fact he could say it. His tone was "subtly conniving" as he asked about the details of black sexuality in a pseudo-scientific language that failed to mask his intentions. It was clear to Griffin that "he was one of those young men who possess an impressive store of facts, but no truths."

Griffin was exhausted by the tedious questions and a long day of walking. He did not want to judge these night crawlers who insisted he pay the price of a ride by submitting himself "to the swamps of their fantasy lives." If that was not galling enough, the "boy ended up wanting me to expose myself to him, saying he had never seen a Negro naked."

Aghast at the request, Griffin kept his silence rather than bursting into a rage of justifiable recrimination. He saw the young man as a "boy" and felt pity instead of anger; the boy's shame intensified with the hitchhiker's silent reprimand. "How could I let him see that I understood and that I still respected him, and that I formed no judgment against him for his momentary slip? For instead of seeing it as a manifestation of some poor human charity, he might view it as confirmation that Negroes are insensitive to sexual aberration."

Before he could speak, the young man came to his own defense.

"I wasn't going to do anything to you. I'm not queer or anything."

"Of course not."

"It's just that I don't get a chance to talk to educated Negroes—people who can answer questions."

"You make it more complicated than it is. . . . If you want to know about the sexual morals of the Negro—his practices and ideals—it's no mystery. These are human matters, and the

Negro is the same human as the white man. Just ask yourself how it is for a white man and you'll know all the answers."

"But there are differences. The social studies I've read . . ."

"They don't deal with any basic difference in human nature between black and white. . . . They only study the effects of environment on human nature. . . . These characteristics don't spring from whiteness or blackness, but from a man's conditioning."

"Yes, but Negroes have more illegitimate children, earlier loss of virginity and more crime—these are established facts."

"The fact that the white race has the same problems proves these are not Negro characteristics, but the product of our conditioning as men. . . . When you force humans into a sub-human mode of existence, this always happens. Deprive a man of any contact with the pleasures of the spirit and he'll fall completely into those of the flesh."

Griffin's final comment was straight out of Aquinas, but the young man seemed oblivious to any wisdom that could not be distorted to his prejudice. He insisted that "we don't deprive you people" of such pleasures.

They argued this point. Griffin made the case that in a segregated system black people were denied access to the better schools, as well as to the cultural institutions (libraries, museums, theaters, concert halls and universities). The young man agreed that it was unfair but argued that many whites lacked access also. Then Griffin made the salient (but obvious) observation that whites were at least given the choice of public access whereas blacks had been denied access altogether, even though they had to bear a proportionate tax burden to maintain institutions that barred their entry.

The young man lamented that he did not know but believed that "a man could do better." He did not know because he did not want to know; it was easier to deny injustice and rationalize the segregated system. His view was illogical, unjust and self-serving. Griffin did not clarify his argument to the young man at this point—no doubt because he was exhausted and thought it pointless. However, in later writings, he articulated a brilliant critique of segregation.

"Take the logic out of civilization," he wrote just after his journey, "and reason is reduced to the squalor of prejudice. All the classic fallacies of logic then become a sort of weird virtue and man seeks by loudness, fear and violence to win cause that could not be won by rational persuasion." Even though the young man attempted a rational approach, whereas the rabid segregationist used "noise, religion, bombast and diversionary considerations—such as states' rights and mongrelization—to cloud an issue that would be seen as absurd if stripped of these trappings," he still professed what Griffin posited as the "credo" of the segregationist. "His credo would seem to be: If the truth makes you uncomfortable, don't change yourself but simply alter the truth to conform to your comfort."

As a Southerner he felt disgust for his fellow whites—not only the blind racist but those "good whites" who either rationalized their illegal system or fell into silent denial. He felt "shame and humiliation to be numbered even geographically among them." As for the arch-segregationists, "make no mistake about it, for although they speak of the good of both races, they base their entire behavior on the conviction that the Negro is an inferior being." And even though "man is technically defined as a rational being," it must be remembered that this "admits of no degrees of superiority except on the basis of individual virtue or accomplishment." Thus, anyone "who judges a whole race to be anything less than this definition is obviously not measuring up to it himself, for this is prejudice rather than rationality."

Griffin's long ride through the Mississippi night was silenced by a rainstorm. As the young driver watched the highway, Griffin watched the rain rushing across the windshield. He tried to turn the abandoned conversation in a positive direction. He declared that "the situation is changing" because black people know for certain that "the only way out of this tragedy is through education, training."

"Thousands of them sacrifice everything to get an education, to prove once and for all that the Negro's capacity for learning, for accomplishment, is equal to that of any other man—that pigment has nothing to do with degrees of intelligence, talent or virtue. This isn't just wishful thinking. It's been proved conclusively in every field." There is a hint of paternalism in this last passage—toward black people and toward the young white driver. Griffin's continual use of the phrase "the Negro"—as well as the reference to "thousands of them"—reveals a bit of slippage into the comfortable attitude of the self-respecting white patriarch.

Across the Mississippi-Alabama border they approached a small, unnamed black settlement. The young man steered the car over to the side of the highway and came to a stop. He turned to the black hitchhiker with an apology. Griffin waved it off as forgotten and assured the white driver that he had taken no offense and thanked him for the ride. He stepped out into the cool mist, which was refreshing, and looked at the unlighted settlement. There was no sign of life, no place to eat or sleep. Then, before this could become a real concern, an old-model car came to a stop. He was "suddenly sick with dread at what this stranger would want." There was nothing else to do except open the door and smile.

CARITAS

The driver was another young white man, stout and "tough-looking" on first impression. He asked where the hitchhiker was headed and, when he was told Mobile, he told Griffin to get in. They drove east in the slackening mist and, as each mile passed, the hitchhiker's stress diminished as he listened to the driver talk in a "boisterous, loud and guileless" manner.

"I could only conclude that he was color blind, since he appeared totally unaware that I was a Negro. He enjoyed company, nothing more. He told me he was a construction worker and tonight he was late getting home to his wife and infant son." During the first hour they delighted in swapping stories about their children.

Since the driver had not eaten, he suggested they stop for a meal. Griffin was just as hungry, but wondered aloud where there might be a place that would serve a Negro. The driver suggested that he could bring the meal to the car and they could eat while they traveled. When they stopped at a roadside cafe, Griffin watched the young man go inside. "I wondered how he had escaped the habit of guarded fencing that goes on constantly between whites and Negroes in the South whenever they meet. He was the first man of either color who did not confuse the popular image of the thing with the thing itself."

Griffin was not only relieved at the man's demeanor but fascinated with how he appeared to have escaped every trace of racism. Through a series of questions he discovered that the man came from an ordinary background and was not highly educated; that he preferred popular music and TV westerns; that his wife was an avid reader and a religious person. He could reach only one conclusion that made sense: that the man's "attitude came from an overwhelming love for his child, so profound it spilled over to all humanity." Apparently, the young man was one of those naturally caring people who had no interest in judging others. Griffin "knew that he was totally unaware of its ability to cure men; of the blessing it could be to someone like me after having been exhausted and scraped raw in my heart by others this rainy Alabama night."

Except for his brief interlude with the man from Massachusetts and the natural courtesy of the woman in the Catholic book store, whites had treated him as if he were sub-human. But this man, whom he referred to as "my young friend," was the most beautiful antidote to the racist poison on the road. He was reminded of Jacques Maritain's "conclusion that the only solution to the problems of man is the return to charity (in the old embracing sense of *caritas*, not in the stingy literal sense it has assumed in our language and in our days). . . . Or, more simply, the maxim of St. Augustine: 'Love, and then do what you will.' "

When they arrived in Mobile, his young friend dropped him off downtown near the bus terminal. They waved goodbye as Griffin walked toward the center of town. Nearing the terminal he noticed an elderly black man seated on a stoop across the street. He went over to get information about lodging.

As they conversed casually, he learned that the elder was a preacher at a nearby mission. After asking if Griffin were a "nice man," he offered to share his own lodging. The preacher led him to his house, opened the door, and flipped on the light switch. The place was clean and simply furnished; the elder was living in two rooms at the front of his daughter's house. While the preacher went into the other room to bathe in a large metal washtub, Griffin remained and made some notes. He looked about the room: its walls were covered with cheesecloth but lacked wallpaper. He surveyed the items hanging from the walls: a calendar with a reproduction of "Christ in the Temple," family photographs, and clothing on hooks.

When the preacher returned, the two men carried the tub outside and emptied the bath water. Returning inside, they prepared for sleep and turned out the light. After a few minutes in the dark, the preacher asked if he wanted to sleep or talk. Griffin suggested they talk, "feeling the depression of the night and the poverty close in on the room." The preacher spoke about the miracles and this "banished the somberness." Later they discussed the South. The preacher had two sons who had gone North to study law, never to return. He had stayed on to be with his daughters and grandchildren, but lamented the breaking up of the larger family.

Then they discussed white people and the preacher said: "They're God's children, just like us. Even if they don't act very godlike any more. God tells us straight—we've got to love them, no ifs, ands, and buts about it. Why, if we hated them, we'd be sunk down to their level."

"A lot of people I've talked to think we've turned the other cheek too long."

"You can't get around what's right, though. . . . When we stop loving them, that's when they win."

They spoke further about the changing politics of the race issue.
The preacher objected to both extremes—the Uncle Toms and the
new militants. He held about the same views as the Reverend Davis in
New Orleans, but he was not part of any group. There was much less
organization in Alabama, which resembled Mississippi more than it
resembled New Orleans in terms of tolerance toward black people in
that era. After the long day and night of hitchhiking, Griffin was
relieved by the sanity and generosity of the preacher, and he slept
soundly.

Over the next three days, November 21–23, he applied for jobs and
researched the living conditions of black people in Mobile. The pattern of inconvenience was the same as elsewhere in the South, and
only one scene about job hunting in Mobile is described in the book.
It is disheartening, to say the least, and reveals a new twist of cruelty.
Griffin went to speak to the foreman of an industrial plant. The man listened patiently as the black applicant recited his skills and creden-
tials. Then he looked him directly in the face and said: "No, you
couldn't get anything like that here."

His voice was not unkind. It was the dead voice one often hears.
Determined to see if I could break it somehow, I said: "But if I
could do you a better job, and you paid me less than a white
man . . ."

"I'll tell you . . . we don't want you people. Don't you understand that?"

"I know," I said with real sadness. "You can't blame a man for
trying at least."

"No use trying down here," he said. "We're gradually getting
you people weeded out from the better jobs at the plant. We're
taking it slow, but we're doing it. Pretty soon we'll have it so the
only jobs you can get here are the ones no white man would
have."

"How can we live?" I asked hopelessly, careful not to give the
impression I was arguing.

"That's the whole point," he said, looking me square in the
eyes, but with some faint sympathy, as though he regretted the
need to say what followed: "We're going to do our damndest to
drive every one of you out of the state."

This attitude cropped up often. Many otherwise decent men
and women could find no other solution. They are willing to
degrade themselves to their basest levels to prevent the tradi-

tional laborer from rising in status or, to put it bluntly, from "winning," even though what he wins has been rightfully his from the moment he was born into the human race.

Once again, the phrase "you people" arises from the lips of a white manager, who supported the segregated system as if it were his duty, his honor to be a member of a superior race. He felt no need to use epithets or to display anger. He did not have to burn down a black church or lynch a Negro or join the KKK; all that was necessary for him to uphold the sacredness of white supremacy was to close another door, firmly but without fanfare. It was a clear example of what would be called "institutionalized racism" in the future. It was the heart of the segregated system and Jim Crow's heart was made of stone.

Those mornings and early afternoons in Mobile were spent making the rounds of advertised jobs and the nights were spent in the charitable company of the preacher. During the late afternoons and evenings, before it was time to meet the preacher near the bus terminal, Griffin walked the streets. He recalled his first visit to Mobile, the seaport from which he had embarked on his journey to France as a teenager. He knew it then "as a privileged white." Mobile had impressed Griffin "as a beautiful Southern port town, gracious and calm."

"I had seen Negro dock workers stripped to the waist, their bodies glistening with sweat under their loads. The sight had chilled me, touched me with pity for men who so resembled beasts of burden. But I had dismissed it as belonging to the natural order of things. The Southern whites I knew were kind and wise. If they allowed this, then surely it must be right."

But this visit was entirely different from the black man's point of view. The "gracious Southerner, the wise Southerner, the kind Southerner was nowhere" to be seen. He concluded that the very "atmosphere of the place" changed drastically with one's perspective: "The Negro sees and reacts differently not because he is Negro, but because he is suppressed. Fear dims the sunlight."

Black Like Me covers the three days in Mobile in less than three pages. It was one of the few places where Griffin contrasts his former white perspective—naive and privileged—with his present black perspective.

On November 24, Griffin left Mobile for Montgomery, walking along the highway through swamp country on a cool clear morning. After several miles he caught his first ride. Unaccustomed to getting rides during the daylight hours, he hoped for the best from the pleasant-looking white man who invited him to hop aboard. When he opened the door to the pickup truck, he saw a shotgun propped up next to the driver. He backed away, but the driver laughed and assured him the gun was for hunting deer. Griffin hesitated, but stepped in and sat down. He learned that the man was in his fifties, married with grown children, two grandchildren, and that he was active as a civic leader in his community. Griffin "began to hope that I had encountered a decent white."

The driver then asked the hitchhiker the same sort of questions until there was a turn in the conversation. After Griffin had said yes to the driver's question ("You got a pretty wife?"), there was a pause. Then "with lightness, paternal amusement," the man asked: "She ever had it from a white man?"

What followed was his worst exposure to verbal pornography, more vile even than the earlier drivers who had, at least, left their lascivious fantasies in check until the night had released them. But this driver spewed forth his lust shamelessly in the glare of daylight. Griffin mumbled inaudibly in an attempt to translate his unwillingness to cooperate in the obscenity. But the bigot would not be denied his lurid inquiry.

He told the hitchhiker that all the white men he knew "craved colored girls," and that he had "had it in every one" of the black women hired in his home and in his business. "Surely some refuse," Griffin suggested cautiously.

"Not if they want to eat—or feed their kids. . . . If they don't put out, they don't get the job."

Griffin was stunned. He stared out the passenger window at the dense pine forest that bordered the highway. The silent beauty of the countryside made a stark contrast to the ugly noises of the civic leader at the wheel. "You think that's pretty terrible, don't you?" asked the driver and, when he got no reply, repeated the question. Finally, the hitchhiker said: "I guess I do."

"Why hell—everybody does it. Don't you know that? . . . Well, they sure as hell do. We figure we're doing you people a favor to get some white blood in your kids."

This "grotesque hypocrisy slapped" him in the face.

In a manuscript passage deleted from the book, Griffin wondered, "What moral and ethical difference was there between this sort of rape by coercion that threatened to starve a person and rape that threatened to shoot or knife a person?" There was no difference, except that such weaponless coercion was likely never to be reported and ensured that the victim would be trapped forever in her silent humiliation. In such a tragic climate of absolute white brutality there was no need to "invent" a Theater of Cruelty—the reality was beyond fiction.

This scene renders absurd the white man's view of black immorality or his horror about mongrelization and the loss of racial purity. "Mongrelization is already a widespread reality in the South—it has been exclusively the white man's contribution to the Southern Way of Life." The mongrels did all the yapping about mongrelization, yet those very white citizens gave the most pathetic cur a bad name. It was no surprise that this pattern of abomination went unreported in the press or was tactfully overlooked by the social scientists of that era. If any of the victims had disclosed these crimes, she and her family would have been targeted for violent reprisal. "Alabama nigger women are good about that," declared the white driver, "they won't never go to the cops or tell on you."

Dissatisfied by the hitchhiker's lack of enthusiasm, the civic leader began to interrogate and question him. "He spoke in a tone that sickened me, casual, merciless. I looked at him. His decent blue eyes turned yellow. I knew that nothing could touch him to have mercy once he decided a Negro should be 'taught a lesson.' The immensity of it terrified me."

The driver nodded toward a tunnel of pines that screened the swamps beyond. "You can kill a nigger and toss him into that swamp and no one'll ever know what happened to him," he declared. The threat was clear: *I can kill you and feed you to the gators and get away with it—that's how much power I have over you.*

Griffin held back his rage. In the original manuscript he expressed that rage, but the line was edited out. "It took all of my control not to reveal myself, not to say the words that formed inside me: *Why you sonofabitch, you're not talking to a scared Negro. I'm as white as you are.*"

Instead of saying it, he remained silent and imagined the driver in scenes with his grandchildren at play, standing to sing hymns in church, visiting with wife and friends on the front porch—everything Griffin had seen when he first decided to risk riding in the pickup truck. This was a portrait of "the amiable, decent American" behind which the vicious mongrel salivated, the Southern mask of the family man, the churchgoer, the civic leader that obscured the rapist from detection. "It was the side he would show no one but his victims, or those who connived with him."

The truck pulled into a dirt road and stopped. "I'll tell you how it is here. We'll do business with you people. We'll sure as hell screw your women. Other than that, you're just *completely off the record as far as we're concerned.* And the quicker you people get it through your heads, the better off you'll be."

Completely off the record? Obviously not. *Black Like Me* not only restores many black voices to the record but exposes this Alabama racist's crimes for the record. Griffin's powerful narrative became a new chapter in the modern history of the Deep South, uncovering the truth beneath the hooded will to white power gone mad.

Griffin returned to the highway from the dirt road and sat on his duffel bags to wait for another ride. There was no traffic as dusk shaded toward night. He began to feel a chill and the need to restore his body with food and drink. Again he walked along the gravel shoulder, this time under the first stars, hoping to find a place to eat or another ride. After a few miles he saw a light flickering through the foliage. Perhaps a car? He hurried around the curve and realized that the light shone from a small store at the top of the hill. Reaching the crest, he waited across the highway from the place and surveyed it for some time. He could see an elderly white couple sitting inside, surrounded by shelves and machines that dispensed drinks and snacks. He approached cautiously, not wanting to startle them. The woman came to the door and told him they were closed. He pleaded that he had not had a meal or a drink that day and that he was on his way to Montgomery.

He could see her hesitation, "her caution and repugnance struggling against instincts of common decency," and felt that the woman wanted to refuse his request. He waited in the cold, thinking that "even animals had to eat and drink." Finally, she said that it would be okay and he entered the store. He bought a package of crackers and an orange soda and then stepped outside. This was devoured quickly and he returned the empty bottle and bought another. Since the only two cans of sardines lacked keys and he was not offered a can opener, he bought a fried pie, a loaf of bread and five candy bars. He stuffed the items in one of his duffel bags and departed.

He returned to the highway, heard a vehicle approaching, then saw headlights. Though he "dreaded riding with another white man," he dreaded being out in the cold all night even more. He stepped into the view of the approaching car and waved his arms. An old car came to a halt on the shoulder and he ran to it. To his relief, "the reflections from the dash light showed me the face of a young Negro man."

The young black driver (unnamed and not described, although his character is evoked through his words and actions) offers not only a ride but food and lodging to the hitchhiker, who becomes the unexpected guest of a family that includes six young children. During the next dozen hours, from about 8 P.M. on November 24 until the next morning, the reader encounters a black family imprisoned by a controlled economic system, living in a two-room wooden shanty without an indoor privy or even beds for the children, who sleep on feed sacks placed on the floor at night.

In the opening scene, the driver discloses his situation to Griffin. "As we drove several miles down a lane into the forest, he told me he was a sawmill worker and never made quite enough to get out from under his debts. Always, when he took his check to the store, he owed a little more than the check could cover. He said it was the same for everyone else; and indeed I have seen the pattern throughout my travels," wrote Griffin. Part of the white strategy, when black people were allowed to work at all, was to keep them in debt; the combination of low wages and high prices at the "company" store, where black workers exchanged their weekly checks for perpetual credit, worked flawlessly and maintained the closed system at a profit.

Griffin asked why the mill workers did not organize and strike for higher wages. The man laughed at the suggestion of such defiance. But if they stuck together—surely the whites would not kill them all. "They could damn sure try. . . . Anyway, how long could I feed my kids? There's only a couple of stores in twenty miles. They'd cut off credit and refuse to sell to us." In the harsh glare of that reality, the hitchhiker made no more suggestions.

Soon after they turned off onto a rutted path that ended at the top of a knoll and he saw the shanty. The wife, silhouetted before the glow of a kerosene lamp, met them at the door. He could hear the children (whose ages ranged from nine years down to four months), expressing their delight at having a visitor. The wife had prepared the meal, and he was invited to join them. Griffin describes the scene in terms as bare as their shanty, but in a tone that turns elegiac.

"Supper was on the makeshift table. It consisted entirely of large yellow beans cooked in water. The mother prepared mashed beans and canned milk for the infant. I remembered the bread and offered it as my contribution to the meal. Neither parent apologized for the meagerness of the food." They ate off plastic dishes, the adults at the table and the children on the floor with newspapers as a tablecloth. He congratulated them on their family and the wife said that they felt "truly blessed."

Griffin watched as the cold fact of their existence transformed into the warmth of intimacy at the family meal. He cut up the candy bars he had brought along for dessert. "In the famework of nothing, slices of Milky Way become a great gift," he observed, as the innocent children consumed the chocolate in an animated celebration.

After supper, the two men walked outside. Under bright moonlight he stepped behind a massive pine at the edge of the woods, recalling a passage from Lillian Smith's novel *Strange Fruit*, about a "Negro boy stopping along a lonely path to urinate." He "felt more profoundly than ever before the totality" of blackness and the "immensity of its isolating effects." He contrasted the book with the reality.

"The transition was complete from the white boy reading a book about Negroes in the safety of his white living room to an old Negro man in the Alabama swamps, his existence nullified by men but reaffirmed by nature." However, his contrast was too extreme. He was not really "old" then at age thirty-nine, and he had not read the novel when he was a boy, but as a young man of twenty-five, in 1945. Nonetheless, he had traveled light years beyond "my youth's wildest imaginings."

On the return trip to the house they drew two buckets of water from the well and carried them inside. They made a second trip to gather wood for the cast-iron stove. The wood was set afire and the buckets were placed atop the stove. When the water was heated the mother sponge-bathed the children while the husband and their visitor shaved. Then each child went over to the zinc bucket in the corner because it was too cold to use the outhouse. The adults spread tow sacks on the floor, feed sacks atop those, and gathered patchwork quilts as coverlets to complete the pallets.

Before getting into their beds, the youngsters asked Griffin many questions about his children and kissed their parents goodnight. Then they wanted to kiss their guest goodnight, too, so he sat in a straight-back chair and held out his arms to the line of children. One by one they put their arms around his neck and touched their lips to his. Amid giggling, they said goodnight and slipped into their pallets.

The parents retreated to an alcove bedroom and turned out the kerosene lamp. They climbed into a creaking bed while Griffin lay down, fully dressed, on a pallet in the kitchen area. He watched the moonlight pouring through the cracks in the shanty and listened to the children drifting off to sleep as the wood burned away in the stove until the cast-iron cooled amid quiet poppings. "Odors of the night and autumn and the swamp entered to mingle with the odors of children, kerosene, cold beans, urine and the dead incense of pine ashes. The rots and the freshness combined into a strange fragrance—the smell of poverty. For a moment I knew the intimate and subtle joys of misery."

He thought of their burden, their union, the parents' courage in "attempting to bring up a family decently, their gratitude that none of their children were blind or maimed, their willingness to share their food and shelter with a stranger." He felt overwhelming compassion for this family and nostalgia for his own. He climbed out of the pallet and went outside.

On that cold autumn night in a pine forest near a swamp, Griffin sat on an overturned washtub and wept—wept silently so he would not awaken the children in the shanty, thinking of his own children asleep between clean sheets in a warm house. He remembered the black children's kisses as soft and innocent as the goodnight kisses of his children, and he visualized their eyes, "guileless, not yet aware that doors into wonderlands of security, opportunity and hope were closed to them"—the very same doors that were open to white children.

"It was thrown in my face. I saw it not as a white man and not as a Negro, but as a human parent. Their children resembled mine in all ways except the superficial one of skin color, as indeed they resembled all children of all humans." Griffin's tears are not shed from self-pity or personal guilt; they are the tears of grief for the lost innocence of every child wounded by racism. No child, neither the black child victimized by a discriminatory system nor the white child deformed by the insidious inculcation of white supremacy, escaped the cultural conditioning unscarred.

Griffin wept not as a middle-class white man or as a "Negro" reduced to poverty by the color of his skin—he wept as a *human parent* for all children, who had to be healed and protected, nourished and nurtured, educated and liberated. "One can scarcely conceive the full horror of it unless one is a parent who takes a close look at his children and then asks himself how he would feel if a group of men should come to his door and tell him they had decided—for reasons of convenience to them—that his children's lives would henceforth be restricted, their world smaller, their educational opportunities less, their future mutilated."

If all parents could know such a horror then they would "see it as the Negro parent sees it, for this is precisely what happens." What parent who loved his or her children could accept such a fate for them? What human parent could knowingly impose such a fate on any member of the human family? Yet it was happening only a few steps away in that shanty where six innocent black children slept on a cold floor and where human parents had little hope that life would get better. But the mother told him they had been "truly blessed" with their children, and "you just have to thank God," she said. And the father "looked at the children the way another looks at a rare painting or a precious gem."

Griffin returned to the shanty and stretched out on the floor to sleep. He was awakened by his host in the middle of the night. Griffin had been having a nightmare and had called out in his sleep. The children slept on undisturbed, and the host returned with the lamp to the bedroom alcove. Griffin lit a cigarette and contemplated his recurrent nightmare.

"White men and women, their faces stern and heartless, closed in on me. The hate stare burned through me. I pressed back against a wall. I could expect no pity, no mercy. They approached slowly and I could not escape them. . . . The nightmare worried me. I had begun this experiment in a spirit of scientific detachment. I wanted to keep my feelings out of it, to be objective in my observations. But it was becoming such a profound personal experience, it haunted even my dreams."

This had been the third time he had experienced the nightmare during his journey, but this was the first mention of it. It suggests his unconscious identification with blackness, of being a Negro victimized by a white mob; it suggests also that the threat of unmasked hatred—and not merely the obscenity of the hate stare—had penetrated to the core of his being. In the nightmare there is no escape from white racism and its punitive violence against his black skin; in the safety of the shanty where he and the black family are consoled by a sense of charity and peace, his dream state is invaded from within.

Griffin was awakened by his host at dawn. There in the lamp-lit shanty, the three adults nodded and smiled but said not a word. The six children slept on peacefully, while the adults shared a breakfast of bread and coffee in silence.

When it was time to depart for work, the husband went outside to start the car. Griffin thanked the wife and bid her goodbye with a handshake. Then he reached for his wallet and offered to pay for the lodging. The wife refused, but he pleaded with her to take something as a gift to the children. She relented and took the money.

At the intersection of the country path and the highway, he stepped out of the car. His host waved farewell and drove away in the opposite direction toward the sawmill. The hitchhiker waited by the side of the highway for a ride that would take him into the unnamed town. Very soon he got a lift from two young white boys. He could see immediately that they were kinder than the older generation, and they let him off at the bus station.

BETWEEN TWO WORLDS

Griffin purchased a one-way ticket to Montgomery. He was not looking forward to another bus ride, but there would be no more hitchhiking. He sat on the curb with the black passengers, warming in the sun for a while, and then went into the segregated restroom. He pulled out a hand mirror to inspect himself. "I had been a Negro more than three weeks and it no longer shocked me to see the stranger in the mirror. My hair had grown to a heavy fuzz, my face skin, with continued medication, exposure to sunlight and ground-in stain, was what Negroes call a 'pure brown'—a smooth dark color that made me look like millions of others."

Instead of avoiding the mirror this time, he concentrated on the changing details of his disguise. He noticed something deeper than color: His face had "lost animation," and in repose "it had taken on the strained, disconsolate expression that is written on the countenance of so many Southern Negroes." His mind had also lost animation, "dozing empty for long periods," thinking of food and water, and spending many hours "just waiting, cushioning self against dread." In finally accepting the "stranger" as himself, Griffin also experienced the internal despair that accompanies the visible appearance. The condition of being a "Negro" had fixed his expression into a mask. His thought processes had lost their characteristic curiosity and liveliness; his mind was little more than a sleeping object.

He was desperate "for something merely pleasurable," something beyond the squalid external reality and the internal humiliation. He found some stolen bit of "joy in the mere fact that I could be alone for a while," safely locked away from "the hate stares, the contempt." There was a water faucet from which to drink, and the act of splashing his face with cold water seemed like a "luxury," as did the smell of Ivory soap, which "livened the atmosphere."

He noticed that some of the stain had come off with the washing, and he wondered when he would be able to pass for white again. He decided to stop taking the pills for a while. Then he removed his shirt and undershirt. His body had "paled to a café-au-lait color," several shades lighter than his face and hands. He wet a sponge and poured dye on it to touch up the most problematic portions of his disguise— the lips and the corners of the mouth.

Refreshed and ready to resume his journey, he boarded a bus for Selma late that afternoon. That evening he strolled around near the Selma bus terminal during a long layover. He sat on a park bench a few blocks away and waited near a public phone booth, uncertain of the local restrictions. Once he saw a black man use the phone, he placed a long-distance collect call to his wife.

In a brief passage cut from the book, Griffin admitted to feeling uncomfortable yet about "a Negro never speaking endearments to a white woman." His discomfort irritated him and he told Elizabeth, "Surely, we've enough sense to overcome this." She agreed, but still the word "darling" stung his mouth; however, with the children he had no problem, because a "Southern Negro can call children 'darling' without flinching." This is the tension behind the scene in *Black Like Me*, which takes an elegantly literary turn in the text.

"I talked with her and the children as their husband and father, while reflected in the glass windows of the booth I saw another man they would not know. At this time, when I wanted most to lose the illusion, I was more than ever aware of it, aware that it was not the man she knew, but a stranger who spoke with the same voice and the same memory." In this scene, the fifth "reflection" and the second one of that day (November 25), Griffin stands between two worlds: the white world he *hears* that confirms his identity as husband and father, and the black reality he *sees* reflected in the glass. But where does he actually exist at this moment? He seems to be suspended in an eerie limbo, an existential absurdity that is not quite either world.

His family is not aware of how he appears in Selma, but the sound of his voice confirms their sense of him as husband and father. They continue to operate from their single perspective, but he perceives the experience in the cross hairs of his double perspective. After the conversation, he feels "happy at least to have heard their voices." These moments of happiness interrupt, in a conscious way, the unconscious mechanism of his despair. He stepped out of the booth into the cool night air to contemplate the meaning of darkness.

"The night was always a comfort. Most of the whites were in their homes. The threat was less. A Negro blended inconspicuously into the darkness." At this point, Griffin quotes the last line of Langston Hughes's lovely lyric "Dream Variation," the source text for the book's epigraph and memorable title.

> *Night coming tenderly*
> *Black like me.*

Griffin's next paragraph expands beyond the literal concerns of black and white in a poetic evocation of spiritual inclusion and universality. "At such a time, the Negro can look at the starlit skies and find that he has, after all, a place in the universal order of things. The stars, the black skies affirm his humanity, his validity as a human being. He knows that his belly, his lungs, his tired legs, his appetites, his prayers and his mind are cherished in some profound involvement with nature and God. The night is his consolation. It does not despise him."

Griffin slept at the back of the bus during the final leg of the trip from Selma to Montgomery. He arrived in the state capital close to midnight, and he would stay the following week there before moving on to Georgia.

Montgomery—which had been the scene of the historic bus boycott, initiated when Mrs. Rosa Parks refused to give up her seat in December of 1955—was marked by an atmosphere entirely counter to the other cities of the Deep South. The sense of hopelessness reflected elsewhere was replaced by the spirit of passive resistance. "The Reverend Martin Luther King, Jr.'s influence, like an echo of Gandhi's, prevails. Nonviolent and prayerful resistance to discrimination is the keynote. Here, the Negro has committed himself to a definite stand. He will go to jail, suffer any humiliation, but he will not back down. He will take the insults and abuses stoically so that his children will not have to take them in the future."

Griffin was not as certain about the mood of the white community. The attitude was "too fluid, too changeable," and the only sense of unity was based on old fears and cherished stereotypes. But which action would the whites choose—a grudging acceptance of change or the habit of violent reprisal? He decided to test this unknown mood with a new strategy: to pass back into white society.

He secluded himself in a rented room in the ghetto for the next two days to avoid exposure to sunlight. He did not touch up his face with stain and took no more medication. He ventured out at night for what was necessary and brought the supplies back to his room. By the third night, November 28, he scrubbed himself "almost raw until my brown skin had a pink rather than black undertone." After examining the image in the mirror, he believed he could pass back into the white world. He found the shift nerve-wracking, because he had to leave the ghetto room as a white man; conversely, if he checked into a room in the white district, but had been exposed to too much sunlight, the medicine in his system would reactivate the darkening process.

In a reversal of his New Orleans transformation, Griffin slipped out of the ghetto late that night to reenter the white world of Montgomery, Alabama. He carried all his belongings and headed toward the other side of town. Along the way he encountered a black teenager near the dividing line of the two worlds. The young man's caution in his presence seemed to validate his "white like me" identity. But it was not until he passed a white policeman in a well-lighted area that he was convinced that the reversal had been accomplished.

Once again he was accepted as a first-class citizen, but the psychic readjustment would not be so easy. He crossed the street to a restaurant, entered and sat at the counter between two whites. The waitress smiled and he felt he had witnessed a trick of magic. However, he "felt no joy in it." All of the smiles and courtesies he had not known as a Negro (and which he remembered too well) turned the "miracle sour." He wondered what sense he could make of it.

The following dozen pages of *Black Like Me* cover his days in the tense capital. A series of parallel episodes brings his double perspective into sharp focus, revealing the tragic ironies and comic absurdities of the "two worlds" he moves between in both the literal and figurative senses.

First, upon waking up as a white man in a plush room of the Whitney Hotel, he writes: "Montgomery looked different that morning" of November 29, and the "face of humanity smiled—good smiles, full of warmth; irresistible smiles that confirmed my impression that these people were simply unaware of the situation with the Negroes who passed them on the street—that there was not even the communication of intelligent awareness between them." His observation is precisely accurate. The black reality was entirely *out of the awareness* of white perception. When he spoke (as a white man) with other whites that day, he heard the same old cliches that reeked of unconscious racism glossed over with the patina of paternalism.

On that same day, he walked through a ghetto area new to him. "I, the white man, got from the Negro the same shriveling treatment I, the Negro, had got from the white man." He realized, of course, that his presence there meant nothing more to black people than their conditioned reflex to whiteness. In either world one was an alien if one was of a different color. It was that simple and also that tragic. The flaw in the human condition was engrained in the cultural unconscious.

Under the circumstances, he wondered if it was worth going on. "Was it worth trying to show the one race what went on behind the mask of the other?" It was not worth trying to show it to them in that place at that time, but it would be worth revealing it in a book to be read later. Only with reflective distance and through his double perspective could a meaningful new awareness be communicated.

There is a second use of this structural juxtaposition in contrast to the tragic sense of the South's two masked societies; it is a comic touch that unmasks the pathetic in both races and both modes. On the night he checked into the white hotel, a Negro porter rushed to carry the duffel bags with a masked smile and a rush of "yes sirs." Griffin felt like telling the porter, "You're not fooling me," but he was "back on the other side of the wall," and there was "no longer communication between us, no longer the glance that said everything." (This "glance" refers back to the porter in the New Orleans bus terminal who rescued him from the white waiting room and directed him to the area segregated for blacks.)

Three nights later, as the "Negro Griffin," the narrator becomes an instant porter in the Montgomery bus terminal. He was there to purchase a bus ticket for Tuskegee and not to pick up spare change. Even though he was wearing no uniform he was waved over by a "large matriarchal woman," calling "Boy, come here. Hurry!" He obeyed her command and, "without thinking," he tells the reader, "I allowed my face to spread to a grin as though overjoyed to serve her. I carried her bags to the bus and received three haughty dimes. I thanked her profusely. Her eyebrows knitted with irritation and she finally waved me away."

The first scene at the hotel portrays the measured obsequiousness of the black porter in a pathetic light. The comic element, illuminated by the white narrator's awareness of role-playing, becomes tinged with the bitterness of a social lie exposed. The scene at the bus station becomes ludicrous rather than pathetic, because the roles are reversed. The matriarch is the one who is out of awareness and, because she is so haughty, she becomes the butt of the joke. Even though Griffin claimed to have reacted "without thinking," he pitched the scene toward madcap absurdity, certainly aware that he was tweaking the pomposity of the woman for the reader's delight and his own.

That tense week in the capital, of moving between two worlds and changing masks in transit, becomes the maddening climax of *Black Like Me*. The effect of his "zigzagging" technique, as he called it, was unsettling and hazardous. It also suggests that Griffin had become bolder, even somewhat reckless, in this quick-changing experiment. The "zigzagging" made for a more complex and compressed test, but the results were the same. He pushed the limits of his confidence in the knowledge that only appearances needed to be touched up in order to pass in either world undetected. It was almost too easy, but beneath the appearances its essence was difficult and sad. The double perspective of being a white man disguised as a "Negro" was redoubled by also passing into the white world as an "ex-Negro"—yet all the time he was the same man. Everyone perceived only "color" and judged by reflex in "black and white" terms. It was frustrating and depressing. Was it still worth continuing? No, the point had been made over and over. He decided to end the experiment.

On December 1, Griffin rode a bus from Montgomery to Atlanta. He was the last person off the bus in Atlanta, and he went directly to the segregated restroom in the terminal. "I had had enough. Suddenly I could stomach no more of this degradation—not of myself but all men who were black like me. . . . In the men's room, I entered one of the cubicles and locked the door. For a time I was safe, isolated; for a time, I owned the space around me, though it was scarcely more than that of a coffin."

He was struck by the irony of being in Georgia now, the land of his forefathers. Jack Griffin, his father, had been born in Texas, but the patriarchal lineage stretched back to the era of slavery. "The town of Griffin was named for one of them. Too, I, a Negro, carried the name hated by all Negroes, for former Governor Griffin (no kin I would care to discover) devoted himself heroically to keeping Negroes 'in their place.' Thanks in part to his efforts, this John Griffin celebrated a triumphant return to the land from which his people had sprung by seeking sanctuary in a toilet cubicle at a bus station."

He rubbed cleansing cream on his hands and face to remove the stain. Then he took off his shirt and undershirt and rubbed his skin nearly raw and looked into his hand mirror. He could pass for white again. He repacked his duffel and waited until he heard no more sounds in the restroom. Then, around midnight, he left the cubicle and disappeared from the restroom into the crowd. He rented a room at the YMCA and slept deeply.

On December 2, he woke early and made a few telephone calls. He called the *Sepia* office to inform them that the long experiment had been concluded. They requested that he take on an assignment in Atlanta to do research into the great strides toward racial understanding being made there. He agreed, but only on the condition that his work there would not be done in disguise. They were clear on that, and he was directed to meet with a photographer assigned to the project at noon on December 4. Since this arrangement left him free for two days, he called the Trappist monastery in Conyers, asking permission to make a short retreat there. The guestmaster accepted his request and, with great relief, he took a bus to the monastery.

When he arrived at the magnificent rural setting amid woods and farmland, he heard the monks chanting Vespers. He was greeted in the courtyard by a brown-robed monk and led to a cell on the second floor. "The contrast was almost too great to be borne. It was a shock, like walking from the dismal swamps into sudden brilliant sunlight." It was also like stepping out of the Deep South of 1959 and into Europe of the Middle Ages. "Here men know nothing of hatred. They sought to make themselves conform ever more perfectly to God's will, whereas outside I had seen mostly men who sought to make God's will conform to their prejudices. Here men sought their center in God, whereas outside they sought it in themselves. The difference was transforming."

The distance between these two worlds—the hypocritical "Christianity" of the racist South and the genuine sanctity of the cloister—was not merely spatial or temporal. It was a spiritual transformation from fragmentation to wholeness. That evening he entered the chapel for the last prayers of the day. He knelt in the balcony to listen to ninety white-robed monks chant Compline. The final chant was the solemn *Salve Regina*, which was so tender that "we felt the crusts of our lives fall away and we rested in the deep hush of eternity." He realized that the same tenderness had been part of the reality of monasteries throughout the centuries, and it was that tenderness he had missed most during his journey.

After the monks had filed out he remained in the darkened chapel—"not praying, simply resting in the warmth where all senses are ordered into harmony, where hatred cannot penetrate." The timelessness was the exact opposite of the anxiety-ridden time he had experienced in the Hattiesburg shanty, which had been relieved only momentarily by his unexpected epiphany there. Here in the chapel it lasted more than an instant and, when he was gone, it would continue as the Great Silence the modern world had never heard. "After my weeks of travel, when I had seen constantly the rawness of man's contempt for man, the mere act of resting in this atmosphere was healing."

Later that night, he showered and washed his clothes in the sink. When he returned to his cell, the guestmaster was there to greet him. They conversed for a while and Griffin confided to the monk his recent experiment. Then he asked if black people ever visited the monastery. Yes, they had, he was told, but not many knew of the place. How did the white guests react? he wondered. The monk explained that the type of white man who came on retreat "would hardly keep one eye on God and the other on the color of his neighbor's skin." Souls, in any case, are colorless, and that was enough for one to know in the presence of the Divine.

After more conversation, the monk left to retrieve a book; it was Maritain's *Scholasticism and Politics*. The monk leafed through the book, found the page he wanted and said: "Maritain has some profound things to say about the religion of racists. . . . You might review this page." When he was alone, Griffin read more than the one page, "startled that the French philosopher could so perfectly characterize the racists" of the South. Then he realized that Maritain was "describing racists everywhere and from all times" and "that this is the religious trait of men who twist their minds to consider racial prejudice a virtue."

He slept deeply but was awakened in the middle of the night when he was revisited by his familiar nightmare. The horror of it subsided immediately in the cloister. It was not welcome there, and he felt embarrassment for having smuggled it unconsciously within and for disturbing the Great Silence of that holy place.

On December 4, he met Don Rutledge at noon. The young photographer from the Black Star agency had driven from his home in Rockvale, Tennessee. Griffin "liked him immediately," describing Rutledge as "a tall, somewhat skinny young fellow, married and [with] a child—a gentleman in every way."

On December 7, after three days of intense work, his notebooks were full. For the next five pages in the book, he summarizes the activities in Atlanta, impressed with how far the citizens, black and white, had gone "in proving that 'the Problem' can be solved and in showing us the way to do it." Most of his research was done in two sections of the black community—the three-block area of the black-owned institutions of finance and industry and a larger quarter where six Negro colleges were located. "A close parallel exists between the two, for most of the business leaders are connected with the schools of higher learning, either as teachers or directors," he had learned.

These two closely aligned sections also contained the churches and homes of the significant religious leaders in Atlanta's black community. As businessman T. M. Alexander expressed it: "If we know anything, it is that if virtues do not equal powers, the powers will be misused." The unification of these primary social institutions formed a cohesive infrastructure that pooled its resources into one unified community.

"In the matter of education, Atlanta has long been eminent," he observed. He made specific reference to Benjamin Mays, president of Morehouse, and Rufus Clement, president of Atlanta University. In his interview with Dr. Mays, he recalled "the look of surprise and vast amusement on Mays's face when I confided to him my journey as a Negro." Atlanta was, and of course still is, the home base of the Southern Christian Leadership Conference, which was organized by Martin Luther King, Jr.

For Griffin, and for countless others—black and white—Atlanta became a symbol of hope. The black community was extremely well organized and the white leadership, by comparison to the rest of the South, was enlightened. Atlanta had taken the higher road, to which Montgomery aspired by forming new black unity in a state yet in the segregated grip of Governor George Wallace. In contrast, New Orleans, even though far ahead of rural Louisiana in 1959, was not as well organized as Atlanta and not as determined as Montgomery. Places like Hattiesburg and, indeed, the entire state of Mississippi and most of the rural areas of the Deep South still resembled the dark ages of previous centuries.

No one could imagine in 1959 what the next decade would bring. Many lives would be lost and many places would become flashpoints in the second civil war. Griffin's life would be changed profoundly by the historical battles yet to be fought during the 1960s, as well as by the unexpected effects of *Black Like Me*.

One of the final dialogues he had in Atlanta was with the Reverend Samuel Williams. Griffin recalled what the professor of philosophy had told him, because it connected so seamlessly with what he had read by Maritain and Dr. King.

> "I spent years," he told me, "studying the phenomenon of love."
> "And I spent years studying the phenomenon of justice."
> "At base, we spend years studying the same thing."

By December 9, Griffin had returned to New Orleans, intending to retrace the terrain of his journey where it had begun. He mentioned the plan to Rutledge and asked his advice about a first-rate photographer in New Orleans. Fascinated by the idea of making a documentary of Griffin in disguise for the *Sepia* series, the photographer decided to take on the assignment.

Over the next five days they returned to many of the scenes to shoot as many images as possible. But the project presented them with some unique problems; a black man being photographed by a white man aroused suspicions. "Whites tended to wonder, 'What Negro celebrity is he?' and to presume that I was uppity." Black people were also curious. "The 'Uncle Toms' think that every Negro should bury his head in the sand," and "they distrust any Negro prominent enough to be photographed by a white photographer."

They invented new strategies to overcome the obstacles and the result was a batch of sharp images and some humorous episodes. The general approach, which was also the simplest, was to meet at the same place and time, pretending not to know each other. Rutledge acted like a tourist taking casual pictures, and Griffin found ways of slipping into the frame. One day they received some unexpected assistance at a fruit stand in the French Market. As Griffin was being waited on by one woman, Rutledge talked to the other vendor a distance away. The woman said to the photographer, "Why don't you hurry up and get a picture of that funny old nigger before he leaves?" Rutledge obliged her while Griffin pretended to be unaware of the game.

Another episode occurred at a fish market where Rutledge asked the vendor if he would pose with a fish. The vendor left Griffin at the

counter and went in search of the biggest fish he could find to comple-
ment the picture. Griffin followed the man behind the counter, as if the
fish were intended for him. The vendor tried to manuever his black
customer out of the picture, finally telling him that customers were not
allowed behind the counter. Just then Rutledge spoke out: "That's
good right there, hold it," and the vendor turned toward the camera
wearing his best smile. Griffin smuggled himself into the frame.

At the shoeshine stand, Sterling Williams was relieved to see Griffin
back safely in New Orleans and delighted to be the subject of several
documentary photographs. Some of Rutledge's finest images from
the series are of Williams and his protegée, including one that
appeared on the back cover of the book.

According to Rutledge, Williams was still unsure that the "black"
Griffin was the "white" writer he said he was and, despite assurances
from Rutledge, the bootblack remained somewhat uncertain. Neither
Williams nor Rutledge ever mentioned this to Griffin. Of course, once
the book had been published there were no lingering doubts.

However, Williams's previous uncertainty casts a different light on
Griffin's assertion that the bootblack shared his secret (of white identity), because while the writer operated under this assumption and
wrote that Williams had slipped into the illusion that Griffin was a
Negro, Williams had, in fact, never believed that Griffin was white! So,
the only real "secret" had been the bootblack's, because Griffin
remained always unaware of his friend's disbelief.

By December 14, the documentary work was concluded. His brief
entry for the last day in New Orleans ends the text of his journey: "I
resumed for the final time my white identity. I felt strangely sad to
leave the world of the Negro after having shared it so long—almost as
though I were fleeing my share of his pain and heartache." He would
soon find out that he was wrong about this, because his share of suffering would return as soon as his experiment became known.

Photograph of the effigy at the Mansfield dump. Griffin's reaction on seeing it was, "It's not a very good likeness." (Photograph by Griffin)

THE AFTERMATH

How difficult it is to put into practice the theories of the spiritual life that one never questions—the returning of love for hate, of tenderness for brutality. Most terrible of all has been this weird thing—I have become a hero-figure in a way that throws into my face the total unworthiness of it. The haters consider me a mortal enemy now, but the crowds consider me a great hero, and I cringe from both.

I live on St. Thomas and Jacques Maritain, on Bach and the great musical masters. My brain is dulled by everything else, closed against the constant outrage of men who cheat against themselves in order to win over other men. Yet, I am dumbfounded to find ever greater certainty in the inherent decency of the majority.

—John Howard Griffin

RETURN

On December 15, the "ex-Negro" departed New Orleans on a jet flight bound for Dallas. He was welcomed at the airport by his wife and their three young children. His parents joined in the reunion that was marked by nervous jubilation and profound relief. They drove south to Mansfield. "We came directly here to my parents' farm," wrote Griffin in his personal *Journal.* "We sat in the living room for a while as my father fixed coffee, smiling all over himself. My mother asked: 'Was it as horrible as I think it was?' I answered: 'Worse than you can possibly imagine.' A shadow crossed their faces but it was no time—and we knew it—to discuss the past weeks. It was time to visit with the children, who fought for places on my lap; time to talk of nothing, for the pleasure of hearing normalcy again."

In the hubbub of excitement with the children, Griffin tried to catch the eye of Elizabeth. They had not been alone, and he still felt anxiety about their intimacy after the long separation. Finally, he got up from the circle of children and said he was going to wash up. As he walked to the bathroom, he heard the laughter of the children pouring out of the house into the front yard. Right behind their voices followed those of his parents, laughing with the grandchildren and guiding them out the door. Then he heard Elizabeth's footsteps approaching the bathroom door.

> A sense of panic flew through me—a moment of fear. She opened the door, stepped in and closed it after her. We stared at one another, completely disarmed, defenseless. "Is it all right?" I asked, hearing my voice—hoarse, weak, full of strain. "Yes . . . oh yes," she said, and was in my arms and then kissing me in a way which left room for nothing but a flood of relief in me. I held her close and whispered against her hair, almost unable to believe that we could have this kind of good fortune in our relationship. "Are you sure?"
>
> "Yes," she repeated, breathing it out with an ecstatic sound.
>
> "I'm so glad," I told her.
>
> "I am, too," she whispered, and then I heard her weeping with relief. She quickly controlled herself, however, and said she'd better get back to the kids. "What would you like for supper?" she asked at the door. It was such a natural question there was genius in it.

Thus ended Griffin's *Journal* entry for the day and night of his return. It marked also a few weeks of intimate union for the family, a private peace that would be erased by the upcoming public storm.

The final seventeen pages of *Black Like Me*—from January 2 through August 17 of 1960—report the story of the aftermath and public reaction to the news of his unique experiment. This was all that Griffin chose to publish, deciding that his complete *Journal* notes were too personal and, at the time, would have invaded his family's privacy. These unpublished pages fill in the gaps and provide an inside view of his family life, creative process, ethical scrutiny, and spiritual reflection. These notes reveal a wounded healer attempting to heal his own wound by loving others. Loving his wife and children, his parents, and a close circle of friends and relatives—that was easy and natural. But to love those who had hated him during his journey or to love the white neigbors who hated him as a traitor to his race—that did not come easily.

Yet, he felt it was his responsibility to love them in the manner of the *caritas* and that, according to the spiritual direction he followed, it was—in fact—required of him. This was especially true for all the whites who hated black people, without knowing why they hated or why they seemed to find it impossible to overcome the dehumanization of an entire race of human beings. This was *not* about how he had been hated, but his very deep human hurt had to be transcended before he could focus on the real issue of white racism. Even though he was inexorably the "subject" of his own experience and the "object" of hatred, he had to discover a way beyond this confusing, fragmented existence to being whole again.

Loving humanity, loving equality and justice, loving peace—this was the *only* way for him. He knew this and tried to live as an instrument of these values—not just to love his loved ones but to love everyone, not only justice for some but justice for all. He was not the composer of this way but its instrument.

He took nourishment from those around him, from the music of Bach and other classical masters, from the words of the philosophers and theologians (from the Greeks and the Catholic saints to the examples of Maritain, Ghandi and Dr. King), and also from the harmonium of nature and the silence of God's Grace.

He tried to keep his balance between the dissonance of re-descending into hell and the joy of being home; between the isolation of the journey and the creative solitude of his studio. He wrote of these contrasts constantly: the saint and the ordinary sinner; the beauty of love and art against the ugliness of hate and chaos; the glories of music and silence instead of the bombast of racism. In all this he considered himself an ordinary man, a sinner who listened and meditated, prayed and wrote.

During these months Griffin split time between home and the studio. His work on the *Sepia* series and the *Journal* entries were typed in the solitude of his barn studio. His "cell," as he called it, was less than seven feet wide and ten feet long—or "three long steps each way." The rest of the barn was an aviary full of parakeets and canaries. The barn was situated within sixty yards of his parents' small house. The country tract was forty acres, with a pasture surrounded by woods, located about two miles north of Mansfield and five miles east of his family's home. To the east of his studio, about fifty yards down a slope, ran a creek.

The studio was furnished with a cot, a wooden table and chair, plus a radio and record player. Despite a heater and a fan, the room was hot in summer and cold in winter. The solitary light was a small lamp. He worked on a manual typewriter and kept a supply of cheap bond paper and ribbons at the ready. Also, he had at least one camera there and another at home. He allowed himself to keep a small stack of books, usually texts of philosophy, theology and musicology, along with a tattered dictionary.

More often than not he worked through the night, listening constantly to music or the songs of aviary birds or the distant sounds of the countryside or everything at once. At other times the aviary was silent, and he opted for the night sounds instead of listening to music. He typed fast and the old standard made a loud clatter as long paragraphs were crammed single-space in the *Journal* or expanded to double-space for his manuscripts. He was an accurate typist and speller and, even during the years of blindness, made few errors. His cell was simple and bare by intention. The room had white walls, a wood floor, two windows and a door. Even with the door and windows closed in cold weather, the cell remained in touch with the natural elements while being isolated from the noise of civilization.

During the last two weeks of December 1959 his work on the series went well. "The work flows," he wrote in the *Journal*. "I stayed here in my studio last night until after four this morning. Then, to the sound of rain against the top of this barn, I went to bed. I failed to bring pajamas, so slept in my wool shirt. Outside, the night turned cold and the sound of rain turned to the sharper sound of sleet."

He thought about "how depressing it had been to sleep in the hovels I occupied as a Negro touring the South; and yet, here I was in one scarcely better (not even as comfortable as some of them) and was blissfully happy." He worked through that night and into the next afternoon, then had a brief visit with his family before returning to continue the work. "In truth, I love this barn, and was happy to be stuck here through the storm. Today, it has continued—so dark I need lamplight. This afternoon snow begins to fall, with a forecast for snow tonight. I settle down to it now, with the luxury of long hours stretching before me, long hours isolated by snow and ice, long hours that will bring no interruptions."

The long entry continues with the "sensation of perfect felicity," a mood that is reminiscent of so many nights at work in his studio, when he rhapsodized about the life of inner solitude. Most often he listened to music but on this night, "no, only the silence, the occasional glance out the window to the grays of the countryside, to the thickly intertwined tree limbs in black silhouette, utterly still, inviting the occasional flakes of snow that drift past."

This solitary stretch reminded him of his student days in Tours, and he speculated about the roots of his continuing "love of dark and stormy days when one can be cut off from things by the weather."

Later he turned out the light and sat near the fire to say his prayers. The steady blue flame of the gas heater held his gaze, while all else dissolved into the background. After finishing the Rosary, he turned on the lamp to resume writing in the *Journal*.

"Strange how when a man is alone, deeply involved with nature, everything—his prayers as well as his functions—all is taken up without separation, without contradistinction into the love of God. There is no dissonance, no conflict between body and soul. All of the elements of each fall into some basic harmony that is his love, his form of worship, his manner of glorifying God." Of course, Griffin was speaking about himself, about his own form of worship—the very work he was writing, the works he had written and would write—all glorifying God. Not just the writing but everything—body and soul, heart and mind—for him became "liturgical" when one was whole and "deeply involved with nature," all of nature—human nature, Mother Nature, the supernatural. "For in this framework, nothing can be contained—it overflows and must pour out in glorification, in a tremendous union with the Source of it all. Not bringing in the source to self, but throwing self outward toward it—until there is abandonment, until self is lost in this concatenation."

After several days and nights alone in the studio, he returned to the family cottage to stay the night. At that time, there were three children: Susan was five, John Jr. was four, Gregory was two years and five months. The fourth and final child, Amanda, would not be born until 1966.

On that night, his glorification overflowed to his loved ones. After the evening meal, he put on one of their favorite recordings, Benedetto Marcello's *Concerti Grossi*, turned out the lights and lit a candle. He wrote about it in the *Journal*, calling the night "perhaps the most beautiful in our family life."

"We sat there in the soft light and listened to this magnificent and tender music, and no one uttered a sound; but what a glowing joy lighted their faces as they would put fingers to their lips to call for silence and smile, or grimace whenever any sound intruded on the music. . . . Then, when the music was over, we slowly came out of the deep calm delight into which it had plunged us . . . slowly we stirred, regretting the need to break the spell, but needing to celebrate more actively." Then they turned on all the lights and made popcorn. He watched his children, feeling as if he "could not bear the warmth, the unblemished happiness of this" after the painful emotions of his journey.

After the children had bathed and slipped into bed, he and Elizabeth lay in the darkness, listening once more to the Marcello and the sounds of their children turning in sleep. Before drifting off themselves, Elizabeth whispered to him that "we mustn't ever lose this." They embraced and, slowly, he watched her slip into a deep sleep. He remained awake until the Marcello ended and the machine turned itself off with a clatter. "It was only then," he wrote, "that I felt not the slightest doubt that no matter what happened, I would take it and be glad, for the one thing I had feared most damaging—my wife's love for me—had not been damaged at all."

What Griffin had not realized and, perhaps, never knew, was that from his wife's point of view, her love for him had never been at risk. Elizabeth's only concern had been for him, for his safety, and she had no fears about his transformation. Whether Griffin had been a "Negro" or not was irrelevant to her feelings for him. In terms of the "race question," it was a matter of her own formation that she was not, as Griffin had been, poisoned by the same racist mythology.

Elizabeth had been raised by her adoptive parents on the same farm on which she was raising her own children. On the Holland farm, where the family had lived in close proximity to black people, there had been no segregation and no attitude of white superiority. For instance, everyone who lived and worked on the farm took meals together—black and white ate the same meal at the same table. Her parents were relatively "liberated" for that era. Her mother was a teacher and her father, who was an insurance agent and a part-time farmer, had come from "mixed" Anglo and Comanche stock. The Holland farm was located three miles west of downtown Mansfield; between their fifty-acre tract and the town was the Negro section. Most of their neighbors and all of the people who worked on their farm were black.

In the Griffin household, which had always been in a city context, the "help" lived elsewhere—usually on the "other side of the tracks"—and the maid or the handyman ate their meals at "the second table," according to the Southern tradition; this meant that black people ate in the kitchen after the white family had eaten in the dining room. Of course, Griffin's own children never saw any of this tradition in their upbringing, and they grew up in a household that was not only liberated from unconscious racism but with parents who were consciously anti-racist. However, in 1959 and 1960, the children had no idea that their father had ever been a "Negro"—only that he had been on a long trip, and that he was home.

They were happy about that and the same high spirits of his return extended beyond Christmas and into the new year. Griffin wrote that their Christmas had been "the finest we have ever had." There had been only one minor flaw in the festivities when, on Christmas Eve, he had wrestled with the assembling of a so-called "Superior Toy" and had "ended up two hours later cursing it and vowing never to have anything to do with such a toy as long as I lived."

Otherwise the *Journal* recorded his progress on the magazine series and he continued to marvel "at the simplest and most prosaic things," remarking that "occasionally it worries me, for it is the child's reaction in the adult." It was the same reaction he had experienced during the initial hours of his experiment. Several times, as he watched his children eat and play and sleep, he was reminded of the six children sprawled across the cold floor in pallets in that swamp shanty. The inequities were painful to contemplate, but it was an image he would not forget. Yet it was the humanity of those children and his own that struck him most deeply, for they were all "part of the universal order that none can go against." For him, "there is constantly renewed harmony in it, a harmony of the most magical sort— old as time but always fresh, astonishing, and inciting us to love the way things are at this universal level of humanity beyond innocence or guilt."

A NEW DECADE

Griffin's *Journal* entry for that first day of a new decade explored contrasts. It was one of those days he relished—"a dark, cold day, misty and hinting of sleet" that most would not enjoy. He made notes as he listened to Bach *Cantatas*, which in any case "jubilantly defy the mood of the day and change it." It was "a new day, a new year," and he felt "like spending the lonely day immersed, lost in work."

"My work, the writing of my experiences as a Negro, takes a turn back into the darkness. By comparison with the literature and the studies of the Dark Ages, the truth of the present appears a monstrous regression." He wondered if the new decade would be darker than the so-called Dark Ages; and if it was to be so, it would be so because black people were going to demand what should not need to be demanded—their God-given equality and their rights as citizens proclaimed by the Constitution. "The whites in the South have simply receded from the human race. They, with all their bullying and refusal to accept the responsibilities of justice, are simply not manly enough to be called man. Their courage has the inverted quality of cowardice. The man who is less than just is less than man."

He was writing about a state of injustice that should not be, but because it existed nonetheless, he was compelled to write about it.

"With pain and great excitement I write the pages I so detest, because I detest delving in corruption; and I have never seen more obscene corruption. And it is foolish. They wallow in their white misery, but will not do the things that will make them at peace. . . . They will not let the Negro breathe, their deep prejudice does not want that, considers it unpatriotic, a sin against one's seed."

"All of this bounces off the wall of Bach, like sickness bounces from the wall of health, or like viciousness from the wall of love," he concluded. "It cannot enter into the felicity of art's great order, because it is without order—it sneaks molelike through the underground tunnels of the soul."

The "aftermath" text in *Black Like Me* picks up on January 2, 1960 (after a gap dating back to December 15, 1959)—and then it goes silent again until February 26. However, on that second day of the new decade Griffin made a visit to the *Sepia* office in Fort Worth. Publisher George Levitan tried to give him a chance to back out of publishing his series. "The only way I'll run it is if you insist," the publisher told him. "Then I think we must run it," replied Griffin, but "wishing with all my heart I could drop it." However, since the magazine was read by so many blacks in the South, he felt it was the only way to let them know that the truth would be made public, and that there were some white people who cared enough to speak out against the gross injustice and, perhaps, contribute to the black movement for change.

The original deadline for the first installment of the series was March 1 for the March 17 issue of *Sepia*, which allowed him two more months to work. However, an unforeseen problem in scheduling at the magazine pushed the debut of the series back one month. The initial installment of *Journey into Shame* would hit the stands on April 17, although news of the story would become known before then in local newspaper articles and through national radio and television interviews. *Journey into Shame* ran monthly, and the final installment would be published in the September 17 issue.

Griffin's work consisted of two related projects. The first was his diary of the journey, and the second was a report on the relevant data he had accumulated. The diary was flowing well, but his attempt to make sense of the reports and statistics—all the data about "race relations"—did not progress. Little by little, he came to realize that the real story was in his diary and not in the data. He knew that his personal truth lay in the fact that he had been awakened to his own unconscious racism.

In this specific context, he was clarifying his awareness of the prejudice that had conditioned his shocking reaction to that black face in the mirror, as well as the mechanism of his denial, rationalization, and the guilt attached to this complex of emotions. He had begun to go beyond the limits of his intellectual concepts and ethical presumptions, which had deluded him into believing that he was free of racism. This act of self-criticism demanded more than clarity of thought; it also necessitated a purging of his emotions and a purification of his spirit.

On the night of January 13, he attempted to outline an ideal of sanctity toward which he believed his life and work had to be redirected. "The man in love with God," began the long entry in the *Journal*, "is assailed by satanic impulses of a depth unknown to most men." He viewed these impulses as developing parallel "in clarity and sheen as his love of God grows, until a point is reached where the two forces threaten to tear him apart." At this critical point of spiritual crisis one is forced to make a choice.

Either one succumbs to the pressure and finds a way to "balance the two forces in nice proportion, and cease all growth"—or one takes a blind leap of faith. He believed the latter to be "the beginning of sanctity; that is to say, the beginning of a higher love, which no man can know in advance of actually experiencing it."

For him, the direction toward sanctity meant that "a brute act" must be made—the act of abandoning oneself to God; otherwise, our "whole existence is haunted by an indefinable longing," which he saw as "the way of the routine practitioner of religion." The brute act, then, becomes a conscious response to the higher order and a rejection of the habitual conformity of the crowd. It is total obedience to the Divine will and a complete breaking away from self-interest and the protective concerns of the personal ego.

Five nights later, on January 18, both the act of writing and the healing solitude helped guide him through the process of clarifying, purging and purifying his entire being. He noted that it was "down to twenty degrees outside," but the work flowed despite the bitter cold. "The silence is profound, but without the loudness it sometimes has. I work, and in the background listen to recordings made in a Benedictine convent—the nuns' chanting exquisitely evoking the strict life of the cloister, its peace, its timelessness."

He was filled "with their tenderness. . . . They go all the way in it, and it is full of mystery—the mystery of the ancient rule; it touches depths that cannot be defined, but that are lost when the rule is lessened, when less is demanded of man's gift to God." He was aware of his own secular cloister and his immersion in the "mystery of the ancient rule." He knew he must demand more—not less—of himself. And again, he was alive in the contrasts.

"The music fills my studio with its ageless serenity, and I find the contrast between the moment and the work (my trip as a Negro and the cruelty of man to man) almost unbearable. I play it deliberately to remind me to love what is still so close and personal." Prior to the journey he had been concerned that his love "would not be great enough to embrace" the black people he would encounter. But he found that "familiarity brought its own love." And now—"how easily I love them as brothers and sisters." But how to find the humility to love the whites?

"My bitterness to find my own people so distorted, so full of hate, has blackened me, and it is the devil temptation. I struggle against it. I pray for the ability to love them for they are sick and their meanness is a sickness that seems almost universally shared."

He would have to heed the wisdom that many black people confided in him—especially the New Orleans elders and the old preacher in Mobile—the mercy and humility of loving one's "enemies" as fellow souls in the eyes of God. "Without loving them, I feel I cannot write properly of them as humans, but will continue to write of them as mere operatives, and therefore in giving an accurate account, will not give a wise or completely true one."

This was his "great uneasiness," aware that as he wrote, he sometimes poured "out my deep distress with my white brothers—then erasing and trying not to call names." He had just finished making the point in his book about the disparity between the way the Southern white lady appears—"so sweet, so decent, so fine—and the way she is when she turns on the vicious hate stare. . . . My greatest shock was this viciousness of the women." His view of the Southern white lady had been formed by the same cultural influences that had formed his rationalized racism. Both views needed shattering, he realized, because glorified stereotypes of womanhood were no more true than racist stereotypes of black people; together, of course, these myths had combined to create the great sexual taboo, which needed shattering also.

His lucidity carried over to January 19, and this "modality remains, the felicity lingers at midday the way it was at midnight—the chants add the patina of what is eternal, as do the views of barren trees and brown pastures, calm in the sunlight." He responded to this healing orientation as if it were a "prolonged prayer" in which "every act participates," including the clatter of typing.

Yet the work was "immensely difficult," and he had to force himself back into it, "because it must be done, but it is a violence of sorts, like forcing a compass needle away from true North and all the magnetism of its nature draws it to that polarization." His "true North" was in the direction of the eternal modality, but he could not avoid the *true South* that now forced him to revisit that troubled territory in the dimension of time.

By January 30 that time had arrived: The experiment was becoming known and he was receiving requests to do radio and television interviews. "I realize the hatred it will bring me in the South and I look on the next months with the worst possible dread. I have the deep conviction that I am on the right side—the side of justice; but it will be a dirty bath, regardless, for the opposition refuses to reason, to debate, to seek truth. They brand and hate, that is all."

Throughout February the workload grew and Griffin's pace quickened to meet its demands. The schedule for lectures and interviews was being set for April and those set for March were being confirmed. His mother and Elizabeth fielded most of these calls at their homes, while he remained out of contact in the studio. He made a two-day retreat at the Carmelite monastery at Chalk Hill south of Dallas, where he was able to regain some of the serenity of the past six weeks through prayer, meditation and the sacraments.

The next day he lectured to a group of adjustment psychologists. "I advanced the thesis of cultures, suggesting we seek those isolates that contradistinguish the culture of a handicapped person from the surrounding culture. Then I correlated this model with that of black people in contradistinction to the dominant white culture." He had observed that while blind he had been treated by the sighted as an object of pity; he had felt this same minority condition as a black man who had been treated as an object of scorn.

In both instances he had been judged by his "condition" and not as an individual. He recognized these attitudes of superiority as being based on the same unconscious cultural conditioning that placed limitations on the sightless and forced greater limitations on black people. Both experiences illustrated that the prejudiced majority had defined the minority condition, and its victims were cast into the social substrata of *otherness*. The intrinsic qualities of a person— black or sightless—were ignored in favor of the extrinsic stereotypes.

During this period, he had received a pamphlet from the Mississippi Citizens Council, "Propaganda in Our Schools," a censorship tract that had inspired several book-burnings in the Deep South. As a veteran critic of censorship, he was outraged by this endangerment of free speech and concerned about the pamphlet's racist view. P. D. East, who had forwarded it to him, sent along a laconic note: "Leave us join 'em. We'll never beat 'em."

Griffin was most galled by one line in the pamphlet. "They cited this line as contaminating: 'I am an Indian and am proud of it.' They also deplore the fact that in this same book, the compilers recommend as supplementary reading a book written by a Negro." Once again, he was struck by the contrast between the racist propaganda and the text of the music he was listening to on the record player (the lament section of the Crucifixion scene in Bach's *B-minor Mass*). "Its appropriateness chilled me. The nails were honest compared to this, and certainly cleaner," he wrote to East. He questioned the absurdity of damning the words of a Native American as "alien propaganda," wondering just "how alien can an American Indian get?" Instead of joining them (the racists), as East had suggested, he decided to forget them for the time being and return to writing.

On February 13, he wrote in the *Journal*: "The depression has left me, despair from the after-effects of the experience, from the shock of seeing kind people's cruel capabilities—and the work has flowed much better now that the shock is over."

Black Like Me picks up the "aftermath" on February 26 with the news that he has accepted an invitation to be interviewed on the Paul Coates television show aired in Hollywood. The book then skips ahead to March 14, when the first of two shows with Coates appeared on television; but several significant internal events during the "unpublished" interim were recorded in Griffin's *Journal* and letters.

He received two phone calls from Washington, D.C.—one requesting that he appear before Congress to brief its members about his findings, and a second from the Department of Justice proposing a series of lectures in April and May. These calls from the nation's capital, along with the national programs already lined up for March, made him wonder about his preparedness in the public arena.

He turned to his old friend and sometime confessor, Father J. Stanley Murphy. Father Stan, as he called him, was a professor of theology at Assumption University in Windsor, Canada, and director of the Christian Culture Series. The Basilian priest had been responsible for supplying Griffin with audio tapes during his years of blindness and was an annual visitor in the Griffin household. In a letter dated October 4, he confided to Father Stan his concerns about going public.

"My story is not sensational, it is an ethical study of an experience lived. I am in a petrifying position of having all possible communications media open to me and therefore of being capable of turning the entire history of our land at this point. Why it had to be someone so deficient, so unwise as me, I do not know." Obviously Griffin felt great anxiety about the upcoming exposure; he had never been on national television, or spoken before Congress, or lectured beyond the local level. He was also somewhat naive in his estimation that the impact of his experiment might "turn the entire history of our land" and, conversely, he underestimated his gift for communication. Perhaps his

Griffin at a book signing in California, 1962.

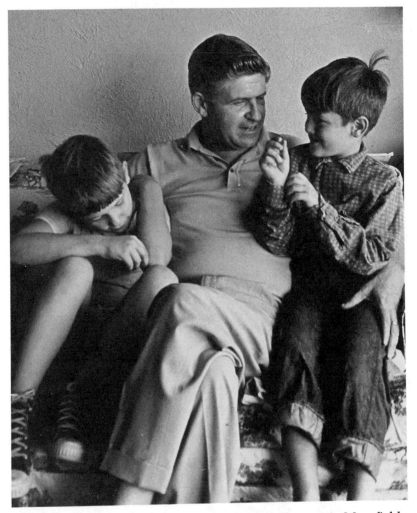

Griffin in 1965 with his two sons, Johnny and Gregory, in Mansfield.
(Photographed by Griffin with an automatic timer)

"story" was not intended to be "sensational," but the media would make it so. However, what he had to say would be controversial and his "story" would have far-reaching effects upon race relations, especially with whites.

He wrote Father Stan that his "first concern is to be a good Catholic, to speak Thomistically (as I do in my book)." He offered no explanation for the meaning of this first concern, because he knew the priest would understand. "Pray very hard for me, because it is possible that my appearances before the whole country can save lives and restore some respect for ethical values that have been tossed down the drain. This will be my plea, in any case," he concluded, "for it is something I feel profoundly, and it may communicate to the viewer. But I am sick that it had to be me and not some wise man."

But what did it mean "to be a good Catholic" and "to speak Thomistically" in Griffin's view? In the immediate context of presenting his "story" to the public, three basic realms—the experiential, the philosophical and the religious—were all involved and intimately interrelated.

First: To be absolutely honest about his experience, including the revelation of his own racism; and to clarify the fact that our racist culture has taught us to judge and condemn black people on the basis of skin color rather than on the basis of their qualities as human individuals.

Second: To articulate, in a rigorously logical manner, how white racism is irrational and illogical; and to critique the institution of segregation for its fallacious "legal" statutes (as well as the extra-legal forms of discrimination) that violate the basic human rights of black people and the ethics of Natural Law.

Third: To plea for the resurrection of justice, peace and Christian charity and the elimination of injustice, violence and hatred; to value the good of humanity over the evil of racism.

In relation to his presentations, he vowed to face criticism "without rebellion, without giving in to temptation to defend myself, to lash out." He believed himself to be an *instrument* of communication but not the *meaning* of that message. He felt, in all humility, that what he had written (or what he would say) had its only significance in the transforming quality of the message and not in the messenger. In this he followed the example of St. Thomas Aquinas, whose last words before dying were, "All I have written seems to me like so much straw compared with what I have seen and what has been revealed to me." Griffin made no claims for his words or deeds, believing that he was merely the medium God had chosen. He felt that what he had done (or might do) was "deficient" and that what he had written or said (or might write or say) was "unwise." And as for seeing himself as being courageous, he wrote: "They speak of me as a man of courage, but I sit here utterly devoid of courage, numb, waiting for the great axe of hatred to fall."

On March 12, he wrote in the *Journal* that "the news has broken." He had just returned from taping the interviews with Paul Coates. Both segments were about to be aired locally the next week. There were stories on the wires of the Associated Press and calls from *Time* and *Life* magazines and national television networks. Meanwhile, at the center of the vortex, Griffin was back in the solitude of the studio, "listening to Bach, waiting to be slaughtered, waiting to see how much they will misquote me, heartsick at what must come; though I expected it."

He prayed that the message would not be distorted. "I pray and offer up all the pain of it to God, and try to act easy around my parents, but I am in mortal fear—the hate merchants, the bigots, the racists have shown me I can expect no more mercy from them as a white man than I could as a Negro. I know I must pass through the Beatitudes—those dreaded ones of being despised, poor, degraded. I pray for charity large enough to encompass the whole thing."

But the experience "makes me mute, bludgeons my brain." He could not write or think. His "great sadness" was not what they might do to him but that "our civilization could come to this." Despite his belief that the greater evil was what happened to black people every day, he could not deny the deep fear that in the aftermath of his public disclosures his wife and children and parents might be the targets for violent reprisals. "In such a state of dread, one must return to the basic teaching—that not my will but God's be done." In his *Journal*, he poured out his concerns.

"The challenge here is to act with sanctity while the public focusses on you; and the only way to act with sanctity is not to attempt it, but to fix all your attention on God. . . . It must be done. The great 'Yes' must be said again; my own strengths must be abandoned to a point where I even appear a fool in public. If I fail to love them that hate me, then no other victory can compensate for it. I will have lost my chance, fallen short." He would not fall short or appear foolish in public, but the upcoming public controversy would exact its price and place a burden on his loved ones.

"But Lord, though my intellect understands and my will is bent in that direction, my whole being cries against it. My appetites cry for the esteem of men. And yet the deadly battle lies here, for our Carmelite manual for novices says that we must avoid the temptation to value the accepted goods of the world, in particular the ideas that it is beautiful to be praised and to be credited with this quality or that merit." In other words, he had to win the battle with his own egotism; he had to overcome the desire to be esteemed and praised for what he truly believed was the work of God—and not his own.

CONTROVERSIES

Black Like Me resumes its narrative of the aftermath on March 14. The two interviews with Paul Coates were aired on television amid heavy publicity in the Dallas–Fort Worth area newspapers. The first phone call after the telecast at the family cottage caused anxiety. Would it be an abusive call? It was not. It was their old friends from ten miles south in Midlothian, L. A. and Penn Jones. There was a long lively discussion and Griffin realized that the Joneses were tying up the line so that no abusive calls could get through. After their hour-long call was finally finished, another ring followed immediately. He hesitated but picked up the receiver. It was his parents, saying the program had been fine. "How full of dread their voices were," Griffin noticed, "but they sincerely approved of what I had said." After that, there was a long silence, and relief that there had been no abusive calls.

Griffin flew to New York the next day. There was an interview that morning with *Time* magazine and another that afternoon with TV host Dave Garroway. In between appearances he returned to the hotel room and phoned his parents. His mother had received the first threatening call—from a woman who did not give her name but did say she was from Mansfield. The conversation began politely but soon the woman became abusive and "succeeded in terrorizing my mother by telling her, 'If you could just hear what they're planning to do to him if he ever comes back.'" This concerned him, because his mother had never been confronted with that kind of brutality. He called Elizabeth, asking that she take the children over to his parents' home and give Penn Jones a call. Jones drove up from Midlothian and watched over the family until Jack Griffin returned from work. (From that night on Griffin's father kept a loaded shotgun by the front door.)

Manhattan was frenetic, exhausting. When he was not doing interviews, he was having conferences with the *Sepia* publisher and its publicist. He got little sleep, smoked more incessantly than usual, and checked with the family by phone. During the period of March 15–27, he made a television documentary with Harry Golden, stayed up one night doing a live radio interview with Long John, and did live shows on NBC and CBS. Back at the hotel the room was populated constantly with media and hangers-on, congratulating him on his appearances. He was not so sure about how he was faring; he felt that the documentary with Golden could have been stronger, but it improved as they went along. The all-night radio show featured phone calls from listeners, but because he was so exhausted he was unsure later about his responses. However, he was particularly impressed with Dave Garroway, who had told him before the NBC show went on live to be as frank and honest as possible and not to worry about sponsors or anything else.

"He kept me on camera twenty minutes and he asked pointed questions that did not evade the issue. Before the interview was over, we were both deeply moved. At the end, he asked me about discrimination in the North. I told him I was not competent to answer. I told him that the Southern racist invariably brought up the point that things aren't perfect in the North either—which is no doubt so—as though that fact justified the injustices in the South."

Griffin recognized the two glaring oversights in his report: First, he had journeyed only through the South, which meant that he had no firsthand knowledge of conditions in the North; and second, he had not been critical of the churches that practiced segregation in the South. At that time, he believed that the churches—and especially the Catholic bishops in the South—would rectify the abuses he witnessed there once they were pointed out. He had been naive about his expectations concerning the Catholic bishops, and it was a sensitive point with him—so sensitive that he vowed to walk off the set if Mike Wallace asked "one wrong question" or highlighted the issue in any way that might embarrass the Catholic church.

He was assured that the newsman would be sympathetic, but he was wary of Wallace's image as a tough inquisitor and had reservations. On the way to the station, he picked up copies of *Time*, relieved that its piece on his experiment had been at least accurate. Then he was driven by publicist Benn Hall to the CBS studios. Led into a back office, he met Wallace, who offered him a seat and a copy of the questions he intended to ask. Griffin sat but rejected the idea of reviewing the questions. As Wallace "fumbled uncomfortably for words," Griffin "took a liking to him." When he hinted that CBS had made a thorough investigation, Griffin was "aghast," because Wallace knew "many things I had tried to hide in order to protect the people involved."

"Please," I pleaded, "Don't mention those names on the air."

"Hell—I'm not going to do a damned thing to hurt them," he said. "Look—I'm on your side."

Griffin was curious how Wallace had found out such information, but the host declined to be specific. As they sat in the office, talk ebbed away, and it was clear that both men were exhausted. Wallace wanted to know how the interviews had been going and hoped to do better. He pulled out a bottle, offering Griffin a drink, but the author declined.

"Look, John—hell, I know you've done nothing but answer questions . . . but will you pull yourself together and really work for me tonight?"

"I'd do that as a matter of conscience anyway."

"You want me to tell you something," Wallace said. "I'm scared to death of you—I mean a man who'd do what you've done—"

"Then you don't know me as well as I thought you did. The truth is I'm scared to death of you."

At that, Wallace burst into laughter and insisted that he had no reason to be frightened. That cleared the air, enlivened the mood, and they felt it would go well. As the stage was prepared, Griffin noticed that Wallace smoked even more incessantly than he did. The countdown began, the red lights blinked on, and they launched into a half-hour dialogue. "He poured intelligent questions into me and kept his face close, absorbing my attention, encouraging me. It was a supercharged moment. I answered, forgetting everything except him and his questions. Fatigue disappeared. Fascination took over. The excitement sustained us. I realized, when the time was up, that it had gone well. And when we went off the air, Wallace shouted, 'Top notch.' It was an extraordinary experience. Never have I been handled more superbly by an interviewer."

Most of the aftermath entries in *Black Like Me* tend to be terse, while the unpublished passages from Griffin's *Journal* evoke the musings of a penitent. The exception to this pattern in the book is the New York scenes, which are vivid and immediate, because Griffin kept a traveling notebook and made fresh notes after each encounter.

He returned from New York on March 28 to work three days with a film crew from Radio-Television Francaise of Paris. It was not his first appearance on French TV, and there would be many more during the decade of the 1960s. Griffin, who was fluent in the language and culture of his adopted homeland, was known to French readers as the best-selling author of *The Devil Rides Outside*.

The text of the book continues the aftermath story on April 1. By that time, news had circulated globally in one form or another, and telegrams, letters and phone calls were pouring in. To Griffin's relief, most of these communications were positive, and there had been no further calls from his Mansfield neighbors. In fact, he thought that the local situation was oddly quiet.

The next morning Griffin was awakened by a phone call from a reporter with the *Fort Worth Star-Telegram*, cautiously asking the author how things were going. Griffin indicated that everything was fine as far as he knew. When the reporter said, "You don't sound too excited," the groggy author began to feel uneasy.

> "Why should I be?"
> "You mean you haven't heard?"
> "What?"
> "You were hanged in effigy from the center red-light wire downtown on Main Street this morning."
> "In Mansfield?"
> "That's right."

The reporter assured him it had happened, then asked for any comment. Griffin was sorry it had happened and told the reporter that it would only give the town a worse name. The newspaper had received an anonymous call about the effigy. When the reporter investigated the situation, the local constable confirmed that a dummy, half black and half white—with a yellow streak painted down its back—had been strung up at the intersection of Main and Broad Streets, from the town's only traffic signal at that time.

The reporter asked a barrage of questions, but Griffin's responses were subdued. When asked what he was going to do about it, he said he would ignore it. Griffin also indicated that he had no intention of taking a look at the effigy, but he did drive over to the dump where he found that the dummy had been removed and hitched to a sign that read: $25.00 FINE FOR DUMPING DEAD ANIMALS. Griffin's only comment about the dummy—which he kept off the record—was to opine that it was not a very good likeness; this was said in private to Elizabeth, and they laughed about it. And that was that.

Nothing was heard from the townspeople during that day. He viewed their silence with disappointment, wondering if they condoned the lynching. His parents and Elizabeth's mother begged the couple to take the children out of town. That evening's newspaper carried a six-column banner headline about the effigy hanging. The family received calls from the Turners and the Joneses, offering sanctuary. Decherd Turner told Griffin to bring his typewriter and current work, because he had set up an office at the Bridwell Library (of the Perkins School of Theology on the campus of Southern Methodist University in Dallas).

At first, Griffin refused the offer from his friend, but, after Turner insisted, he accepted and also agreed to lecture to the SMU student body. The family stayed one week at the Turners' home in Dallas, and Griffin's parents also left to stay with friends outside Mansfield.

On April 7, the *Star-Telegram* ran an accurate follow-up story on the effigy hanging, which also reported that a cross had been burned on the lawn of the black church just down the lane from the couple's cottage. The cross-burning incensed Griffin immensely more than the effigy hanging, because it was aimed at the black community and not at him.

The family returned to Mansfield on April 11, deciding to hide no longer. A huge stack of mail awaited them, all of it from out of town and most of it favorable. Griffin's parents returned to their home also and received several phone calls threatening their son's life. "They have terrified my mother," wrote Griffin to Father Murphy on April 12, "and the worst of it—to see those I love so forlorn before the cries for my blood." He asked the priest to "pray for the haters; this is all I know to do." He had prayed "for a sufficient love to encompass them, and it has been given me, thank God."

There is another gap in the book between April 12 and June 18. During this time frame, Griffin embarked on a lecture tour under the auspices of the Department of Defense, for whom he would file a report similar to those filed with Congress and the Department of Justice.

The first installment of *Journey into Shame* hit the newsstands nationally on April 17. Local calls increased thereafter and even more mail poured in. Elizabeth kept up with the influx of mail and Griffin's parents took their phone off the hook. He returned from the lecture circuit in early May, recording his reactions to the April issue of P. D. East's newspaper in his *Journal*. "In the South, teachers, school principals and other black people have described their indignities when they tried to register for voting; and others tell of threats, reprisals and the intimidating techniques brought against them," while at the same time in the nation's capital, "the Southern senators lied themselves bald, saying the Negroes in their states are not discriminated against."

Meanwhile, in his studio, he went on listening to Bach and wondering about "the perversity that allows men and women to show cruelty of this nature to others." On May 4, he read that the Central Texas Division of the Citizens Councils for Segregation had met in Dallas, asking for a boycott against all businesses that in any way served black people. "One wonders if these men are really of such retrograde minds that they believe this. Their attitude of white supremacy, suppression of the Negro, and deprivation of rights has given more 'aid and comfort to our communist enemies' than any single propaganda factor," he wrote in the *Journal*.

"This is the Communist's most cherished line of attack—that in America, the land of the free, a large group of citizens are not free to exercise their rights. They use this fact consistently to show the weakness of our system—and it is an immensely effective weapon they use against us, because it is true thanks to the racists. . . . What can we conclude except that the racists' concern about our playing into the Communist's hands is utterly spurious and that the racists put the national interest far below their personal and regional interests. Either they are invincibly ignorant," he concluded, "or they are the most un-American group we have—their sheets of patriotism to the contrary."

By mid-May, Griffin had delivered the completed manuscript of *Journey into Shame* to the offices of Good Publishing in Fort Worth, even though the second installment would not appear in *Sepia* until May 17. Then he returned to the lecture tour, speaking at colleges and universities and giving radio and TV interviews. According to James C. Evans, who coordinated the tours, Griffin was the most significant voice in race relations at that time; he asked him "to go on trying to create a conscience and an understanding"—especially in the white community—as long as his health held up. Griffin continued even though this period was marked by several flare-ups in his diabetic condition; undoubtedly, the hectic pace of touring, plus stress and exhaustion, had conspired to lower the level of his immune system and raise the blood pressure level.

On May 20, he took the opportunity of a brief time in the studio and a bit of good health to catch up on correspondence, writing Father Stan, Decherd Turner, and the Gillespie sisters. He thanked Turner for the chance to speak at SMU and to meet "people of that calibre" (the professors and students of the Perkins School of Theology). Then he wrote about the recent problems of P. D. East. "This is a bad day, and in truth you are the wailing wall, Decherd." He was "torn up by a letter from East, in a terrible depression." Griffin recognized in his own case that a "person cannot go on forever being despised," but that it was worse for his Mississippi colleague, because East did "not know how to 'offer it up' to God." East did not have Griffin's balm of religious training and the glory of music.

He wrote to Father Murphy that "these are the busiest days I've ever known . . . lecture four and five days a week, make tapes, films." As usual, he opened up to his long-distance confessor concerning his spiritual struggle: "I live close to the sacraments, but am not man enough to take all this. This work shows too much inhumanity, too much sadism, too much of man committing spiritual suicide." At least he felt blessed, because he could "return home to the arms of my wife and children, completely devastated, wanting to flee the whole business." In addition, he had the continued support of friends like the Joneses and the Turners. "Decherd remains a life-saver. What a wise man he is."

Yet, as he was experiencing hatred from the whites in Mansfield, he was moved by the decency of the white communities around the country to whom he lectured. "Forgive the complaining," he wrote in closing. "I am simply unable to stand this look at hell, this mammoth sin against the spirit." That night he wrote a "note in haste" to Sallie and Hannah Gillespie, beginning rather than ending with an implied apology. "It has been so long, but our life is one of extremes, always busy." He wrote of Mansfield as a place where "we are despised and every dirty harrassment they can think of is being brought to bear against us. . . . The ignorance of these people who are ruining themselves and a great segment of our white children— the unmasked evil of their intentions and desires has turned my heart sick for them."

Meanwhile, the family was making plans for a permanent escape. "Mother and Dad are selling out here and going with us to Mexico. It is the only solution—the only way to get sufficient peace to go back to my regular work." The plan was to move to a village near the city of Morelia in the State of Michoacán, where Griffin's older brother, Edgar, owned a house.

Griffin concluded his lecture tour in early June, anticipating their retreat to Mexico. By June 10, they had not departed, due to problems that had prevented the sale of his parents' property including, of course, their home and the old barn that had been his studio since 1947. This unexpected delay would be a gift, however, because it enabled him to be with his family and to work in the studio.

June 16 marked his fortieth birthday. He wrote about the day in his *Journal*. "Delicious moment when I woke up yesterday, went and got coffee and then heard from the other room my children's singing of 'Happy Birthday.' " But he decided there was too much work to be done to take the day off. He drove over to the studio and worked at turning the *Sepia* series into the book that would become *Black Like Me*. When he returned that evening, there were gifts and Elizabeth had baked a "superb" chocolate birthday cake. Since he had given himself a new Leica camera, he spent the evening taking pictures while learning the instrument.

On June 19, Emancipation Day and also Father's Day, *Black Like Me* picks up the narrative after a nine-week hiatus. He wrote that there were six thousand letters from whites in the Deep South and only nine had been abusive; he concluded that the "average Southern white" was frightened more by his white neighbors than by black people. Among the letters was a note from Curtis Bok, Justice of the Supreme Court of Pennsylvania, who enclosed a speech he had made at the Radcliffe College Commencement of 1960. Griffin thought that Justice Bok's speech "put it clearly," in his "Angry Old Man" tone, which is quoted at length in the book.

The book's coverage stops at this point and does not continue until August 14, eight weeks later. But on the night of June 19, Griffin wrote in his *Journal*: "The threat is there, just beneath the surface of existence, almost unconscious in my awareness, but always there—always there in the possibility that they could come to this studio, prowling through the woods, and see the light at my open windows. This strange awareness of my not belonging here haunts me, keeps my nerves on edge, keeps me heartsick."

He contemplated Emancipation Day, visualizing black people "dressed in their best, attending their churches for all-day sessions, celebrating their freedom from slavery, all in feeling the inside thing, knowing that they are not free after all, that they are celebrating a myth." Again he saw controversy in the contrasts, the beauty of black people thanking God against the evils of white racism, the sense of "nature contrasting its health, its magnificent peace to the troubled men, the sick men."

Then he began to focus on the question of when—or if—the threats that had been communicated in various indirect ways would be carried out. Isolated out in the country, out of earshot of neighbors and with his parents staying with friends again in Dallas, he wondered: "Is tonight the night they have decided on? Is it tonight when they come to show the rest of the world what they do to men who dare question the mob's prejudices, who suggest we are no longer Americans so long as we force a segment of our citizens to remain on the junkpile? Is tonight the night the shotgun blasts through the window? Is tonight the night they have marked on the calendar to drag me out and castrate me as they have promised?" He waited, feeling like "a perfect target," illuminated in a bright barn window and surrounded by darkness, by the climate of fear and hatred . . . but they did not appear that night.

EXILE

Nearly a month later, on July 14, the racists had yet to fulfill their promise. That night, after weeks of working alone in the studio, he stayed the evening with his family. After they had gone to sleep, he watched the Democratic convention coverage on television, staying up late enough to enjoy the nomination of Senator John F. Kennedy. "During the speeches of the Southern bloc," he noted that he had never "heard such double-talk, such delusive reasoning as was brought forth against the civil rights platforms." Then he realized that it all had a familiar ring after all. "They screamed Constitution, Bible and freedom in their demands to maintain segregation and racial discrimination"—and, as usual, "they cried for the right to be wrong."

During the next two weeks, Griffin became involved in the preparations for their departure to Mexico. As he packed up his studio, his thoughts were not on present threats or even the immediate future. "After thirteen years in this barn office, I try to sort my books—books gathered over the past twenty years of life. Strange to go back over them, to dig them outside and decide what to give, what to sell, what to keep." It was 105 degrees that afternoon, overpowering "the best efforts of an old, old fan that once cooled my Grandfather's store in South Dallas." Griffin does not mention this in his long *Journal* entry, but it was his maternal grandfather, Samuel Clements Young, who had introduced the boy to books. Every night the old man read from *The Harvard Classics*, passing them on one by one to his grandson and, finally, bequeathing him the set. He packed the set to leave with Penn Jones, editor/publisher of *The Midlothian Mirror*, for safekeeping in the newspaper office. All of Griffin's manuscripts were entrusted to Decherd Turner.

He gathered "things forgotten, things not seen in years or, again, many that I got while I was blind and never saw until I went through the storage boxes today. They range from magnificent volumes, like the *Paléographie Musicale* from Solesmes to our little two-franc school volumes of Moliére and Hugo. All represent periods of momentary enthusiasm that flared and then cooled to affection that remains to this day. Each was once held between my hands with that excitement nothing else can quite parallel. . . . The experience of taking out and examining these beautiful things becomes almost unbearable—the evocations are fresh, stripped to their essences, and the essences were good, indeed terribly good for all of it was discovery, marvel, delight."

The Gestapo had forced his first departure from France, and blindness had forced the second, in 1947, the year he had moved into the barn studio. Now he was being exiled again—this time by the local racists; or, at the very least, because the mood was too dangerous for his young children and his elderly parents. For him, this departure was the most bittersweet and no more so than on this day, because he reminisced about other worlds he had been forced to abandon.

That night he wrote a letter to Jacques Maritain, who had written him about the serious illness of the philosopher's wife, the poet Raïssa Maritain. He poured out his affections for the old friends. "Above all, know that you are not alone, that everywhere in the world you are loved. . . . How to say thank-you to two people who have (after St. Thomas) been the greatest formative influence since one's adolescence? How many others are spiritually your children in this sense? Many more than you imagine. How many others, ordinary types like myself, have taken fire thanks to you, and have worked day and night in the 'Thomist' liberation? I know of a number—and authentic ones—who have taken this lamp, lighted by you, and have gone into the shadows to illuminate, by their art or their science, the obscure corners of the world."

He also wrote Father Murphy on that night of August 4 to let him know about Maritain's "very distressing" letter. "Jacques speaks of Raïssa's falling ill in Paris; better now but with a long and dolorous convalescence ahead of her. . . . Lord, when you think what this man has given the world; what some poor beggar like myself owes him in formation, and then to be impotent to do anything to make things easier for them." He told Father Stan that he had worked "harder than ever in my life" on the two versions of his experimental journey, "and with more love and a greater feeling of desolation than ever." These would be the last letters to friends that he would type from the barn studio.

A few days later, on August 9, he made his last *Journal* entry in his "cell" of thirteen years, typing on a bare table and surrounded by sealed boxes. The first portion of his entry was a jubilant description of a sudden rain storm "after weeks of drought, all the more wondrous because nothing led us to expect it," making the "senses sing with the pleasure of being cool, of feeling energy return to dehydrated nerves and muscles."

However, after the mail had arrived that day at his parents' near-empty house, nerves were once again rubbed raw. "Dad brought the mail, with that long-suffering expression of patience on his face, of pain and anguish; another no-return-address letter, another threat, another promise. I tore it open and read it. The writer tells me 'they' have definitely set the date for August 15. 'So fuck your wife good, you half-nigger bastard,' it says, 'because after August 15 you won't have balls or peter. Your time is up. You are marked.' "

He stuffed the letter in a pocket and showed it to no one. However, his father was able to read the postcard that had arrived in the same batch of mail. Scrawled in pencil was the simple message: "August 15 is the date." At that moment, Griffin's mother walked into the room and responded to "the mournful, terrible glance" on her husband's face (even though she had not read the postcard). She blurted out: "Well, let's go *now*! Let's pack up and drive away."

Six days later, on August 13, Lena and Jack Griffin drove to Taos, New Mexico, to spend a few weeks with Sallie and Hannah Gillespie. Later they would travel on to Mexico to meet their son's family in Morelia.

On August 15, Elizabeth and the children boarded a flight to Mexico City. They were met by Robert Ellis, who had known the Griffins since 1953, and his wife, Rosa, a native of Mexico. After more than three hours in customs, a kindly clerk intervened on behalf of the Spanish-speaking Ellises and allowed the weary Texas family to pass through the gates.

Griffin stayed on alone in Mansfield, living at the family cottage. He sold the last of his parents' furniture and traded his English Ford in on a new 1960 Chevrolet Corvair. The final entries in *Black Like Me* are dated August 14 and August 17. The earlier entry makes clear Griffin's "other" reason for staying on alone—that he had waited for August 15, "until the bullies had a chance to carry out their threats against me." But that day and the next passed without incident.

The final scene of the book describes his last day at his parents' property, cleaning out their empty house. He had hired a black youth to help him, one of the sons of a neighbor he had known for several years. He was dismayed by the young man's perception that all whites hated black people, "except you, Mr. Griffin, and a few other people like the Hollands."

When the work had been completed, Griffin remained on to collect the last of his personal possessions, then drove away from his parents' property for the final time. He returned to the family cottage on the Holland farm to sleep that night.

Black Like Me closes with a warning that was to become prophetic for the 1960s. "If some spark does set the keg afire," he wrote, "it will be a senseless tragedy of ignorant against ignorant, injustice answering injustice—a holocaust that will drag down the innocent and right-thinking masses of human beings." The final words are: "Then we will pay for not having cried for justice long ago."

Early on the morning of August 18, he loaded up the little Corvair with all that he could squeeze into the passenger compartment and the trunk. Elizabeth had already taken six large suitcases that contained all their clothes. He loaded up the photographic equipment, a record player and boxes of albums, a recorder and tapes, enough cookware and utensils to begin a new life. It was his intention at that point to relocate permanently in Santa Maria del Guido, a little village on a mountainside overlooking Morelia. The plan was to remodel the old hacienda owned by his brother and to send the children to a French lycée in Morelia.

Packed to capacity—with only a tunnel between the rear-view mirror and the back windshield—he drove out of Mansfield, heading southwest. He felt a mixture of emotions that blended into a "tremendous heaviness I could not shake." He wondered how "a man should live here so long and make so little impression on it that when he left he merely vanished—as I was doing—without so much as a handshake." Obviously, he had made more than a "little impression" on the citizens of Mansfield, but it was not the sort of impression that inflates one's self-esteem!

After a hot day and 450 miles, he arrived in El Paso and laid over in a motel. The next morning Griffin drove to the border check, passed through customs, and then crossed the bridge over the Rio Grande into Mexico.

AT THE CROSSROADS

I have had a life that I loathe for these past years—I mean the public life. But I have had to go in conscience and also because I am under spiritual direction. We have had one racial crisis after another in this decade and I have been able to function in these crises, but all that time I have been away from my desk, away from my true vocation.

—John Howard Griffin

THE PUBLIC LIFE

The relati obscurity and stability of Griffin's life before he made his journey through the Deep South were shattered by the publicity surrounding the *Sepia* series and the harsh events of the aftermath in Mansfield. The exile in Mexico restored some of his creative solitude and family intimacy during the last half of 1960 and into early 1961. After nine months across the border, the family returned to Mansfield in the spring of 1961, but Griffin had not intended to remain in Texas for long. Upon their return, the family cottage on the Holland farm was occupied by renters and there was no choice except to move in with Elizabeth's mother in her large, rambling farmhouse, which was a short walk to the west of the cottage. While living several months in the home of Bess Holland, Griffin realized that returning to Mexico or moving elsewhere would be financially impossible until sufficient royalties could be earned from *Black Like Me*, which was scheduled for November publication.

Since his barn studio had gone with the sale of his parents' property, Griffin set about turning the Holland's storage shed into a new studio. The "little white house," as it was called, was a wood-frame structure with a tin roof situated far enough west of the big farm house to ensure privacy. With a loan from his parents, he remodeled the shed, which was twice the size of the old barn studio, into a work space. He installed a wood-burning stove and an air conditioner, upgrading the new studio from the bare essentials of the old. By August, the family had resettled into the cottage and the artist had completed the remodeling work.

On August 20, he received an advance copy of *Black Like Me* and noted it in his *Journal*. "The book arrived yesterday evening from Houghton Mifflin. Always a strange moment, to see one's work printed into this format, complete—a year of labor that weighs less than a pound; and yet few pounds of any substance have produced the explosion this has, the repercussions, the changes in our life and status." What he did not realize then was that the "explosion" of the *Sepia* series would be as sticks of dynamite compared to the atomic blast of *Black Like Me*.

However, throughout that autumn he relished the solitude in his new studio, working intensely on a new book he hoped would eclipse the horror of his "journey into shame" with a magnificent ode to joy. That book was *Scattered Shadows*, his spiritual autobiography about blindness and sight-recovery. He believed that it would become his most significant work of non-fiction and that it would lead him back to the writing of fiction.

In the new studio, looking out on a sunlit pasture, he wrote of his sightless years in the barn studio, the period he knew to have been the most productive as a creative writer. This was a return, also, to earlier chapters about France, about his spiritual awakening at the Abbey of Solesmes and the long, inexorable fading of eyesight. It was the story of his leap of faith, the struggle toward religious conversion, the writing of five novels and the publishing of two, the unexpected joy of marriage and children, and the miraculous gift of sight restored.

This felicity of solitude and family intimacy lingered throughout the winter, but it would melt away with the snow when spring arrived. *Black Like Me* began to stir, slowly at first, during that winter of 1961–62; but the good reviews and an effective promotional campaign sold out the first printing—and the title hit the best-seller lists and climbed near the top. Suddenly, or so it seemed to him, private life vanished in the glare of the limelight.

Griffin was flooded with interview requests and newspaper reporters, with invitations to lecture and teach, with movie offers and proposals to write for national magazines. He signed with a New York agent, a London agent to handle British rights and all translations, and with the Redpath Agency to book his lecture tours. He agreed to a paperback deal and a film contract. By the end of the year, *Black Like*

Me had been published in England and Canada to excellent reviews, and the book had been distributed in fifty-eight English-speaking countries. At the same time it had been translated into French, German, and Polish, and was well-received in Europe. (It would go on to be a two-million-copy best-seller in France, where it remains in print after thirty-five years.) Signet brought out the paperback edition in late 1962, and it would sell over five million copies during the decade.

Griffin lectured across the country the second half of that year and all through the 1960s, touring nearly three weeks each month. Basically, his lectures were a retelling of the *Black Like Me* story and, since he knew it intimately, he spoke without notes. One of his main speaking strategies was to focus on the member of each audience who appeared to be the most skeptical. If that doubting listener's expressions changed toward understanding and acceptance, he felt that the message had been communicated. Whenever black people were in attendance, he encouraged them to speak out during the discussion sessions after each lecture. Often, after he had received a standing ovation, the white members of an audience would not accept the comments of black audience members, even though they were saying essentially the same thing Griffin had presented from the podium. This pattern of white resistance and disapproval to the remarks of black people at his lectures revealed, in a new way, Griffin's observation that blacks and whites were responding from separate points of view based on wholly different sets of experience.

Griffin noticed the same pattern when he began doing crisis intervention work in many Northern cities during the mid-1960s. Often he was called in as a liaison to mediate between the black and white communities in urban areas. "I came into those meetings as what was called an 'ex-black man,' " he wrote. "It was a very peculiar role in which I was cast, a role that was enormously frustrating, because what I perceived had been a degeneration of very basic communications." This lack of communication had been clear to Griffin even before the Deep South journey—as early as his involvement in the Mansfield school desegregation crisis of 1955–56. It was a constant theme in all his writings and lectures on racism.

"I had the profound personal humiliation of sitting in the presence of the black man and the white man, realizing that almost any black man sitting at the table had to know infinitely more than I did, and express it better than I could—the kinds of things, sadly enough, that still tended to give offense to whites if a black man said them." He was plagued by the same questions asked over and over by whites, making him feel that either they did not really want to know the truth, or that they had been so thoroughly indoctrinated by the unconscious racism of white society that they were unable to perceive it. "The tragedy of this situation was that the white leaders who had brought me in (to bridge the gap between the races) nevertheless felt that they lived there and knew better and said I was being 'unduly pessimistic' . . . and then within weeks of my departure the very explosions I had warned about happened."

Crisis-intervention work, as well as lectures, also brought Griffin back to the Deep South. He became part of an underground network that included many of the high-profile leaders and activists, but also independents like himself. He deliberately did not belong to any organization and said little and wrote less about this network, until he made some of it known in his 1977 epilogue to the second edition of *Black Like Me*. "In a sense we led absurd lives in those days of terrible tension," forming "a kind of loose confederation, without organization, exchanging information, helping one another." The most dangerous areas remained in the Deep South, because the racists (and even members of the Ku Klux Klan) held positions of authority in local governments, police forces and county sheriff departments. "In one year we lost seven friends and colleagues" to murder, and "Dr. King and Dick Gregory became almost fatalistic in accepting the fact that they were dead men and that it was only a matter of time before that fact became a reality."

With characteristic humility, Griffin never referred to himself in these same terms. "They and many, many others acted with a bravery and heroism almost incomprehensible to most men. They went into areas of extreme danger." He knew that such action was "possible occasionally, but it is almost impossible to keep it up," Griffin concluded, because "the human nervous system will not stand it."

One night in Atlanta, Dr. King and Dick Gregory and Griffin made a pact. They agreed that since violent death seemed inevitable, they would ignore their fears and fight on for equal justice. Dick Gregory was assaulted and jailed several times, but he remains with us today, still witty and insightful and even wiser. Griffin was spared the jailings, and he was not called upon to make the ultimate sacrifice that Dr. King and Medgar Evers and too many others suffered. But he did experience a brutal beating at the hands of the Klan one night on a deserted dirt road in rural Mississippi. They left him for dead. He survived and recovered, but he did not speak of the incident publicly. He mentioned it only once in his *Journal*, in a long discussion about torture and violence, written December 12, 1975.

"The deepest damage to the victims of torture is not the physical pain inflicted but the sudden devastating moment when one perceives that one is at the mercy of men or societies in which mercy simply does not exist. It was particularly, though, in the studies dealing with the after-effects on the victims of torture, that I began to see the universality of these effects. . . . I remember my own torture: the beating—and it was not the physical pain that penetrated in any greatly destructive manner. What did penetrate was when I heard them say, 'Get his kidneys,' and they rolled me over and stomped the kidney area. That I have had to face in order not to be destroyed by it. I would not have been at all surprised if they had shot me or bludgeoned me to death. . . . But they went one step deeper into depravity—they deliberately and even cunningly left me to live maimed and I am sure with the idea that I would die much more slowly, but surely. The lasting damage came not from anything physical at all—it came in that moment when horror swept over me at the words, 'Get his kidneys'— not horror either (I am sure of this) for what they were doing to me, but horror that men who had 'left their humanity at home' were doing this thing, horror to be in the *presence* of such human degradation."

Griffin's *Journal* entry does not discuss the exact time and place of this event, except to clarify that it did not happen during his Deep South journey. He sensed something of this horror—this absence of mercy—in the description of the hate stare in *Black Like Me*, feeling "the sudden soul-shrivelling terror," and "realizing that there was nothing there to which you could appeal for mercy." But he had not then connected this horrible lack of mercy with the concept of torture, although those hate stares and their threat of violence erupted in his nightmares (during the actual journey and after).

Extensive travel, especially in the South, presented basic problems and risks. On several occasions he was tailed by state troopers and county deputies in officially marked vehicles along highways and bytrails through the Deep South—often all the way to the state line, where the lawmen turned and disappeared. Whenever he was followed he avoided stopping at the homes of black friends, never picked up white hitchhikers, and always adhered strictly to the traffic rules. When he checked into a hotel or motel he made every effort to change rooms upon arrival, because other activists had been discovered and beaten. He knew also not to be in the company of a woman, unless he knew her well or other friends were present, because false charges of rape had been made against activists as well. If he needed to use the telephone he went to a public booth to avoid a tapped phone in a rented room. In any case, he would speak in a form of code to avoid detection. This sort of stress was unhealthy, and it took its toll, especially upon one with an acute diabetic condition. It reminded him of the experiences in the French underground and military combat training, where he had learned to listen for and avoid danger. But the effort was nerve-wracking and exhausting.

When he was able to return home for a week each month, it took a day or two of rest to relieve the stress and to ease the sense of para-noia and anxiety. When the phone rang, which it seemed to do con-stantly, he was always jarred into asking himself: Who's that . . . what next? Yet, even with so little time and energy, Griffin managed to pro-duce a large volume of commentary on racism and censorship, religion and ethics, music and art. He wrote book reviews on race issues for *Saturday Review*; personal essays on culture for *Ramparts* (the radical Catholic magazine that twice published two chapters from *Scattered Shadows*, in 1963 and 1966); and he was also selling his photography to various print media. In addition, over eighty excerpts from *Black Like Me* were being anthologized, translated and used in educational texts.

As he continued the intense pace of lecturing and writing, his famous book was also being made into a movie; and during this same period his civil-rights work was being recognized in the media and by various awards committees. In 1963, the book was published in Italian, Dutch, and Portuguese. The following year it appeared in Norwegian and the film version premiered in New York. The black-and-white movie featured Tony-award-winning actor James Whitmore in the title role, supported by a distinguished cast of char-acter actors (Will Geer, Roscoe Lee Brown, and Richard Ward, in the role of Sterling Williams).

Unfortunately for Griffin, the production was as poor as Judith Crist said it was in her review for the *New York Herald Tribune*. The most powerful film critic at the time wrote that it "is a good-will ges-ture gone wrong—gone so far wrong in form and content, in fact, that its high purpose and noble intent are all but perverted. . . . The seri-ousness and good intent of those involved in the film cannot be denied, but the incredible mixture of sex sociology they have come up with smacks with opportunism and ineptitude." The monstrous flaw was the director's lack of vision for the material (Carl Lerner, a film editor, was making his debut as a director and co-scriptwriter)—it was confusing where the book was clear, shrill where the book was controlled, and sentimental where the book was empathetic. In an interview concurrent with the Crist review, Griffin lamented the tone of Whitmore's characterization. "He plays it angry all the way through," observed Griffin. "I couldn't behave that way when I was doing it in real life. I'd have been killed. But Whitmore became so out-raged, he couldn't control himself."

But 1964, despite the failure of the movie, ended on a successful note. Griffin was presented with the first *Pacem in Terris* Peace and

Freedom Award by the Catholic Interracial Council, shared with the late president of the United States (John F. Kennedy). Previously, the book had received the Anisfield-Wolf Award in 1962 and a citation from the National Council of Negro Women for the *Sepia* series in 1961.

Griffin's banner year, however, would be 1966, because he achieved international acclaim during a period of personal joy. Elizabeth gave birth to their fourth and final child, Amanda, and that same summer the family moved from the crowded cottage in Mansfield to a spacious rented house in Fort Worth. Their new home, which afforded him studio and darkroom space, would be their residence for the rest of Griffin's life. That same year he was awarded Canada's most important international prize, The Christian Culture Award, and his seminal essay on racism ("The Intrinsic *Other*") was read all over Europe as part of the influential anthology *Building Peace*, Father Dominique Pire's guide for avoiding war. Griffin lectured at the Nobel Peace Laureate's famed University of Peace in Huy, Belgium, where he had dialogues with the leading thinkers from Africa and Asia, who edified his work on the global patterns of racism.

The decade of the 1960s was far and away Griffin's most public period. He gave more than eleven hundred lectures; served as a bridge between various minority communities and the white power structure in thirty-two U.S. cities; and made countless secret trips to crisis areas, especially in the Deep South, without fanfare and at his own expense. His work with the media was equally prodigious, including numerous programs for National Public Radio in Washington, D.C., twenty-one documentaries for the Paris-based network of French National Television, a series of radio projects for the Canadian Broadcasting Company in Toronto, and literally hundreds of media appearances around the world.

With the exception of *The John Howard Griffin Reader*, a 588-page compendium of his fiction, non-fiction and photography, all of his published work related to the subject of racism. Even his *Reader* featured excerpts from *Black Like Me*, as well as later works on racism that developed new and controversial themes—not the least of which was Griffin's criticism of institutionalized religion.

RACIST SINS OF CHRISTIANS

Black Like Me catapulted Griffin to the crossroads of the international discourse on race, but his subsequent work stirred even greater debate. As if his critique of the segregationist ideology had not been controversial enough, his attacks on the institutionalized racism of the churches created even deeper acrimony.

He considered his own reluctance to expose the separatism and discrimination of the churches to have been one of the major limitations of *Black Like Me*. "I did not write about the churches for two reasons," he explained. "First, I was so deeply shocked to be driven away from churches that would have welcomed me any time as a white man that I did not know how to handle this and I feared I might be committing an injustice. Second, in my naiveté, I was certain that as soon as these conditions were made known to church leadership, the matter would be corrected."

But instead of stimulating any changes, he heard outright denials and dubious rationalizations from white priests and bishops. He was told that Negro Catholics, for instance, preferred their own churches, especially in the South. In other regions, where churches had been desegregated, he was told that black parishioners understood why it was best to take a pew at the back and to let the whites take communion first. The white clergy indicated that black people wanted it that way. However, when he spoke with black parishioners, they said that these practices had not been due to their preference, but that they accepted them out of respect for the churches.

Griffin discussed this issue with Thomas Merton, who was not only aware of it but was writing about it in his "Letters to a White Liberal"—which would become part of his 1964 book *Seeds of Destruction*. The Trappist monk and priest, who had admired *Black Like Me*, encouraged Griffin not to hesitate writing his critique.

Griffin responded to Merton's words as if they were a command to his personal vow of obedience and wrote an essay about the episodes left out of *Black Like Me*. It was a scathing critique of the Catholic church entitled "Racist Sins of Christians," and it was published as the August 1963 cover piece by *The Sign*, the most popular lay Catholic magazine of the day. It caused a widespread debate, but this time the stale denials and elegant rationalizations of the Catholic hierarchy were met by a wave of support from the laity and the clergy, both black and white. This led Griffin to further research and a series of conversations with black theologians, priests and nuns.

One of his conversations was with a young black priest from rural Louisiana. His outspoken "Dialogue with Father August Thompson" was published in the Christmas issue of *Ramparts*. It was a bombshell, stirring headlines like NEGRO PRIEST SAYS SEGREGATION MAKES SECOND-CLASS CITIZENS (*New York Times*), FEAR AND FAITH IN THE DEEP SOUTH (*San Francisco Chronicle*) and NEGRO PRIEST

SAYS SEGREGATED CHURCH EXISTS IN THE SOUTH (*The Catholic Messenger*). The entire dialogue was reprinted in *The National Catholic Reporter* and anthologized by Catholic book publishers.

It had been one thing for Griffin to speak out against discrimination, but Father Thompson's revelations were about an actual Southern Negro—who happened also to be a Catholic priest with a black congregation that had experienced racism and separatism from the institutional hierarchy itself. In fact, the priest's bishop attempted to suppress the publication of the interview, but Father Thompson would not be silenced; he had the support of Merton, Griffin, Jacques Maritain and others.

At one point in the published interview, Griffin asked "about claims frequently made by whites that Negroes, never having known anything else in the South, become inured to all of these undignifying things." Father Thompson retorted, "How can any man ever become accustomed to getting cheated?" Then he elaborated on this point.

"When a body is never fully fed, it never stops being hungry. It is the same with a man's spirit—it hungers, hungers after dignity, freedom and love; and it never stops hungering after these things until it is finally crushed. . . . The Negro has never become accustomed, and he will never become accustomed to being treated as less than fully a human being." Or as an American or a Catholic in the fullest sense either, he pointed out.

Griffin asked how black priests were perceived in the South. "Well, let's say that in some areas, we Negro priests might be called second-class Christs." Father Thompson's phrase stunned Griffin. "We know that we do have a profound scandal of second-class Catholics, but when it is the scandal of a 'second-class Christ' it becomes inconceivable. . . . This must burn you very, very deeply—"

"As a priest it does, because it degrades the priesthood. And that's why I try to do everything possible to right it. . . . I'm not saying either that Negro Catholics want any kind of special treatment," concluded the priest. "They feel they are getting special treatment right now, and that is the trouble. All they want is to be treated exactly the same as any other Catholic."

Six years after their dialogue, Griffin's ongoing critique of the racist sins of Christians culminated in a collaborative book, *The Church and the Black Man*, which had Father Thompson's input. "The words of a black priest," Griffin wrote, "have guided me through the preparation of this book." That guidance included Father Thompson's warning: "For the love of God, please don't make this just another white man's book about black men. We've had about all of those we can stand."

The Church and the Black Man, published by small imprint (Pflaum Press) because no establishment publisher would risk being associated with such radical views at that time, was anything but a "white man's book about black men." The large-format paperback, including many photographs, carried the unusual credit line "as seen by John Howard Griffin," in order to accentuate the visual aspect and to downplay his white authorship; and, in fact, only about 60 percent of the text pages are his. The book's intellectual discourse, then, is a confluence of voices—a few white, most black, and all radical. It charts the strategic shift between the civil-rights era of the late 1950s and early 1960s and the black liberation movement from the mid-1960s up to the time of the book's publication in 1969.

"For approximately a decade," Griffin declared, "black Americans persevered in the dream of non-violent resistance. But its success always depends on the conversion of the hostile white force. An indication of the dehumanizing character of racism on racists themselves is surely found in this failure of love and redemptive suffering to cure the wounds of racism. Non-violent resistance appeared to have failed. In fact, racists redoubled their efforts in the name of patriotism and Christianity, to suppress not only black people but all non-racists."

However, Griffin went on to record his personal feeling "that non-violence did, in fact, make profound changes in that it did touch and move many individuals; but these changes were intimate, surrounded by confusion, filled with fears of reprisals and character assassination." He felt deep regret that the racial violence and the "racist attitudes have finally driven black men to abandon many of the old dreams we shared, dreams that were good; and to embark into this period of transition that so bewilders men, but in which we are *beginning to see our first real hope.*"

Only by giving up the "dream of integration" could black thinkers move toward a philosophy that was entirely their own. This was the development of black consciousness as opposed to the "fragmented individualism" that denied black identity in the pursuit of white goals; a consciousness that transformed "black" into a sign of beauty and dignity, rather than internalizing the negative images and stereotypes. This was a return to the celebration of sisterhood and brotherhood, based on self-determination, that was turning the black community's white-imposed separation into a space of unity.

"Black thinkers—usually unknown to white America—began to structure and analyze the weaknesses of black America," Griffin pointed out, "and since their philosophical analyses conformed to their lived experience, much of it was immediately understood," and the old dream was laid to rest. This did not mean relinquishing the struggle for equal rights and justice but to perceive it as a form of political *desegregation* of cultural institutions and not as a form of social *integration* with whites. In this sense, "integration" was a misnomer, because it had always meant the melting down of diverse ethnicities into a crowd of pale mediocrity; when the rich stew was boiled too long in the "melting pot" it was reduced to a denatured gruel.

"Black Power rose to the surface at a time when this land faced a confrontation that appeared inevitably to lead to violence and to genocidal suppression of black people," wrote Griffin. But "Black Power rose, if men could only perceive it, as almost a *stroke of genius* that could avoid violence, that could turn the burning resentments and the energies they engendered, into healthful and constructive channels. Black Power, thus understood, implied not the advocacy of violence—as so many whites think—but the alternative to that kind of fruitless confrontation."

Regarding the question of violence, Griffin quoted Reverend Albert Cleage, who viewed this question as simply "irrelevant" and observed that black people "were rather weird creatures in America dedicated to non-violence in the midst of a nation as violent as America is, has been, and will be." The black theologian went on to say that "we were separate and yet we dreamed of integration and therefore did not utilize the separation to our benefit, but permitted it to be utilized for our exploitation."

Like "integration"—the phrase "black separatism" was a misnomer also. Blacks had always been separated—by whites from whites; ghettos had not been created by black people any more than segregation or slavery had been their invention.

The most common criticism of Black Power was that it amounted to a form of black racism (or reverse racism). This was a false analogy, because black people had not lynched whites or burned down white churches or blocked white voters from the polls. Racist attitudes, hate stares, epithets—from anyone to anyone else, regardless of color—are capable of causing emotional pain. But without the power to physically injure or kill another *with impunity*—as in many segregated areas of the Deep South during the 1960s, which were tacit forms of a police state—a racist attitude remains just that, an attitude and nothing more; merely an ugly personal trait but not the codified expression of a cultural institution.

The Black Power concept, like the non-violent civil-rights concept, contained inherent flaws. The quest for "black identity" was significant, but it became confined to a declaration of black solidarity against "white identity" that rendered it more rhetorical than actual. And unfortunately, the same seeds of male domination in white society were carried into the movement and black women were excluded from most leadership roles. An even deeper problem for the black liberation movement was the fact that it generated little real power, because it never gained equal footing with the entrenched white system. Perhaps, if the black leaders had been more unified in their ideologies and more organized in their strategies and tactics, greater advances might have been made.

However, any critique of the entire black liberation movement during the period from 1955 to 1975 must be viewed not as a matter of "progress"—from a white capitalist perspective—but as a process of revolutionary consciousness-raising that lighted the cause of justice within a system that had cast a supremacist shadow over the very democratic principles and religious ideals it espoused.

"What is more disedifying than a religious man with no sense of justice?" asked Griffin. "Thomas Merton says such men do not imitate Christ, they merely parody Christ." Clearly, *The Church and the Black Man* was a radical critique of those who had parodied Christ and a passionate affirmation of those who had imitated him. But white America did not see it that way, if it saw it at all.

The book achieved immediate obscurity. Reviewers either ignored it or dismissed it as Black Power rhetoric. The one major promotional chance hinged on a television appearance, a brief spot for Griffin on "The Today Show" that reached four million viewers on NBC. The response was tremendous, but not in book sales. Instead, Griffin received a massive wave of abusive phone calls and hate mail.

The only similarity between *Black Like Me* and *The Church and the Black Man* had been the volume of hate mail each had generated. And there was another sad irony: *Black Like Me* was being pulled from the shelves of small-town libraries due to the "objectionable" language it contained, and a lawsuit had been filed in Wisconsin, based on the contention that the book was "totally objectionable, obscene and perverting" when "intentionally directed to 13-year-olds."

Griffin was bewildered by the white backlash, which had also claimed that his lectures were "a deliberate, plotted plan to subvert the minds of young children" by an author whose name was associated "with persons who are communists." This was the sort of harrassment that went with the public arena, of course, and it was not new to Griffin—but he never got used to it.

Yet, Griffin held the belief that he had been called to sacrifice his artistic solitude and to obey the cause of justice. He answered that call and expected to go on answering it, despite the damage to his precarious health.

Then, in the spring of 1969, he heard a different call.

Griffin in the family cottage on Holland Farm, photographed in 1966 with a self-timer. He is in a wheelchair after surgery on his feet.

Trappist monk Thomas Merton, photographed by Griffin at the
Abbey of Gethsemani in Kentucky. After Merton's death in 1968
Griffin was asked to write his official biography. In 1969 and 1970 he
spent many months living in Merton's hermitage, where he took this
self-portrait.

LEGACIES

The violent legacy of the 1960s took a terrible toll on the American psyche, including Griffin and those friends and colleagues who had survived the senseless waste of human life. The roll call of the dead was long, too long: Martin Luther King, Jr., and Malcolm X; Medgar Evers, Vernon Dahmer and many remarkable civil-rights workers, black and white; President John F. Kennedy and Senator Robert F. Kennedy; and, of course, the horrific "body count" of Vietnam and the urban riots.

But equally painful for Griffin were the losses of Pope John XXIII, Father Gerald Vann and Father Dominique Pire, poets Raïssa Maritain and Pierre Reverdy and novelist Lillian Smith. Without question, however, the unexpected death of Thomas Merton hit him the hardest.

At the time of Merton's accidental electrocution in Bangkok, on December 10, 1968, Griffin was halfway around the world on a lecture tour of the eastern United States. He did not hear of it until the next day. He was devastated, asking why Merton and not himself. He had not expected to live longer than his friend and fellow artist, who was gone at age fifty-three. For Griffin, it had been "only with the awareness that there were people like Merton who didn't have to be out in those alleys which gave me the strength to do it; otherwise I couldn't have done it."

He would go on lecturing and writing about racism during the 1970s, but at a pace that would not and could not compare to the madness of the previous decade. America in the 1970s would move toward the repressive "law and order" stance of the Nixon administration. This had already been evident from the white backlash of the 1967 riots and the election of the Republican ticket in 1968. The discourse on race would be different in the new decade, and that was clear even before the assassination of Dr. King on April 4, 1968. The evolving struggle would be carried on by the Black Power advocates and not by white liberals.

Griffin was relieved to be able to retreat into the background, because he had great respect for the black liberation movement, and he encouraged other white activists to do the same. However, even if the political landscape had not been altered irrevocably, his failing health would have kept him on the sidelines. Because his ethical view had been clarified by the new black thinkers, and his poor health demanded a curtailment of constant traveling, Griffin was predisposed to accept the call he received—in the spring of 1969 from the Merton Legacy Trust—requesting that he become the "official" Merton biographer.

Griffin had already been a contributor to the Merton legacy when, as early as 1963, he had photographed the monk for the purpose of making an "official" portrait to be distributed by the Abbey and also to be used by publishers. During succeeding visits after 1965, when Merton had been allowed to move into a hermitage in the woods, Griffin had made a large archive of the monk in various activities and of the surrounding grounds of the hermitage and the monastery.

It was during these visits that the two artists became close friends and Merton's fascination for photography was stimulated. Griffin loaned him a camera, while Gregory Griffin, already a prodigy under his father's tutelage, took over the joyful task of processing Merton's film. This relationship through the silent, visual medium of photography—among two famous men and a remarkable boy, who were all fine artists—continued privately for several years as a creative parallel to Griffin's public existence. His last portrait of Merton was made in 1968, and the Alpa camera "loaned in perpetuity" accompanied the monk on his journey to the Far East. Many months later, in 1969, the camera was sent back to Griffin with Merton's last images intact.

From this archive of photography—Griffin's prints of the monk and his surroundings, and Merton's prints processed by Gregory—came the beautiful visual collaboration entitled *A Hidden Wholeness*, published by Houghton Mifflin in 1970. Griffin had anticipated that it would be a "silent book," but his commentary about Merton's brief artistic adventure as a photographer accompanied the images after all. As soon as the prints had been made and his text completed, Griffin sent these materials to his publisher, and he began researching the "official" biography, which had also been contracted by Houghton Mifflin.

From August of 1969 until June of 1972, Griffin lived in Merton's cinder block hermitage about one week each month, totalling 168 days. During this period he was assisted ably by Merton's secretary, Brother Patrick Hart, and edified by the many fellow monks who had known Merton over the years. He considered the work in the hermitage a joy and the solitude there to be "the highpoint of my life." Besides making notes about the voluminous research materials, Griffin also kept a daily journal. "I try to approximate Merton's schedule in my own research," he told an audience at The Thomas Merton Studies Center in 1971. "I keep a running journal of my own experiences in living and researching this material—in other words, a complete journal of the writing of this work." That complete journal has yet to be published, but a shorter version was issued posthumously as *The Hermitage Journals*—in 1981 by Andrews and McMeel in a cloth edition and reprinted as a Doubleday Image paperback in 1983. It was not Griffin's last published book, but it was the final manuscript he would send to a publisher.

The Hermitage Journals tracks a search for Thomas Merton through the materials he was studying (most significantly the monk's own private journals) and the many interviews he did with witnesses (particularly Merton's fellow monks). But even more important, Griffin recorded the impressions of being alive in the actual space of his subject, aware of the natural rhythms and simple rituals of solitude. "Since Merton perceived the connections in many diverse elements of his life," wrote Griffin, "I simply do what he did—put down everything and wait for the connections to come in their own good time. . . . The truest and deepest sense of wholeness comes when the solitude itself is truest and deepest, when you are emptied of all the junk of self and simply function as a part of nature and silence and odors and feelings, at your own natural rhythms of spirit and body, with nothing to distract you from a sense of union with what Merton called 'the Christ of silences.' Tom made the point again and again in his journals that he did not come into this solitude and silence of hermit life *seeking* but rather he came here because this is where he believed Christ wanted to find him."

By the time of his seventh visit, in February of 1970, Griffin realized that he had come to that solitude just as Merton had. Each arrived not to find the fulfillment of some literal preconceived plan of hermiticism or, least of all, to discover the "self"—but simply to be alive and open. "I am openmouthed with bewilderment that God should flood me with such fine gifts, and I utter prayers of thanksgiving for Tom for being the instrument that brought me here to be where Christ obviously wanted to find me, in the silence of these woods, at this time."

He compared his journal in the hermitage to the journal he had kept as a disguised black man. This "is the happiest work I have ever done in my life, the most satisfying, the deepest adventure. *Black Like Me* was crushing and depressing as lived experience. *Hermit Like Me*"—the humorous name he called his journal—"is enthralling as a lived adventure . . . nourishing in the most robust and jubilant way; overwhelming in its graces."

Griffin also clarified what his journal in the hermitage was not. It was not some false reincarnation of Thomas Merton, "because we are vastly different men, though similar in our love of the silence and solitude." Several years later, in an interview, Griffin reiterated this point by telling Thurston Smith this story: "When I was doing the biography of Thomas Merton, a student who was writing a doctoral thesis on him said: 'Before I start, I want to tell you I want to be exactly like Merton.' I said, 'Then you don't understand anything about Merton, because Merton would have tried to help you be exactly like yourself.' Love does not possess but frees the other to be what he or she really is."

The Hermitage Journals was a return to Griffin's solitary path, which he had been called to sacrifice on the physical plane at the crossroads of public crisis. But those 168 days and nights in Merton's hermitage had been the deepest solitude he had known. "Here one was alone without the slightest sense of loneliness, and the longer it lasted the more profound grew the felicity, the sense of freedom, the faith, the loving. . . . And yet I wondered how could one find such solitude in the world for a sufficiently long period to learn what it had to teach. . . . The creator and all of creation are one's constant companions, day and night, in all one's occupations. Living in that solitude, I often thought of Cassian's 'We pray best when we are no longer aware of praying.' "

During that three-year period when Griffin made eighteen retreats to the hermitage, he also traveled around Kentucky to interview Merton friends. There were several other research trips—to New York and New England in 1969 and to Prades, France, in 1970. Everywhere he traveled doing research he photographed the places and the people Merton had known.

By mid-1971, Griffin's advance for the "official" biography had been spent. Besides the support for a family of six, there had been more medical bills and travel expenses than he had anticipated. He began then to accept some of the lecture invitations he had been refusing. He instructed his agency to advertise the new lectures with the following remarks: "I'm a firm believer in Black Power, as I believe any man who wants the good of the total community must be. It is a tragedy that non-violence didn't work. The black man was trying to cure his white brother with it, but the white man wouldn't be cured. Non-violent resistance has done more than we realize, though. I think history will show that it accomplished an enormous thing in men's souls. It didn't fail, it just didn't complete the job. Black Power is a progression from it. It's the black's assertion of his humanity, and it requires us to confront one another as equals."

In June of 1972, he made his final visit to Gethsemani, which is the last entry in the published version of *The Hermitage Journals* (on the feast day of St. John the Baptist). "My feast day, and never was a day more glorious—absolutely still, sunlit, cool." He was reminded of lines from Merton's translation of the Chinese Zen master, Chuang Tzu: "When the shoe fits, the foot is forgotten; when the belt fits, the belly is forgotten." The sage's words caught the morning and Griffin's sense of oneness with it. "It is like that here this morning with everything—everything fits, and the *self* is forgotten."

However, when Griffin returned home, the *self* was remembered once again with the news of Robert Casadesus's death. Contemplating the death of his musical mentor and friend of thirty years, Griffin wrote: "I stood there with the phone in my hand, full of the most terrible anguish over the loss." He felt "a terrible sense of my own weakness and vulnerability . . . and of the deaths of that whole group who were so profoundly involved in my life: Merton, Reverdy, Casadesus, Gerald Vann, Dominique Pire; and how Jacques [Maritain] and I remain, and Jacques barely in life; and I felt the greatest confrontation with the death of my existence, as though the grave were stalking me in the deaths of these friends."

The published version of *The Hermitage Journals* ends with this excerpt written in Fort Worth, but Griffin would make a nineteenth retreat to the hermitage in 1972. In the unpublished *Journal* entry of October 2, he reflected at dawn. "I am aware that at home my wife and children sleep still in their rooms and that the greater part of me is there with them. But you cannot divide up parts like that, because more than 'just the remainder' is here with me in this forest, in the profound felicity of this silence, this solitude, these early morning hours. . . . I pray 'without praying' for my family and friends in these hours when nothing seems rushed, particularly this morning for those who have died this year—Robert and Jean Cassadesus, Saul Alinsky, P. D. East, because in this place and time, everything is open and you do not have to dole out this and that in the way of affections, love, prayers. . . . Here, those things that are merely 'time consuming' are no longer so—they enter into the whole and become other dimensions of the same freedom."

But such periods of wholeness, felicity and freedom would be rare for Griffin throughout the remainder of life. Never again would he experience that kind of expansive solitude or sustained creative energy. He had done more in those three years than he would be able to do in the eight years left to him. And all this had been accomplished despite several surgeries to save his feet from amputation and a series of operations to reconstruct his jaw. This had necessitated many months in bed or in a wheelchair and also the growing of a beard to cover the facial scars.

By the end of 1972, his salt and pepper beard was full and neatly trimmed. For the first time—at age fifty-two—he looked older than his years; all his life he had appeared younger (and healthier than he really had been). The specific disease was osteomyelitis, an inflammation and eventual deterioration of the bone marrow, which was insidiously common in severe diabetics. It would continue to ravage him internally, so that either constant pain or heavy sedation would thereafter be his alternating conditions of consciousness.

On April 28, 1973, he received news that "our beloved Jacques is dead." He recalled what one of Maritain's closest friends had told him in

1947. "Pierre Reverdy, the great French poet who first introduced me to Jacques, warned me that they would all die and leave me alone; and they all did—and now none are left." However, he was able to console himself with the thought that his youngest child, Amanda, was one of Maritain's godchildren. "Odd, I realize that the feelings I had for Jacques, particularly in the later years, were identical to those I have for Mandy: a kind of very pure tenderness without any impediments, conditions or restrictions, a tenderness that seeks nothing but simply exists as a privilege to the heart ... this is what has erased death in Jacques' case, filling me with such peace instead of the grief I anticipated."

Throughout the next month he worked on a large archive he had made of the French philosopher, photographic images that would become part of Maritain's legacy. He made notes about their long friendship and recalled a conversation with his old mentor that he had not written about. He had told Maritain that he had been "obedient to you insofar as my actions have consistently been the incarnation of your thought," which Griffin believed to be the work of the Holy Spirit in Maritain. Then "I explained that such a vow permitted me to function in a way that helped me overcome my cowardice," he told the astonished philosopher. *Black Like Me* had been possible, he insisted, only because "I could act under obedience without ever thinking of the consequences in a way I could never bring myself to act from any other motive, that even love of truth and justice, love of humanity, could not overcome my cowardice." This particular conversation was kept private in Griffin's *Journal*, but what he did reveal about his friendship with Maritain would become part of a book published in late 1974 entitled *Jacques Maritain: Homage in Words and Pictures.*

During the fall and winter of 1973, Griffin endured the pain of efforts to keep the osteomyelitis in check, the constant interruptions that were always a constant of a large household, and his futile attempts to pay the bills. Finally, in the spring of 1974, he reentered the public arena, joining the staff of *Sepia* as an editor and feature writer. The job afforded a decent income, but it also meant traveling again, so the collapsible wheelchair became part of his baggage. He made several trips to the Deep South, updating the magazine's continuous coverage of changing race relations.

After eight months at *Sepia*, some financial relief came in the form of several grants, and he was able to leave the daily editorial work and return to the Merton biography. He continued to write historical pieces about the civil-rights era for the magazine, signed on for several lectures on Merton, and taught classes at Loretto Heights, as he had done every year, in exchange for Susan's education at the Catholic college in Denver.

In March of 1975, he made a series of tapes with John Reeves, covering his life as artist and activist. Griffin's words, along with readings of his books by actors, were combined masterfully into a five-part radio program that aired many times over the Canadian Broadcasting Company and, later, throughout the states over National Public Radio affiliates. It was the most comprehensive "oral history" ever done on Griffin, and it would be his final collaboration with John Reeves.

By April of that year the grant money had run out, but Griffin managed to stay afloat by doing lectures on Merton (and racism) and writing articles for *Sepia*. He wrote two excellent historical pieces about the murder of Vernon Dahmer and the assassination of Malcolm X, tying the 1965 killings to later events—the release of the KKK members who had burned down Dahmer's home and the recent books about the plot to eliminate Malcolm X. He also wrote about the current situation in race relations for European readers; in his editorial for the Dominique Pire Foundation, he was critical of the "benign neglect" of the Nixon administration.

"With the 'law and order' politics of Nixon, we soon became aware that almost all of the programs for inner city help were to be killed," he wrote, citing the impounding of funds "to sabotage the inner city special schools, the scholarship funds for American Indians and a great many other programs that had given minority people hope. Few realize that one of the reasons for the eruption at Wounded Knee was the cut-off of 22 million dollars in scholarship funds."

Griffin also became part of the most controversial debate of the mid-1970s—what he called academic racism—in which white scholars claimed that black people were genetically inferior. His piece was about Dr. William Shockley, a Nobel Prize winner in the field of physics, who tried to solicit the author's help in recruiting blacks to submit to blood tests and intelligence exams in order to "prove" a racist premise. Griffin refused to cooperate with the scientist because, as he wrote in a letter, "you are expressing highly inflammatory unproved theories that can result in overwhelming grief to too many people . . . also, you have made a historical error in comparing your situation to the silencing of scientists in Nazi Germany. I heard them. No scientist advocating theories of racial superiority were ever silenced by the Nazis. It was those who protested against such theories who were silenced."

Griffin would revisit this debate—from the early exposure to Nazi anti-Semitism to the recent exchanges with the scientists during the 1970s—in an upcoming project proposed by a young editor at Macmillan. David Reuther invited Griffin to write a personal overview of racism as a book for young adults. Griffin agreed to the idea because he was impressed with the job Reuther had done on the young-adult biography of Thomas Merton, written by his friends Cornelia and Irving Sussman. However, he could take on the project only if an advance upon signing could be made in time to relieve the financial stress he felt once again in late 1975.

An agreement was reached, and he began work on the project that would become his most comprehensive book on racism, *A Time to Be Human*, published in the spring of 1977. He would dedicate the book to Roland Hayes, the great black tenor whom he had photographed and interviewed for *Sepia*, and he would take his title from Merton's translation of Chuang Tzu's words that would be the book's epigraph. Griffin chose the ancient sage's lines because they sounded so aptly modern: "When men do not get twisted and maimed beyond recognition, when they are allowed to live—the purpose of government is achieved. . . . From the time of the Three Dynasties men have been running in all directions. How can they find time to be human?"

The ancient sage was not only modern, he was universal. What could be more "twisted" than racism, and who could have been more "maimed" than the victims of racism, both black and white?

A VERY LONG DYING

By the spring of 1976, Griffin was well into the new manuscript, working steadily until his father's heart condition worsened in early April. Jack Griffin died on April 13 of cardiopulmonary arrest due to congestive heart failure, just a few months before his eighty-second birthday; his son would die the same way, but he would be only sixty. "He died mercifully at 3:15 last Tuesday, in his sleep," wrote Griffin about his father. A week later, he noted that "things gradually come nearer normal, though I am still obsessed almost constantly by Dad's death."

By the time he traveled to a writers' conference in Minnesota in July, Griffin had a completed first draft. He began revising the text and did not stop until it was finished and off to the publisher on September 8. He had to write a brief preface and submit his photographs before collecting a second check. By October, everything was done and he was amazed that "God had given me the energy to do it."

From October 20 to November 20, he went on an extended tour of lectures, speaking in Detroit and Rochester, as well as in three Canadian cities. At the airport in Montreal, he experienced severe chest pains but traveled on to Rochester to end the tour. He became more congested but did the lecture and finally arrived home in "terrible shape," according to his own account.

His regular physician, Dr. Ross Kyger, put him through a complete examination and a battery of tests. Diagnosis: Griffin had endured a severe heart attack and permanent damage had been done. Prognosis: The next attack would likely be his last unless he remained bedridden, with constant observation and an immediate rush to the hospital at the first sign of trouble. Incredibly, he would live almost four more years under this prognosis and endure many more attacks and several surgeries.

The most absurd contrast—between the public's perception of Griffin, as the author of *Black Like Me* and the courageous crusader against racism, and his own private reality as a virtual shut-in being cared for by family and friends—could not have been greater and more evident than it was in 1977.

The famous public personality was a subject for *Newsweek's* "Update" column in February; *A Time to Be Human* received favorable reviews as a "sequel to *Black Like Me* for children" in *Publishers Weekly* (February) and *The New York Times Book Review* (April); and the second edition of *Black Like Me*, which included his epilogue about race relations since the publication of his classic, received glowing and even reverent reviews in the big-city dailies around the country. In addition, several positive reviews about both new books, considered together as the "then and now" statements on racism in America—for white adults especially—spread the news. Both books, published and promoted by establishment imprints like Macmillan and Houghton Mifflin, created the impression of a major publishing event.

To some degree this was true, for not many authors had two cloth editions in one season published by mainstream companies—plus excellent reviews for both and a media call for interviews and author profiles. Certainly Griffin was not as "popular" or as "famous" or as "controversial" in 1977 as he had been in the 1960s. But *Black Like Me*, in its mass-market paperback edition from Signet, was still being taught in public school systems and in university classes, was continually kept in stock by bookstores, and was promoted from time to time in positive ways (Griffin's lecture tours with their attendant publicity) and in negative ways also by news of book-bannings and censorship campaigns throughout the 1960s and into the 1970s. Without question, Griffin was not anonymous to the American public and his controversial best-seller was remembered by millions (and being read by a new generation).

All the elements for a commercial success were put in motion and, much more significantly, the intrinsic ethical value of Griffin's perceptive assessment in "What's Happened since *Black Like Me*" (his epilogue to the second edition) and the coherent and lucid analysis of his personal experiences with prejudice in *A Time to Be Human* were capable of stimulating thoughtful dialogue. Together these two testaments constituted a serious and insightful "summing up" of his views on racism, as well as being a meaningful historical overview of 1959 through 1976 in the area of race relations in America and beyond.

What was missing in all of this, of course, was the physical public presence of the author himself. Griffin was too ill to travel cross-country, even in the most superficial promotional manner; and, of course, resuming his lecture tours, at any level, was impossible. He was under doctor's orders not to leave the house, to avoid all visitors (besides family and a select group of friends, who were with him strictly to care for his physical and spiritual needs), and to turn over phone call answering and correspondence to others.

He was permitted to write and read, to partake of the sacraments, to be with loved ones for brief periods only. He continued listening to music, watched an occasional television program, and typed or wrote in his *Journal*. Every attempt at writing new pages of the biography, or even revising earlier drafts, left him exhausted and utterly frustrated. He turned away completely from the world outside his intimate circle, refused all public overtures, and did not want to know how the "new" books—which he considered part of his old life—were faring with reviewers and book buyers. He turned the family budget, which had always caused him great anxiety, over to Elizabeth. She handled everything she had always handled and everything else as well—the household, the children, the business of his "career" and the immediacy of his daily needs; she screened visitors and phone calls and mail. When she was overburdened, the children pitched in, friends came to her aid, and Griffin's mother helped. Father Curtsinger brought Griffin communion almost every day. When Father McKillop was in town, he served as Griffin's confessor, offered Mass and communion; when he was back in Canada he kept in close telephone contact. Griffin became deeply dependent upon everyone and, even though he fought against that dependency, he had no other choice but to accept it.

For him that year was quite literally "the dark night of the soul"— his most extended period of excruciating physical pain, emotional torment and spiritual doubt. He suffered numerous brushes with death and thought he would not live out the year. There were several congestive heart failures, a mild stroke, and losses of consciousness. For a time he lost the use of his right hand and all sensation in his legs; his hearing was permanently impaired and the feet would not heal.

Even as early as January 13, 1977, he wrote that "the congestive heart failure has left the heart permanently damaged. . . . Everything is working against everything else (diabetes, osteomyelitis, arteriosclerosis, etc.). And now the immediate danger is high blood pressure, which increases the danger of stroke or heart attack. I have to be very cautious, must have stress and tension minimized."

On January 31, Father McKillop "got me through as complete a general confession as anyone could ever make. It took us three days!" On March 16: "Another terrible attack—myocardial infarction, and I have been virtually dead to everything, all feeling (except anguish), all life, all mind." July 10: "I force myself to make these notes. Never have I felt closer to death. I have no feeling in my legs or arms, and inside only a feeling of desolation and waste—except for a spark of love that glows, but even that seems almost out—no, not out, just buried in this extreme physical attrition. . . . I listen for the beloved, and hear no voice. That is part of this condition—waiting, waiting. . . . I say Yes and offer this up."

During 1977, he managed to type seventy-three pages in the *Journal*—pages illuminating the depths of guilt and the stratospheres of innocence, revealing a tremendous will to live and love coupled with lapses into despair and thoughts of suicide. It was a record of the intense experience of dying amid doubts that such a record had any value. "How poorly I express myself in all of these things. I throw down these notes to clarify them for myself. It is distressing now, because before I could tell myself—'Someday I'll go back and straighten all this out—express it clearly' and now I know I never will."

In the summer of 1978, after many delays and revised plans, the Merton Legacy Trust and Houghton Mifflin demanded that he return his materials from the biography project so that they could be handed over to a new "official" biographer. After nearly a decade of work, he had been unable to complete it. "This has been almost an unendurable burden over me in these last two years of growing helplessness," he wrote on July 17. "I will not be able to work any more, and have finally decided that it is no longer reasonable for me to hold up this work. I have outlived the prognosis but that cannot last much longer—the degeneration is steady and, except for moments of reprieve, I cannot bear the continued responsibility for anything to do with a work so massive."

In this long letter to Cornelia and Irving Sussman, he made it clear that he had reached the point of accepting the reality. "I have no inclination to grieve over this. It is transparently God's will. Even though it may seem an inexplicable waste in human terms, I am no longer able to feel it is. . . . Nothing is lost as far as I am concerned except the satisfaction of having completed a work of my heart. I am confident that if it was not meant for me to do this work to the end, then it will be done better by someone else. It is not a question of giving up, but of recognizing the truth as it is."

Thereafter, he would concentrate only on his *Journal*, typing intermittently, with long periods of silence. His notes for 1978 and 1979 amounted to about sixty pages, a mixture of simple observations and a few profound insights. In 1979, one of his legs was amputated and the other was in danger of being lost. He received holy communion every day from Father Curtsinger, and, when Father McKillop visited him, he would make brief confessions to his Canadian friend.

In 1980, he gave up typing but continued to make notes in longhand. "It has been a period of learning about weakness . . . and losing that clutter about any strength. Those are illusions on which we build our lives. In the long testing, they vanish and you learn to count on mercy." Mercy, in the sense of the *caritas*, would be his central theme—as it had been for years in connection with other themes— until it became his only fascination. "And once all the illusions are gone, when soul, mind, body are stripped of them, then mercy comes in abundance though it is often difficult to perceive except in the actions of friends. A new kind of truth, as bare as your weakness, comes in the voices of friends, and in their actions; it comes in things that surface and that you are allowed to glimpse."

Finally, mercifully, Griffin's earthly life ended on September 9, 1980. Elizabeth, who knew intimately the medical terms for what plagued her husband, told the media that "he died of everything."

During that long dying Griffin never experienced a mystical vision of eternal bliss. His moments were lived on the human plane, expressed in the subtle nuances of compassionate voices and in the merciful gestures of healing hands. His place was there, there in the painful body cared for by loved ones; but it was also here, here in the silence where Christ found him.

CRITICAL PERSPECTIVES

I think the main theme of my work centers around this prison of cultural formation that almost always leads a man of one culture to believe that he is intrinsically different from men of other cultures. And profoundly different, he believes, and therefore superior in his aspirations, needs, responses to stimuli. This is one of the most difficult problems involved in racism. We tend to think that the victim group somehow likes it that way; that its members respond to frustration, for instance, in a manner totally different from us. And along with this goes that other tendency to view members of all other cultures as merely underdeveloped versions of ourselves. I think we have to struggle to grant every person the maximum amount of freedom and so I loathe every kind of totalitarianism. I loathe anything that impugns the intrinsic right of every human being to fulfill his or her potential. There is no such thing as an inherent right to impugn someone else's rights; and it is an utter distortion to claim the freedom to deny someone else's freedom. This attempt to gobble everyone up, to make everyone conform to our individual or group prejudices, our religious or philosophical convictions— and seeking to suppress them if they do not—is the deepest cultural neurosis I know.

—John Howard Griffin

TEXT AND CONTEXT

The text of *Black Like Me* includes several episodes that had not appeared in the magazine series, *Journey into Shame*; these episodes, as well as the crucial scenes in both texts, were expanded and reshaped into a style that was more novelistic rather than journalistic.

Also, Griffin cut or edited down some of the more polemic portions from the *Sepia* articles when he developed the series into the book.

Black Like Me was completed during Griffin's period of exile in Mexico. The book had the benefit of being written in a relaxed context—at both a geographic distance from the tension of Mansfield and at a psychological distance from the stress of the journey and its aftermath. Griffin did not have the time constraints of a harsh deadline, and, of course, he had established that the book would be in the form of a journal.

The manuscript was shipped to Houghton Mifflin from Mexico in December of 1960. The contract was signed on May 7, 1961, and the cloth edition was published in the autumn of that year (November 1961). To Griffin's surprise, the first edition went through several press runs and sold nearly 100,000 copies. "I thought, and my publishers agreed," Griffin remarked, "that this would be an obscure work, of interest primarily to sociologists." Instead, it became a moderate bestseller in cloth and stirred debate in literary and academic circles.

The first-person narrative in the form of a journal was Griffin's most natural mode. He was a dedicated journal-keeper and, from 1950 until his death in 1980, his *Journal* totaled more than three thousand single-spaced typed pages. His two published novels, *The Devil Rides Outside* and *Nuni*, were composed as first-person journals also; the only difference was that the novels were written in present tense while *Black Like Me* was written in the past tense. In addition, many of his short stories and personal essays took this same first-person journal form.

However, as we know, *Black Like Me*, was not originally conceived as a journal but as a sociological study. "This began as a scientific research study of the Negro in the South," writes Griffin in the Preface to *Black Like Me*, "with careful compilation of data for analysis." But he put aside the data and wrote the journal of his own experiences. "I offer it in all its crudity and rawness. It traces the changes that occur to heart and body and intelligence when a so-called first-class citizen is cast on the junkheap of second-class citizenship."

His editor at Houghton Mifflin suggested that he cut this last paragraph of the Preface because it was too harsh, but he chose to let it stand. According to Gerta Kennedy's notes on the original typescript, it is one of the few suggestions he did not heed; in nearly all other cases, he had agreed with her and had made cuts or revisions in accordance with her excellent comments.

He was unwilling to cut this last paragraph or soften its harsh tone, because he believed that it expressed honestly the experiential truth of his journey. He faced this issue in the opening sentence of the Preface—although he concludes the second sentence with a flash of defiance. "This may not be all of it. It may not cover all the questions, but it is what it is like to be a Negro in a land where we keep the Negro down."

Clearly, the author was including himself in this indictment. But who else deserves inclusion in this collective "we" of his accusation? Many whites did not consider the book to be a true account of a Negro, but only the confused impressions of a white man playacting. "Some Whites will say this is not really it. They will say this is the white man's experience as a Negro in the South, not the Negro's."

Griffin had anticipated that some whites would doubt the validity of his findings without even reading the book. This had happened when the news of the *Sepia* series had outraged some white citizens of Mansfield before the first installment appeared in print. He dismissed this objection in advance: "But this is picayunish, and we no longer have time to atomize principles and beg the question. We fill too many gutters while we argue unimportant points and confuse issues." He had taken the risk of alienating potential readers by challenging them not to prejudge his book or to reject the authenticity of his experience out of hand. Rather, he encouraged everyone to focus on the essential issue.

"The real story is the universal one of men who destroy the souls and bodies of other men (and in the process destroy themselves) for reasons neither really understands. It is the story of the persecuted, the defrauded, the feared and detested." This universal story of persecution—man's inhumanity to man—has been told in countless variations by every culture in all historical epochs—right up to the present.

"I could have been a Jew in Germany, a Mexican in a number of states, or a member of any 'inferior' group," he insisted. "Only the details would have differed. The story would be the same." *Black Like Me* is, of course, the historical record of what it was like to be a Negro in the Deep South prior to the civil-rights era of the 1960s. It is also an intensely lived experience, evoked by the immediacy of his vital, vivid prose, that has kept open a window on that historical time and place.

Griffin's odyssey lasted a total of six weeks, from the evening of his arrival in New Orleans on November 1, 1959, until the day of his departure on December 15. Of the journey's forty-two days, Griffin was in disguise a total of twenty-eight days, plus those days he alternated between identities.

The famous photographic record by Don Rutledge of the Black Star Agency documents only the re-enactment phase of the experiment. There were no photographs of the "Negro Griffin" at the beginning or during the middle of the journey, when his pigment was darker and when he was bald. These sharp black-and-white images by Rutledge reveal the author with less than an inch of hair (rather than bald), appearing as if the "burr" haircut was intended (instead of having been the result of several weeks of returning growth).

A BRIDGE OF DIALOGUE

The reviews of the Houghton Mifflin cloth edition, which were overwhelmingly favorable, boosted a slow-selling title in late 1961 toward best-seller status by the spring of 1962, when it was published in Great Britain by Collins. Cyril Connolly, writing in *The Sunday Times of London*, was impressed by the controversial and original nature of the book. "Some actions are so absolutely simple and right that they amount to genius. It was an act of genius on the part of Mr. Griffin to decide to dye his skin and live as a Negro. Why did nobody think of it before?"

None of the American reviewers called Griffin a genius, but some were equally laudatory. "With this book," said *Newsweek*, "Griffin easily takes rank as probably the country's most venturesome student of race relations. It is a piercing and memorable document." *Publishers Weekly* called it a "shocker" and declared that "this book will generate emotion."

The Saturday Review of Literature considered it "a moving and troubling book written by an accomplished novelist. It is a scathing indictment of our society." (In 1962, that magazine gave Griffin its annual Anisfield-Wolf Award "for dealing most creditably with social and group relations.")

One of the most thoughtful responses came from Ralph J. Gleason, who wrote in *The San Francisco Chronicle* that "as a basic text for study of this great contemporary social problem, *Black Like Me* is essential reading. The existence of a whole sub-culture, a whole separate and unequal world is demonstrated. The unbelievable concern with sexuality of the ordinary Southern white is related with grim reality. The daily terror of being black in a white and hostile society is graphically revealed. . . . It is a social document of the first order, providing material absolutely unavailable elsewhere with such authenticity that it cannot be dismissed."

"This fully detailed journal of this odyssey," wrote Dan Wakefield in *The New York Times Book Review*, is "a brief, unsettling, and essential document of contemporary American life." Wakefield was one of the few reviewers to point out the significance of Griffin's bold decision to publish his journal instead of the data he had accumulated. "The courage and intelligence of that decision—one which runs counter to the current style—resulted in one of the few books that do more than take us across the familiar and arid landscape of generalizations and statistics, but convey the feel, sight, sound, and sweat of what the abstractly titled 'Negro problem' is all about." Like Gleason, he had considered the book to be "essential" to "contemporary" understanding of race relations.

John McManis, writing in *The Detroit News*, echoed Wakefield's point about publishing the journal rather than the data: "The book is gentle in tone, but it is more powerful and compelling than a sociological report, more penetrating than most scientific studies."

The New York Herald Tribune declared that the "new book may serve as a corrective to the blindness of many of his countrymen." In general, the New York print media, as well as the major newspapers north of the Mason-Dixon line, tended to laud the book because it reflected racism in the South. Behind this response was the attitude that the South was deeply trapped in the disgrace of segregation, violent racism, and a residual slavery mentality, while the cities of the North tended to be more liberated. This was before Dr. King went North, but it was *not* before the early essays of James Baldwin or the angry speeches of Malcolm X.

Then how was *Black Like Me* received by the print media in the South?

The reviews were mixed, and the overall discourse varied widely from state to state. For instance, the book got excellent to rave reviews in the big-city dailies in Texas, but Griffin's home state had not been on the map of his Journey. (The obvious exception was the aftermath portion about Mansfield, site of the effigy hanging, as well as the school desegregation crisis in 1956.) The tone of these metropolitan newspapers was similar to the northern press: "Shame on the Deep South, but it can't happen here!" This was true even for the Fort Worth and Dallas papers—both cities less than thirty miles north of Mansfield—which interpreted those events as if Mansfield were part of the Deep South and not North Texas.

East of the Lone Star State the response was less than enthusiastic. Except for the heavy coverage in *The Atlanta Journal-Constitution*, no other reviews appeared in the state of Georgia. Very little word came out of Louisiana and Florida, and the entire press corps of Alabama and Mississippi ignored the book completely. (The only exception in Mississippi was P. D. East's review in his own Hattiesburg-based broadsheet, *The Petal Paper*, which he reprinted from the pages of the Midwest magazine *The Progressive*.)

Under the headline ATLANTA PRAISED / RACIAL INSIGHT PROBES DEEPLY, Ed Hughes wrote a rave review of the book and the city in *The Atlanta Journal-Constitution*. "His story is one of the deepest—perhaps too deep for some—penetrating documents yet set down on the racial question," declared Hughes. "This account gives an insight into Negro culture than cannot but jar the firmest preconceived notions." As a basic affirmation of Griffin's insights—primarily for the edification of white readers and from the author's viewpoint as a disguised "Negro"—Hughes's statements seem harmonious. But his next statement strikes a dissonant note: "It gives Negroes a view of their own shortcomings, and in what direction eventual hope lies." Suddenly, his first two sentences take on a different meaning, as if *Black Like Me* constituted a critique of Southern blacks rather than an anatomy of white racism. Basically, Griffin had made two criticisms of black people in the book: first, that the black community in New Orleans lacked unity, and, second, that some blacks seemed to be motivated by self-hatred (in particular, the sad figure of Christophe on the bus, fawning over the whites and castigating fellow blacks). The first criticism was hardly a revelation to the black elders in New Orleans, who agreed with the author. To some degree, Griffin found that lack of unity throughout the journey, yet believed that Atlanta's black community had forged just such a necessary unity. His discovery that there existed a hierarchy of color in black culture wherein the lighter the skin the more honorific the status, that the more one acted "white" the better, and that many blacks seemed to believe the mythical claims of white superiority was not news in the black community.

In other words, Griffin's observations about black behavior were illuminating to white reviewers and readers but obvious to black thinkers of that period. It might have been "too deep for some" (like white racists and moderate white book reviewers in Atlanta) but perhaps somewhat superficial to contemporary intellectuals in the black community.

"Atlanta has gone far in proving 'the problem' can be solved," Griffin wrote in *Black Like Me*, believing initially that Atlanta was "showing us the way to do it." Hughes's review paraphrased Griffin: "Atlanta's hope, he says, comes from Negro unity, from the quality of Negro leaders in education and business, from the enlightened leadership of Mayor Harsfield and from Ralph McGill."

Griffin had been complimentary toward the mayor and toward McGill, the publisher of the Atlanta newspapers; but he discovered the greatest hope and placed the most emphasis on the remarkable accomplishments of the city's black leadership. When, a few years later, McGill declared that victory had been won in Atlanta, Griffin and the black leaders of the city were appalled at the publisher's naive and highly self-congratulatory declaration. In addition, McGill had been an avowed enemy of Dr. Martin Luther King, Jr., and his Southern Christian Leadership Conference (whose home base was in Atlanta); he had not given any credit for the "victory" to King but instead had published stories about the communist infiltration of the SCLC based on false reports fed to his paper by the FBI.

However, at the time of Griffin's visit to Atlanta in 1959, McGill's animosity for King had not yet surfaced. In addition, we must remember that Griffin was not in black disguise during his days in Atlanta, so he did not experience conditions firsthand; also, the black leaders with whom he spoke (King was not one of them) tended to accentuate the tolerance of the white establishment and the unity and progress of the black community. Thus, his impression of Atlanta in the book lacks the deeper insights of earlier experiences (as a disguised Negro) in other Southern locales and, also, the edification he would receive from King, Dick Gregory, and other black leaders a few years later. For the moment, Atlanta was seen as the progressive model of the New South.

Dorothy Johnson, however, offered an immediate challenge to the South, including "enlightened Atlanta." Writing in the monthly publication of the Southern Conference Education Fund, *The Southern Patriot*, she reviewed the book from the organization's central office in New Orleans. "This book should be required reading for all segregationists and moderates," she began, "and even for those who think victory is almost won." Johnson wrote that the book "is hard to lay down, and as you read you become terribly ashamed of your white skin. . . . I beg you to read this book as soon as you can and to urge everyone else to do so. If this does not move the hearts of those who have denied dignity to human beings, it is hard to believe anything will."

Several other reviewers were impressed with the book, but all expressed the most common criticism made by whites. "Could he really 'know' what it was like to be a Negro?" asked Dave Branch in the *St. Petersburg Times*. Branch doubted it, but did not doubt that Griffin "could know what it meant to walk two miles for a glass of water that he could have gotten in any drugstore when he was white." It was at this level of inconvenience that most white reviewers identified with Griffin (and, by association, with blacks). But these inconveniences merely marked the surface of inequality, as Griffin remarked many times; and the response of Southern reviewers seemed to hold the book at this same level. However, Branch closed by saying that the "book is about simple justice. It suggests that any white man who thinks the Negro in the South is secure and contented should try being one."

Dorothy Miller was certain about the question of the author's "Negroness" in her review for *The New South* magazine. "No white person can know what it is really like, day in and day out, childhood on up, to be a Negro, just from taking one short journey." And "more than that," came the criticism usually associated with a white's impossibility of being black, "Griffin can escape, and does. . . . Can the real Negro escape?"

Miller's critique had turned on Griffin's prefatory dismissal that "some whites will say this is not really it. They will say this is a white man's experience as a Negro in the South, not the Negro's." She found it "difficult to dismiss this objection as easily as Griffin does" and insisted that the book " *is* the story of 'a white man's experience as a Negro' " —but not the actual reality of a black person—"because Griffin, no matter what his color outside, is a white man inside, with all the white man's conditioning and experience."

It is a complex point that revealed the defensiveness of both author and reviewer. Objectively Miller was correct; however, she overemphasized her point to the detriment of the book's central issues and, in particular, white racism. Of course, by having dismissed the expected criticism in his Preface, Griffin had overstated his claim of having experienced black reality. To the extent that his temporary change of skin had been the sole impetus for the discriminatory treatment he had received, Griffin had, indeed, experienced something very much like the daily reality of black people—at least in a measure that was beyond the ken of any other white person.

It is, perhaps, ironic that the first publication of Griffin's experiment appeared in a monthly magazine edited by a black staff and published primarily for a black readership (*Sepia*'s circulation was 61,975 in 1960). Certainly the series *Journey into Shame* was not lost on its readers, whose letters were positive in the sense that they appreciated that a white man would speak out from such a unique perspective and that his "discoveries" conformed closely to their daily knowledge. However, several black readers—as well as Griffin himself—expressed their perplexity that the series was listed under the genre of "Adventure" on the contents page. The author was embarrassed by the text on himself also, which described him as "truly a bold and fearless man behind his modest exterior."

There was one friendly notice published in *The Cleveland Plain Dealer* about the *Sepia* series by Rey L. Gillespie, the only black journalist to comment. But as for the black press, there was no word on the series and only one brief review of the book in *Negro Digest*.

The unnamed reviewer responded to the book in succinct and lucid terms. "It is impossible for a white man to truly know the anguish, the degradation, the sense of frustration and despair which gnaw at the soul of the Negro in America," wrote the black journalist. "Empathy, however sharp or genuine or sincere, cannot put a white man in the Negro's place for, deep down, the white man understands that he is free and the rules governing the Negro's life simply do not apply to him." The review was not intended as a rejection of *Black Like Me*, because the writer went on to say that it was "an appalling report of man's inhumanity—institutionalized and sanctioned—to his fellow man. And, while it can only succeed in approximating the horror of the Negro's situation, the book should be must reading for all whites and for those numerous Negroes who like to pretend all's right with the world."

This brief commentary made emphatic a point that had been argued or implied in several reviews by white southerners—that no white man can know truly what it means to be a black man. This anonymous black writer, then, verified from his own experience that *Black Like Me* could "only succeed in approximating the horror of the Negro's situation."

Griffin never responded to the review in *Negro Digest*—either in print or in his *Journal*—although a photocopy of the brief commentary had been forwarded to him by his publisher. Griffin made no recorded comment about the remarks of Malcolm X either, but he had read his autobiography and wrote a piece about Malcolm for *Sepia*. (In *The Autobiography of Malcolm X*, during his pilgrimage to Mecca, Malcolm had edified several Muslims who had read *Black Like Me* and exclaimed that it had been "a frightening experience." Malcolm had replied: "Well, if it was a frightening experience for him as nothing but a make-believe Negro for sixty days—then you think about what *real* Negroes in America have gone through for 400 years.")

Griffin realized that skin color alone could not magically open a door to the deeper recesses of black reality. However, having experienced the journey at the human level—rather than merely at the political or sociological levels—he believed that his suffering from the effects of racism, however brief in duration, was exactly like that of black people in all its human essentials. He continued to lecture and to characterize his experience as "when I was a Negro," and, a few years later, to call himself an "ex-black man." He considered these issues secondary. The important thing was to communicate the reality of white racism and its discrimination of black people on the basis of color. This public position was integral to reaching a large audience that tended to be white, educated, and of the middle or upper economic classes; and, since 70 percent of his listeners were students, they had some training in dialogue. Thus, he began to reach the ears of fair-minded whites in a way that opened a new bridge of dialogue between the black voices he had heard and the white community.

His Deep South journey had confirmed what he had learned during the Mansfield school desegregation crisis, and this was further confirmed by his travels in the North. "My long stays in the inner cities convinced me again that this was a land with two groups of people possessing two entirely different sets of information and experience. The majority did not know, had no idea, what was going on in the minority communities. They viewed everything from the outside and from their own perspective." Griffin brought whites a new perspective, and the student population responded more openly than did the older white audiences. He found that the younger whites were courageous enough to listen, to really listen to a different view in the spirit of honest disagreement and thoughtful reflection.

Griffin communicated the simple truth of fraternal dialogue—that monologues merely separate, that only dialogue can unite; that monologues are deafened by their own cacophony of contradictions, while dialogue harmonized the common connections; that monologues prompted blame and denial, but dialogue awakened healthy self-criticism.

Naturally, most of his lectures were attended by black people as well as whites, and the university audiences usually included a larger proportion of black students and professors than did his church and civic lectures. Increasingly, blacks would approach him after a lecture to say that what they had heard sounded as if "a black man were speaking out of a white man's mouth." His response was to say that he preferred to be thought of as "simply a human being," and to remind them that he was *not* a spokesman for black people or anyone else except himself.

"Whites have sometimes argued that I felt this degradation more deeply than black people because it was new to me, whereas black people had known nothing else all their lives." He believed this argument to be based not on real experience but on one's projection of stereotypes. "This is utterly untrue," Griffin declared, for prejudice "burns any man, and no person ever gets accustomed to it that it does not burn." It had burned all the black people he had observed, spoken with, or befriended. And just as he had seen what racism did to black people, he had seen what anti-Semitism had done to the Jews during World War II. Of course, having merely witnessed what had happened in Europe when he was a young man had not affected him as profoundly as what he had experienced with his change of skin color. "Such whites say it the way they have *seen* it," he clarified in contrast to the fact that "I say it in the way I have *experienced* it."

He observed a similar pattern in all prejudice, whether racism or anti-Semitism, the superior attitude of the sighted toward him during his sightlessness, or even in the censors who had branded his work as pornographic or communist-inspired. It had always been the pattern of the ignorant condemning anyone or any group because it did not match the so-called norm of the majority. In terms of white racism, he argued that "I can explain why they can say that"—that blacks are intrinsically different and inferior—"and why I can say I never met a black who fit the stereotype insofar as authentic ethnic characteristics are concerned. White people have always said: 'We'll treat black people right as long as they stay in their place.' But if you pinned whites down on this point, most could not say what that 'place' is, but every black person knows—it is squarely in the middle of the stereotype. Whites created the stereotype to justify their racism and then forced black people to act out the stereotype."

Before the *Black Like Me* experience, Griffin held many of the same stereotypes to be true without questioning their inherent logical fallacies, believing blacks "led essentially the same kind of lives we whites know, with certain inconveniences caused by discrimination and prejudice." His deepest shock came with the gradual realization that it was not a matter of inconvenience but rather a matter of a total change in living. "Everything is different. Everything changes. As soon as I got into areas where I had contact with white people I realized that I was no longer regarded as a human individual. In our experiences as whites, whenever we meet a stranger, an aura of mystery exists between us until the stranger discovers what kind of a person we are and until we discover what kind of a person that stranger is." One's sense of a stranger in this instance—the scene of two white people meeting—suggests the possibility of discovery, for the unknown is not threatening or alien but a matter of casual socialization.

However, "when a person is imprisoned in the stereotype others hold of him, that aura of mystery is wiped away," and a simple encounter becomes fraught with tension. Instead of a white person perceiving a black person merely as a person, "all of white society looked at black people, saw the pigment, and immediately attributed to all the characteristics of the stereotype."

Jacques Maritain and John Howard Griffin in 1966. (Photograph taken by Griffin with self-timer.)

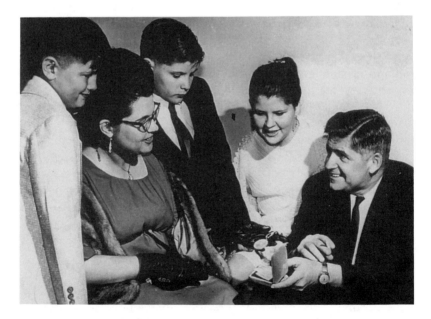

Griffin family admiring father's medal, awarded by the Christian Culture Series of Canada.

Griffin in Toronto during his seminars for the Thomas Merton
Institute in 1976.

Griffin at the Festival of Life Conference in Ottawa, Canada, 1977.

"Surely one of the strangest experiences a person can have is suddenly to step out into the streets," wrote Griffin, "and find that the entire white society is convinced that an individual possesses qualities and characteristics which that person knows he does *not* possess." He was not referring to the fact that he appeared to be a Negro to whites when he was in disguise; rather, he was saying that anyone who is viewed as a stereotype rather than as an individual must feel this strangeness, regardless of how often it happens. "I am not speaking here only of myself," he pointed out. "This is the mind-twisting experience of every black person I know." But until Griffin had created his disguise, he had not realized how perplexing this sense of being perceived as a one-dimensional stereotype instead of as a multi-dimensional person could be. Of course, what is strangest of all, is that such stereotyping persists.

Ultimately, all questions about the authenticity of *Black Like Me*—like the questions about his motivations for attempting to become a Negro—cannot be "answered" in any definitive way; complex subjectivity cannot be distilled to a precise point of objectivity.

Yes, he was a white man in disguise, and, yes, beneath that appearance of blackness dwelled a privileged member of Southern society deeply conditioned by the mythology of race. But Griffin was not an ordinary Southern white male, or his crossing the line would have been in search of fantasy rather than truth.

Yes, he was a "make-believe Negro," but what happened to him was not fiction. Most significantly, how he responded to what happened—to what was done to him and to those black people he encountered—awakened him and changed his life.

Yes, *Black Like Me* only approximates "the horror of the Negro's situation," and it is true that we "cannot put a white man in a Negro's place for, deep down, the white man understands that he is free," pointed out the reviewer in *Negro Digest*, "and the rules governing the Negro's life simply do not apply to him."

Yes, Griffin could escape—and did. But could he have escaped the pursuit of the two bullies in New Orleans, or would it have been wise to push aside the bus driver's arm that kept the black passengers from the restroom facilities at the bus stop in Mississippi? Could he have escaped by saying, "Hey, time out now, I'm only playacting, I'm really white like you!" to that white driver of the bus?

While being chased by the bullies in New Orleans, was his terror "make-believe" or would it have been real only if he had been an actual black man? His fear was real because it was human fear. When he backed down from the threat of that bus driver, was he feeling fake fear and contrived humiliation or were his feelings exactly like those of the black passengers? Yes, he could escape *eventually*, but not by becoming white in an instant.

Stokely Carmichael, the civil-rights activist and early proponent of Black Power, once remarked that *Black Like Me* was "an excellent book—*for whites*." Griffin could not have missed this comment, because it was printed in bold type (and in English) on the back cover of the Swedish edition of *Black Like Me*. But he never took issue with such comments during the 1960s and 1970s because he agreed with that assessment.

However, a generation later, during the mid-1980s, and certainly now, thirty-five years after the book's original publication, that opinion is incorrect. It is wrong because today's readers of *Black Like Me*—most of whom are students in grades six through high school—have no direct knowledge of racism or segregation as it was experienced in the 1960s, regardless of their ethnicity. There has been voluminous testimony over the years—from students and educators both black and white—attesting to the fact that the book opened their minds to the evil of racism and evoked compassion in their hearts for fellow human beings.

A UNIQUE POINT OF VIEW

Griffin's unique point of view in *Black Like Me*—initiated by his encounter with the "stranger in the mirror"—evolved slowly through subsequent experiences, both external and internal, until he developed a compelling double perspective by the time he began alternating black and white identities in Montgomery. The first shock of seeing something more than a disguise—of confronting an image radically *Other* than expected—caused him to recoil from that glaring face and to declare that he "did not like the way he looked." Suddenly, the man in the mirror is a stranger to himself, for he "could feel no companionship with this new person," and the "Griffin that was had become invisible."

But even in the midst of shock and confusion, Griffin was able to step back and to glimpse a paradoxical reality: "I became two men, the observing one and the one who panicked." In this scene we hear the voice of the *observer* describing the panic of the *observed;* or the *white* mind perceiving, by way of mirror reflection, the *black* body of appearance. This first glimpse of the "black stranger" marks the inception of a liberating point of view, a unique double perspective, that he would later clarify and refine in its application. At this point, however, it was yet a game played with a mirror and a disguise, only a two-dimensional image perceived by a three-dimensional eye. But Griffin had taken the first step.

The second step was to enter into a process of purgation, a prolonged suffering beyond shock and denial. He had to learn to observe, with critical detachment, each stage of healing—through fear and anger, despair and guilt—until the wound of his racism could be understood objectively. The "self" had to be forgotten, along with any concern for white "identity" and all of the privileges it afforded. Generally this would be a lifelong process, but in Griffin's situation the healing was accelerated by his becoming "a man born old at midnight into a new life."

The healing process and the adaptations of his dual point of view to existence as a black man were parallel experiences, which are reflected in the subsequent encounters with the mirror throughout the book. This classic literary device reflects his state of mind as he moves from denial toward acceptance of the man in the mirror. We see his wound healing as he interacts with black people, who accept him as a human being, while simultaneously we see his perspective sharpen as he endures the inhumane treatment of most (though not all) whites, who react to his skin color only.

The reactions of whites vary from outright hatred to degrading paternalism to total indifference. Instead of rationalizing the behavior of his fellow whites, he is appalled by their moral degradation and merciless cruelty; but he learns to take their punishment as a way of understanding how black people feel and also to experience the racist mentality from the other side, so that he might analyze it.

Griffin's six-week journey, although brief compared to a lifetime, was exactly six weeks longer than any other white person had experienced. His change of skin enabled him to experience aspects of black reality that no white person, including himself before New Orleans, could have imagined.

He learned to observe—with reasonable objectivity—the behavior of whites in reaction to his appearance, as if his "blackness" were absolute proof of inherent inferiority, immorality, laziness and every other stereotype about black people with which whites are inculcated. He witnessed this racist syndrome with a sense of detachment and a depth of insight he had not known previously.

He listened to black people, who expressed their inner thoughts and feelings without fear of reprisal, because they had accepted him as a black man into their community. What he was privileged to hear, no white person would have been trusted to hear. And what he learned about black reality, beyond the obvious inconveniences he had expected, was that "blackness was not a color but a lived experience."

Most significantly, he faced his own racism and accepted the scrutiny of his own harsh self-criticism in order to deprogram his prejudices. He accepted also the painful purgation of his shame in order to cleanse his spirit.

The book's complexity of vantage points and intersecting realms— black and white, intrinsic and extrinsic, subjective and objective, intellectual and emotional, physical and spiritual—combined to transform a limited scientific experiment into a dynamic personal witness. Through his creative act of insight, *Black Like Me* transcended the conventional limits of cultural perception and opened a fresh vision of human rights.

Black Like Me, as he said in his Preface—"traces the changes that occur to heart and body and intelligence" of a black man living under the power of white racism. But what he did not say directly, although it is implied in the overall spirit of the work, was that his experiment was inspired by religious ideals and pushed forward by his vow of obedience to those ideals. His journal of heart and body and intelligence was also a journal of a soul.

THE SPIRITUAL DIMENSION

Black Like Me was rarely spoken of in religious or spiritual terms, because Griffin—even in such a nakedly personal document—kept his vows private. Yet he lived it as a spiritual quest, and that was exactly how Jacques Maritain responded to it. "I want to tell you of my profound admiration for what you have done," wrote the philosopher in a 1961 letter to Griffin, "and my joy that you have accomplished an action so great, which is a magnificent expression of love, and which will have a sure and beneficial effect on souls." The philosopher's letter had a beneficial effect on Griffin's soul, because Maritain had been one of his guides in the area of human rights.

In an interview with Thomas P. McDonnell, published in the January 1963 issue of *Ramparts*, Griffin revealed that his experiment had been done "without Maritain's knowledge but at his inspiration and at Aquinas's (after reading St. Thomas on justice and Maritain on racism)." In particular, he had been struck by Maritain's statement "that all that can save us is a return of authentic charity and metaphysics, and that some must be prepared to be martyrs for the love of humanity."

Griffin's experiment had tested his faith and vows as a devout Roman Catholic just as profoundly as it had tested the validity of his simple premise. "The book was a nightmare to me," Griffin confessed, but the response to the book had been a great surprise. "I have never received so much mail on a book. Out of some six thousand letters from Southern whites alone, only nine have been abusive; most have said they *wished* they could do something, but fear reprisals." But even "more astonishing have been the letters from many of the world's great and famous thinkers, altogether unsolicited," he told the interviewer.

While he expected the book to stir controversy in some academic circles, he was not expecting a significant public response. "I knew that the work posed a serious problem for ethicists, but I felt the problem was infinitely less important than the problem I wanted to discover: What it is like to be a Negro under discrimination and what it does to the soul of a man." The academic discourse focused on the ethical questions but the public was taken by the exposed hypocrisy of Southern gentility. To the academics it was controversial and to general readers it was sensational. But what about the spiritual dimension? What does discrimination do "to the soul of a man"? Only one writer explored this realm of *Black Like Me* when it was published.

Cornelia Jessey Sussman's essay "The Penitente" appeared in the pages of an obscure but excellent Catholic magazine, *WAY of Saint Francis*, in 1962. Griffin had never heard of the magazine or the essayist, and he did not read the piece until she sent him a copy of the magazine, in 1963. He wrote to her immediately, beginning the letter: "Dear Cornelia," and saying up front: "We may as well start with first names, because I sense this will be a friendship of long duration." He was right. She and her husband, Irving Sussman (also a writer for the magazine), became two of his dearest friends and his most voluminous correspondents during the 1970s.

Griffin insisted that he had made it a habit not to read "anything at all about myself, especially critical writings. . . . So that solves all of that mess, and I urgently recommend the same detachment to you and all other writers." But he had read her piece, because the title attracted him and tnere was nothing in the design to indicate that it was about him or *Black Like Me*. "I was not at all sure what it was about; it sounded familiar and then suddenly electrifyingly so. But dear Lord, how beautifully you write. Here was someone who understood at great depth what this was all about. And I read and was overwhelmed both by your understanding and the beauty of your writing."

"The Penitente" does not mention *Black Like Me* until the final page, and Griffin's name does not appear in the text at all; readers were directed by an asterisk after the book's title to a footnote at the end of the piece. To have been a footnote to an essay about himself delighted him, because he often said he preferred to be an anonymous author, sighting the unknown composers of the Middle Ages, whose names were not attached to the great masterpieces of Gregorian Chant, as his ultimate ideal of selflessness. In fact, Griffin's first published story, "The Big-Time Stockman," which appeared in the February 1952 issue of *Southern Agriculturist* some eight months before the publication of *The Devil Rides Outside*, was credited to "Lew Smollett" (one of several Griffin pseudonyms).

With *Black Like Me* he became anything but anonymous, of course. But "The Penitente" focused its attention on the work and not the man; or, more precisely, the essay was about the spiritual dimension of the penitent. "It is hard to 'have religion'—to put on Christ, to bear the Truth, carry it, fall under it, get up and go on wearing it until you are marked by it forever; and it is imprinted on your body. . . . And no gentler, easier ways were open to him for the learning to love Christ in the habit of a dark skin. Maybe there is no easier way? For anybody?—does the black man have to love his brother in the habit of a white skin, have to carry the white cross until he is imprinted, this, too?"

Cornelia Jessey Sussman recognized the selfless feature of Griffin's experiment, but, more important, she understood the necessity of suffering. "In New Mexico long ago," she concluded, "a traveler might see on the Northern mesas at Easter a man offering himself to be nailed to the cross; sometimes this Penitente died. To put on Christ, to wear the Truth, is *that* hard. Not social or economic problems to be analyzed, not even a matter of human rights is involved in this act— but *only suffering as a mystery of love*, to be lived, identified with, something anyone can do without medication. One Southern penitent went the whole way, white, like me."

It is clear why Griffin was moved by the insight and beauty of her essay and, to this day, no response to *Black Like Me* has been imbued with such poetic elegance and spiritual perception.

The only other response to *Black Like Me* that has explored the spiritual nature of the book was published nearly twenty years after "The Penitente"—in *Sojourners*, in 1981—and, unlike the earlier essay, readers have the opportunity to read it, since it remains in print as part of *Cloud of Witnesses*, a remarkable anthology available from Orbis Books. The essay in question, "A Life of Radical Empathy" by Robert Ellsberg, traces the religious path of Griffin's life and major works briefly but comprehensively. His remarks about *Black Like Me* are incisive.

"Griffin's gesture was a radical effort at human empathy. Even after twenty years it retains its power, for, in spite of its subsequent publicity, it is a gesture which has been rarely, if ever, imitated." Since *Black Like Me*, there have been a few parallel experiments, but none has had the impact of the original. In every other case, the well-meaning imitators have paid homage to Griffin, but none has matched the great risk or profundity of the modern classic. The only subsequent experiment to approach it was the 1969 book *Soul Sister* by Grace Halsell; its primary significance is that the author, a white Southerner also, was the only woman to attempt such a risk; and, unlike Griffin's book, *Soul Sister* travels North as well as South.

Ellsberg does not mention Halsell but does give us a penetrating commentary on Griffin. "*Black Like Me* is a profoundly radical book, and at the same time it is deeply spiritual. Its concern goes beyond a particular set of social/political/economic conditions to the underlying disease of the soul. It is a meditation on the effects of dehumanization, both for the persecuted and the persecutors themselves—sadly, a universal story, and one that is a long, long way from a conclusion." There is no sense that Ellsberg's essay minimizes the conditions of the book's actual historical context, but that the "disease of the soul" goes deeper than segregation in the 1960s or the social/political/economic context of 1981—right up to our day, because this soul-damage has persisted unchanged over time.

"Griffin changed nothing but the color of his skin—and that was everything. Suddenly doors closed, smiles became indignant frowns, or worse. . . . It is not only the burden of poverty, violence, and humiliation that blacks must bear; it is the knowledge, the terrible knowledge of the possibilities for evil in the human heart. What must such knowledge do to a person's soul?"

Griffin was no stranger to the evils of the human heart, which were borne in on him during his youthful days in France under the Nazi occupation. He witnessed not only the destruction of bodies but the damage done to souls. In a magnificent letter to novelist Lillian Smith, he recounted a story related to his underground activities, about his efforts to give medical treatment to soldiers wounded in the war. "Often, by three or four in the morning," he wrote on December 20, 1961, "runners would come for us, and we would stagger to the railroad to dress the wounds of soldiers returned from the front—almost every night under the black-out lights of the railroad station we would work for an hour or two bathing, bandaging, feeding the shattered bodies of the Senegalese troops being used for cannon fodder by the French."

The medics crawled in and out of cattle cars where the wounded soldiers lay on straw, providing them with the dry bread and red wine that were the only available sustenance. He saw in the bodies of those black soldiers—obviously considered as expendable to the French as the Jews were to the Nazis—what he had seen in the sad faces of the Jewish parents who turned over their children to him with the hope that he could take them to safety. What he saw, in the context of war, were the victims of prejudice, whose eyes had perceived the evil in human hearts—an evil not only capable of murder but devoid of mercy.

But Griffin had seen something else also, and it had come as a personal revelation. "I witnessed the Christ in each of those mangled and stinking black bodies; one saw them for an hour and never again, and one had to open one's heart to a tremendous abandonment of love for them or else die of disgust and terror—there was no halfway about it, no nice balance or sanity or fastidiousness," continued the long letter.

"There in the torn bellies was the total wisdom of theology—the wisdom of charity in the old sense of *caritas*; empathy, love of the thing, holiness in the universality of pain felt and pain allayed and the gratitude or hate (it made no difference) that shone from these eyes of strangers as we probed them for shrapnel and hurt them to help them and handled their bodies as one does a baby's."

It was in this "universality of pain" (of war, racism, dying) that he perceived the "wisdom of charity"—in this case as the consoler, the young medic—whereas later he would experience, in his prolonged periods of physical pain, the blessing of charity from others. This is what mattered—not the "niceties of choice, the inanities of meaningless little cut-and-dried arguments, the intellectualizing of all these things—this is what haunted the rest of my life."

He had been haunted both by the merciless cruelty and the selfless charity that were counterpoints in memory. He had seen the terrible soul-damage in the eyes of those Senegalese soldiers and those Jewish parents, but also the caring tenderness in the eyes of the medics he worked with and the freedom fighters he joined in the underground, whose souls were damaged too. He had seen it in the expressions of fellow soldiers and native villagers under siege in the Pacific war. And when he was blind those eyes appeared in his darkness until, finally, as he lost all visual images, they disappeared as eyes but left scars on his memory.

This haunting returned in dreams and reappeared in the eyes of the black people he encountered on the Deep South journey. He recognized that soul-damage in his own eyes, too, reflected in those mirrors. "That is what I could not tell in *Black Like Me*," he confessed to Lillian Smith, "but what permeated this whole experience. I was reliving what I had once before lived. . . . The racist mentality, this horror—this is what was behind *Black Like Me*."

He trusted the novelist, because he knew her work to be both painful in its sense of loss and its supreme mercy. "Rather like you, I suspect, my reasoning was to follow, *Fides quaerens intellectum*, as a search for understanding after the horrible alternatives of love or no-love had been thrown full into my consciousness and burned there forever. And I saw all of this, as you saw it, in its final resonances, in the racism of the South's demagogues"—characterized by Smith in her autobiographical book about her native South *(Killers of the Dream)*.

Griffin realized, as he believed she had realized, that it was necessary to be critical of the South—and "that even a tiny and tasteless cry was better than no cry at all."

Killers of the Dream and *Black Like Me* were anything but tiny or tasteless cries. Rather, they were the prophetic voices of two first-rate novelists with Georgia roots, who cared more for humanity, and particularly about the lives of black people in the Deep South, than any other white Southerner before or since. Reviewing Smith's book when it was reissued in 1962, Griffin wrote: "Twelve years ago, with prophetic vision, she wrote *Killers of the Dream*, a book about the South and segregation. In it she showed that those who embraced the strangely shallow dream of white supremacy were killers of the greater American dream of a society based on freedom, equality and justice. Now the book has been updated and it has no warmed-over-hash character, largely because of the superb vitality and validity of the original; also because it is a highly original work of art, distilled, concentrated, terrible, and beautiful."

Smith's autobiography of growing up in a prosperous white family of the Old South tradition contained all the elements of a magnolia gothic—except for one dissonant note. The intelligent girl began to question those who had "so gravely taught me to split my body from my mind and both from my 'soul,' taught me also to split my conscience from my acts and Christianity from southern tradition."

"Most of all," commented Griffin, they taught her that a "Southern White Woman is Sacred—a sacred reality who must be protected from the lion that raged beneath the thin layer of domestication nurtured in the Black by the White." In her re-creation of the traditional experience, Smith ripped away the false white veil of separation. "She cut through the layers of falsity and arrived at the inevitable conclusion," observed Griffin, that "the Southern White Woman was not the *only* sacred reality," for "every human creature was a *res sacra.*" And once she saw that the consequence of treating any person as less than a sacred reality gave evil limitless power over good, she was terrified. "Are we," she asked, as "the nation that first embarked on the high adventure of making a world fit for human beings to live in— about to destroy ourselves because we have killed our dream?"

In the updated version of her book, Smith answered her own question. "Time has run out: we must right now adjust ourselves to the speed and quality of world events, world moods, world psychology or face probable extinction as a free nation." Smith had observed the white side of the racial coin tarnished by "our demagogues at home and in Congress wailing about mixing and mongrelizing . . . and still giving communism credit for every brave, intelligent, decent act done by a southerner."

Like Griffin, Smith had been branded a traitor to her race, because she had turned up the black side of the coin to the light and attempted to clean the white side of its slime. But the white racists wanted to keep the black side down, wanted to keep the white dream as a nightmare for black people; they had no interest in self-cleansing and no courage for awakening. For them, the American Dream was a one-sided coin and, if it was not pure white, they had the commies and the niggers and the traitors to blame.

But that was not Lillian's dream, not the sacred dream she dreamed on her side of the coin; and that was not Martin's dream, not the beloved dream he dreamed on his side either. From the "other" side Dr. King had envisioned a "beloved community," and it shone exactly like Miss Smith's "high adventure" in the light. Her dream was "written with a vehemence that is the overflow of her vast compassion," said Griffin; and Dr. King's dream was spoken with an equally passionate conviction. But what to do about the hateful white racism that punished anyone, white or black, who dreamed of a community that was beloved or believed in a reality that was sacred?

"Martin Luther King's first problem," wrote Griffin, "was to inspire black people not only to persevere in their battle for freedom but to limit themselves to a single weapon—the weapon of Love: to return love for hate; to embrace a truth strange to modern ears but which black people's lives had uniquely prepared them to understand— that unearned suffering is redemptive." Dr. King asked thousands of black people, and white people also, to do "that rare thing—to make themselves subservient to an ideal (the Christ Ideal) in the face of opponents who made ideals subservient to their prejudices."

But Dr. King had a second problem, according to Griffin, which was "to place the Christ Ideal in firm opposition to segregationists who were persuaded that they themselves acted from the noblest Christian motives and who felt it wholly within the framework of Christianity to smear, terrorize, kill or do anything else to protect the traditional system from anyone who sought to alter it."

Griffin's discourse on Dr. King's philosophy was part of an article he wrote in 1963—not long after he had written the review of *Killers of the Dream*—several months before he began working on his critiques of institutionalized religion. It is clear how Smith's book and King's actions and speeches resonated with Griffin's own sense of the "Christ Ideal" of dismantling one's prejudices in the light of the *caritas* and led to his insistence that the churches—founded on these same Christian ideals—desegregate the parishes and dismantle their racial hypocrisies. The church was, after all, the sanctuary of *res sacra* and the center of any beloved community.

Since he had been born white into the Southern tradition, he knew that side of the racial coin, Lillian's dream—and the killing of it. He had come to know, also, the other side of the coin, Martin's dream—and the nightmare of racism that clouded it. He embodied, then, both sides as "lived experience" by having risked his life on the edge in *Black Like Me*. By having transformed *I* into the *Other*, he had witnessed the criminal inequalities between black and white worlds while simultaneously discovering the perfect harmony of essentials and the sacred reality of being human.

Epilogue

But in the fund of the Spirit what matters most is not what we do but what is done to us.

—Gerald Vann, O. P.

John Howard Griffin lived a long dying, which he contemplated during those last years as a double reality. He viewed the merciless pain and physical disintegration as only one level of truth—to be accepted simply as what was and as what must be.

However, "if all that is my reality," he wrote in 1978, there is another reality that makes mine also slightly different." That other reality, which was not separated but coupled in the embrace of wholeness, was perceived "in the fact that God has sent me a great richness of friends so that the emptiness of trying to live is mitigated by the fullness of that love, which seems a direct and real expression of God's love."

He believed that "because of the blessings, this is a time of the most powerful richness and the most terrible wretchedness of my life. The fact that they happen to coincide is the greatest blessing of all." The spiritual realm did not erase the bodily pain or emotional stress or mental anguish, but it gave him the courage to transcend the trap of meaninglessness.

"I don't know how other people work on faith," he told Thurston Smith in 1977, "but for me it was an almost existential choice. There was no other way to go many years ago. I tried to do the will of God as well as I could, and the first thing I discovered was that this didn't automatically make me a lover of God." Griffin was referring to his decade of sightlessness, when he experienced spiritual crises that were resolved only by immersing himself in writing as a gift to God.

"The second thing I discovered is that most often people interpret the will of God through their own desires. I found that never really worked for me; the will of God rarely coincided with any desire of mine!" Griffin's allusion here was to his ardent desire for artistic solitude and family intimacy and the deep loathing he felt for the public life that *Black Like Me* demanded; yet he obeyed the call of justice, as we know, and accepted the inevitable exposure.

Then he spoke of his most recent discovery: "Toward the end, I've come to the realization that all that I believed was right and all of it was truth. That I was right about the reality of faith. That's been an extraordinary revelation to me." The rightness had come with his first "yes" to God, uttered in 1947 at the Abbey of Solesmes before his eyesight was completely gone.

That was when he discovered his solitary path, even though many crises would obscure it and violent crossroads would seem to obliterate it. In truth, it was there, but he had not perceived it at first, because it was an inner path that would be revealed in the darkness of his spiritual struggles during blindness.

Griffin's resistance to the idea of conversion was reflected in the mirror of his first novel, *The Devil Rides Outside*. The unnamed narrator, an American student of musicology who does research in Gregorian Chant while living in a monastery, does *not* make the great leap of faith. However, in *Scattered Shadows*, the autobiographical text that covers his actual stay at Solesmes, Griffin made it clear that he did say "yes" there and then, but admitted that his affirmation had been whispered with great fear and trembling.

Subsequently, Griffin made his commitment "official" when, in 1951, he was converted to Catholicism. But even after his marriage in 1953 and the birth of the couple's first child in 1954, he agonized over his unworthiness, doubting not God but himself. That period of agony was reflected in the mirror of his second novel, *Nuni*, which was completed during the year he was paralyzed by spinal malaria. Again, he immersed himself in writing and in the novel's narrator.

"I am aware perhaps that I am putting the problems of my life into the lap of Professor Harper and I am desperate for him to solve them," wrote Griffin in his *Journal*. "I am stripping him of everything that men generally consider necessary to a man's ability to function at the human level—family, friends, even clothing, and plunging him into a world he is ill fit to live in. With me, the prospect is similar, though I never mention it aloud. First my blindness, then this paralysis and loss of mobility, the uncertainty of the prognosis. It must drive us to turning into vegetables of frustration or it must drive us to God or an equivalent thing above and beyond us, to abandon ourselves finally, after all the self-delusions of seeming abandonment, to the great "yes" (as the French call it), to the *fiat*, and only after passing through can we begin to live again as functioning human beings."

Like Griffin, Professor Harper must find the faith to believe in a silent God, while stripped of everything and stranded on an island of absolute solitude. The professor immerses himself in the larger reality of the island universe and lets go the delusions of self-interest and the preconceptions of the culture that had conditioned him. Harper like Griffin, then, goes deeper into the spiritual realm than had the student narrator of the first novel. In the end, the professor risks everything for the life of an innocent native girl-child, whereas the musicologist had been unable to do so; what the student denies—selfless love—the professor embraces. Thus, each narrator reflects, in artistic terms, the reality of his personal struggle; and each novel maps, as fiction, the inner path he followed toward spiritual liberation.

In *Black Like Me*, we can trace a textual map of Griffin's actual journey, and we can peer into a series of mirror images that reflect his real struggle. The stripping-away process in *Black Like Me*, as he slowly lets go of egocentric self-interest (white identity) and the stereotypes of cultural conditioning (white supremacy and privilege), allows him to become entirely immersed in the experience while, simultaneously, he observes his changing behavior.

The dramatic risk of "becoming a Negro"—the aspect of the experiment that seems to affect readers most—was, for Griffin, secondary and external compared to the primary, internal challenge of dismantling his prejudices and cleansing his soul of sin. The writing of the book was a stage in that process of purgation; and, by allowing it to be published, he offered to the public his personally shameful disclosures in print and, later, from the lectern. Certainly the bold experiment took courage, but telling his story honestly took greater courage.

Yet, when Thurston Smith evoked the risk of *Black Like Me* in their interview published in *U. S. Catholic*, Griffin revealed what the book had not.

"Well, you've made some fantastic gambles in your life. The obvious one was putting that drug into yourself and changing the color of your skin. That was a risk unparalleled."

"But what people don't really know is that a long time before this I took another great gamble—what the French call simply *le grand oui*, 'the great yes.' The gamble was for God. That means leaping off that cliff and never knowing where you're going to land, but you have the faith that you're going to land somewhere."

"What are you referring to?"

"My conversion in a sense. But it was more than that for me. I took the initial gamble but it's not the one that lasts. I go through reconversion every day."

By going through "reconversion every day" Griffin meant saying "yes" to God and offering everything, literally everything, in faithful adoration. At one time it had meant his works of art and acts of social conscience, and all along his path it had included contemplation and prayer and the suffering of physical pain. Near the end, with only a residue of energy remaining, he offered what was left—the very wretchedness of his dying.

The once robust, well-groomed artist and activist had been reduced to a skeletal, white-bearded invalid. Only his eyes—once blind and again failing in those last years—retained their passionate intensity and loving warmth. His *Journal* of that period reflected the inner reality of a dying man nurturing an undying faith, a naked mercy and innocent wisdom.

Griffin contemplated his dying with the same honesty and insight that had illuminated his social critiques and journals of solitude, his visual portraits and musical epiphanies, his fictional characters and the real connections with loved ones. These same lucid qualities are evident in his meditation on suffering, which he had written during his time at Merton's hermitage. Entitled "The Terrain of Physical Pain," it is a powerful essay of only twelve pages, composed as a third-person narration to create a balance between the philosophical observations and the experiential content of its subject. The essay's meaning could be drawn only from intimate experience with suffering, but its message would be lost without the author's ability to translate that reality into universal terms.

Physical pain and human suffering are as universal as racism and death, but the intensity and duration of pain vary in relation to each person's ability to cope and adapt. For some, "new and vague truths begin to emerge," he wrote, "truths difficult to formulate—and the sufferer perceives that much of what he experiences, much that is most profound in his experience, simply lies beyond the realm of ideas." That is why speculations about the problem of pain, uttered by those who have not suffered, "sound false, off-key to the sufferer because they rarely conform to his own lived reality."

Griffin understood the stereotypes about suffering, which were part of the same cultural conditioning that promoted the mythology of race; he knew, also, that the attitudes about suffering were more damaging to the one in pain than the reality of pain itself. He recalled how the sighted had explained blindness to him, how he had received the same "pep talks" during prolonged illnesses, and how well-wishers were ready to send him off to his final reward in those last years.

The very best that the sufferer could hope for in relation to those around him was "an attitude of union" with the few who had the wis-

Griffin in Canada, photographed by Bill Wittman in 1977.

dom to keep silent and to treat the sufferer as a human individual and not as a condition. But no matter how insightful or unaware those around the sufferer, the solution to the problem of pain resided ultimately with the person in pain.

Related to Griffin's sense of a "double reality" in the context of dying (and the dual perspective developed in the *Black Like Me* experiment), "The Terrain of Physical Pain" elaborates a similar faculty—that of living simultaneously on two planes of awareness.

"This faculty to act at once on two planes can be dissipated when it becomes merely an attempt to escape. . . . No, it must be the contrary—an acceptance and an awareness of the reality that exists in pain and that sometimes becomes obsessive in pain, and then the growing ability, from the same root, to stand off and become the observer; and then again, passing on to the observation of other things until at length and in the natural order of things, the observing self comes to the realization that self, even in pain, is less interesting than other objects of contemplation."

If the sufferer does not discover a fresh perspective, he or she will fixate on the self as victim (why me? why not another?), blame the body as mortal enemy, and then become obsessed with either playing the role of stoic hero (which is a way of rationalizing the reality into a stereotype others can admire), or attempting to escape the pain through massive sedation (which is a form of denial).

The critical break from this enslavement to suffering begins with a step away from self-interest and meaningless subjectivity toward an observing moment of cold objectivity. The effort to do so will be arduous, but the result—initially brief—will open a wider horizon. Eventually, according to Griffin, the sufferer develops the realization "that pain in the body can cure things which are not of the body," and that the observer's new point of view "brings clarity to intuitions, unclouds perceptions and opens up the whole area of intuitive knowledge" that "can replace cultural distortions" and subjective delusions about the nature of suffering.

Neither the pain nor one's awareness of it will disappear, but its resonances are not wasted. This radical shift in perspective allows the sufferer "to be used as a sort of filter for experience, to accept the experience imposed without even judging its value, allowing it to enter, allowing it to teach, and then letting it come back out in some form of expression—prayer, silence, music, contemplation, art."

Griffin believed that certain creative masterpieces (the poetry of St. John of the Cross or the late quartets of Beethoven) "tend to happen despite men rather than because of some purely human initiative." These masterpieces, which cannot be explained by reason, evoke "experience, often in the form of intense suffering, that has been accepted, handled, then released."

The sufferer, who becomes intimate with the universal resonances of pain, will recognize intuitively a hidden connection with the infinite mystery at the core of such masterpieces, accepting that this act of contemplation is enough. And perhaps, according to Griffin, the sufferer "may even learn an ultimate wisdom—not to care about results" but to care only about "submitting to the action and allowing results to take care of themselves, in the knowledge that if God does not allow suffering to evaporate uselessly, then that suffering is being used and how does not matter."

If the sufferer learned this "ultimate wisdom," Griffin believed the effect of that knowledge "turns the sufferer into a giver, into lover, into consoler," because extended "experience with physical suffering has taught him that he can bear what he has borne," but that "he cannot bear it when others suffer." He saw this not as a matter of guilt but as a renewal of innocence—a radical transformation of the sufferer's self-pity into a selfless empathy with the suffering of humanity. "It constantly reawakens him to mercy and to an authentic pity which will bring in their wake a melting of the callouses of indifference and unconcern for others."

Griffin had seen men and women "pass through the ultimate human tortures (at the hands of madmen) and emerge with everything burned out of them except a limitless capacity to love," which "transformed [them] into luminous human beings." He had seen, also, those who had endured interminable suffering, "totally immobilized and locked in pain," yet capable of igniting "an authentic and curative pity that sometimes seems to blaze" from them. Griffin was united with them because he had known equally intense pain, yet he felt even deeper empathy for those loved ones who had eased his own suffering. He wrote of this in his *Journal* but clarified it best in "The Terrain of Physical Pain."

The final result of this expanding perspective teaches the sufferer "that others fear this unknown, that others suffer his sufferings, perhaps even more tormentedly because they do not know them with any precision." The sufferer, then, becomes the consoler of those who are spared suffering "but must witness his suffering."

This dynamic process, rooted in experience, transcends psychological syndromes, philosophical proofs and theological speculations, because pain is real and not merely an idea about reality. "The ultimate and true effects of suffering," Griffin concluded, "can only occur, from the sufferer's viewpoint, in the very silence and solitude from which they spring, beyond the realm of ideas."

Each person called to suffering must discover, step by step, an inward path that no cartographer has charted and in a direction toward which no compass needle has pointed. "These effects—wisdom, giving, mercy, love—produce their own ferment." And this "ferment" reveals these mysterious effects only in silent communion with the infinite.

The sufferer, "who has allowed these realities to come through the experience of suffering, in their own time and with their own priorities, knows that somehow and without any special action of his own initiative, that the ferment of these effects will be returned to the world in some form which is ultimately redemptive."

This redemptive quality of suffering cannot be measured quantitatively—just as faith cannot be proved by tangible results. Yet he experienced the truth of these effects in the solitude of his own suffering, believing that any sufferer, "if he has been deeply enough wounded, will remain reawakened to mercy and to that whole mysterious cycle of replenishment in which he has allowed himself to be used, to be an instrument."

After he had accepted the loss of his Merton biography, Griffin understood that his "acts of faith and hope no longer lie in writing books, but in keeping contact with a few beloved friends, studying and praying as much as I can, and by growing plants with the incentive of living to see them blossom."

His final meditation on dying, like the essay on pain written a decade before, was not about death—it was about being alive. He had "died" many times during the late 1970s, often suspended unaware that his lungs had ceased breathing, that his heart had stopped beating, that his pulse had gone silent. But a loved one had always been there in time to revive him by administering CPR and placing a capsule of nitroglycerine under his tongue. So dying was nothing, it had become commonplace; but living, that continued to be fascinating.

Near the end he was "refusing to count the days or weeks or months, refusing to think that soon I will die or that some medically inexplicable healing might occur." Instead, Griffin was "being obedient to the doctors and, insofar as I can discern it, to the Holy Spirit, hanging on to love and some kind of innocence, trying to have enough presence of mind in the bad hours to go on saying 'yes' and meaning it."

Notes

Unless otherwise indicated in the text of *Man in the Mirror* or in these notes on sources—the passages by John Howard Griffin are quoted from the current Signet paperback edition of *Black Like Me*. All citations are made in reference to the chapter headings in the book and *not* to the page numbers of this text.

BLACK LIKE ME

The thirty-fifth anniversary edition, with Griffin's 1977 Epilogue and an Afterword by Robert Bonazzi, was published in 1996 by Dutton Signet, a division of Penguin Books USA Inc. of New York. It is a Signet paperback of 192 pages. This is the exclusive English-language edition, authorized by The Estate of John Howard Griffin (Elizabeth Griffin-Bonazzi, Executor) and it is distributed by The Penguin Group worldwide.

Black Like Me was published originally in a first edition cloth printing by Houghton Mifflin of Boston in 1961. It was reprinted as a Signet paperback in 1962 by New American Library of New York. Houghton Mifflin brought out a second edition cloth printing in 1977; it was reprinted as a Signet paperback the following year. Both editions included the Griffin Epilogue for the first time.

Journey into Shame, the magazine series upon which *Black Like Me* was based, was published in *Sepia*, a national monthly produced by Good Publishing Company of Fort Worth, Texas. The six-part serial ran monthly in April, May, June, July, August and September of 1960 (Volume XII, Numbers 4–9).

The book has been translated into many languages, but only the French edition remains in print. Marguerite de Gramont's translation, originally published by Gallimard of Paris (1962), was issued as a paperback as late as 1996. The other languages and their years of publication are as follows: German and Polish in 1962; Italian, Dutch and Portuguese in 1963; Norwegian (1964); Hungarian (1966); two separate Japanese editions in 1967; Danish and Swedish in 1968; and the final translation, in Czechoslovakian, appeared in 1976. There was also an unauthorized Russian version published in 1970. A Braille edition was produced by the Wellington Braille Club of New Zealand in 1967, in cooperation with William Collins Ltd., the publishers of the British Commonwealth edition of *Black Like Me* (1962). A Canadian edition was published by Thomas Allen Co. of Toronto, also in 1962.

PREFACE

Griffin's opening remarks are from *A Time to Be Human*, his final book on racism, published by The Macmillan Company of New York and Collier Macmillan of London in 1977 (102 pages); here-after cited as *ATTBH*. The 1975 interview was conducted by Cornelia Jessey Sussman and Irving Sussman and published in *WAY of Saint Francis*, a Catholic magazine in San Francisco. The 1978 interview was conducted by Studs Terkel and published in his book *American Dreams: Lost and Found*, Pantheon Books, New York, 1980; hereafter cited as *AD*. Among some of the white activists who aimed at liberating their own of racism were Saul Alinsky, Father James Groppi and Jonathan Kozol.

THE PATH

The Unanswered Question: Griffin's comments about why he wrote *Black Like Me* are from a 1966 interview with Robert Bonazzi, *Latitudes* magazine; also from *ATTBH*.

A Southern Childhood: The 1970 interview was conducted by John Egerton and published in his book, *A Mind To Stay Here: Profiles from the South*, Macmillan of New York and Collier Macmillan of London, 1970. Bob Ray Sanders's remarks are from a conversation with Robert Bonazzi. Other Griffin quotes are from *ATTBH* and *AD*.

A Classical Education: Griffin's discussion of "mongrelization" was written in 1962 and reprinted from his *Journal* in *The John Howard*

Griffin Reader, edited by Bradford Daniel and published by Houghton Mifflin of Boston in 1968 (588 pages); hereafter cited as *JHG Reader*. This compendium included excerpts from Griffin's novels and non-fiction books, short stories, articles, personal essays, and a folio of photographic portraits.

A Stranger in Strange Lands: Griffin's discussion of *otherness* is from his essay "The Intrinsic *Other,*" originally published (in French) in *Building Peace*, edited by Dominique Pire and published by Gerard & Co. in Belgium, France, Switzerland and Canada in 1966. The English-language version of Griffin's essay, translated by the author, was included in his *JHG Reader* and has been reprinted often. The passages about how Griffin was wounded in the war and his subsequent sightlessness from the injury are quoted from the unpublished manuscript *Scattered Shadows*.

Blind Vision: During Griffin's decade of sightlessness, from 1947 to 1957, he wrote several novels, but only two were published. *The Devil Rides Outside* was published in cloth by Smiths, Inc., of Fort Worth, Texas, in 1952 and reprinted as a paperback in 1954 by Pocket Books, Inc. of New York (596 pages). The novel was revised by Griffin and published in 1953 by William Collins, Ltd., of London (511 pages); this shorter version was translated into French in 1953 and Dutch in 1954. His second novel, *Nuni*, was published in cloth by Houghton Mifflin of Boston in 1956 (310 pages). A British edition was brought out that same year by The Riverside Press of Cambridge; and a German translation was published in 1958. Both novels were condensed in the *JHG Reader*. Griffin wrote a forty-page monograph about blindness (for the sighted)—*Handbook for Darkness*— that was produced by The American Foundation for the Blind and distributed free of charge. His comments about livestock breeding are from an interview with Milt Hopwood published in *Fort Worth* magazine in June 1974; the observation about blindness and racism was written in 1964 and published in the *JHG Reader*. The sixteen-page field report he wrote with Theodore Freedman was published in 1956 by the Anti-Defamation League of B'nai B'rith (*Mansfield, Texas: A Report of the Crisis Situation Resulting from Efforts to Desegregate the School System*).

Becoming the Other: The scene of Griffin's sight-recovery, from *Scattered Shadows*, was published under the title "Is This What It Means To See?" in *The Spirit of Man*, an anthology edited by Whit Burnett and published by Hawthorn Books, Inc., of New York in 1958. The excerpt from Griffin's unpublished novel, *Street of the Seven Angels*, was entitled "Chez Durand" and published in *New World Writing* (#12 in a series of Mentor paperbacks), New American

Library, New York, 1958. Griffin's history of the Staked Plain region of West Texas, *Land of the High Sky*, was published in 1959 by The First National Bank of Midland (212 pages). The final quotation of this chapter—about Griffin's "pilgrimage *par excellence*"—appeared in a review of *Black Like Me* by Anne Freemantle in *Commonweal* (1961).

REFLECTIONS IN THE MIRROR

The Experiment: The monograph *Racial Equality: The Myth and the Reality* was published by the University of Iowa, Iowa City, in 1970 (28 pages). It is a transcript of a lecture Griffin delivered at that university in 1969; it was made available on microfiche in 1979 by Columbia University's Butler Library.

The Mirror: Griffin's discussion of *otherness* is from "The Intrinsic Other" and *ATTBH.*

The Mentor: Griffin's comments on mentors are from the 1966 *Latitudes* interview.

Dialogue and Distance: The book J. P. Guillory was reading was *The Devil Rides Outside*. The piece Griffin told him to read, in order to find out who the author really was, was a version of "Is This What It Means To See?" published in *Reader's Digest* (September 1958).

The Hate Stare: The quotation by Edward T. Hall is from the Preface to the second edition of *The Silent Language*, an Anchor paperback, published by Doubleday, Garden City, New York, 1981. The original cloth edition (Doubleday) was published in 1959; Griffin had read it and corresponded with the cultural anthropologist before he left for New Orleans. Florence Henderson was the woman who cashed his traveler's check at The Catholic Book Store. He sent her a copy of *Black Like Me*, and she wrote him a letter, dated 9-11-61: "I want to say 'Thank you' although I regret from the bottom of my heart the situation that makes so ordinary an act newsworthy."

Mississippi Justice: Some of the information about the Mack Parker lynching was found in Margaret Mansfield's excellent monograph on *Black Like Me*, published in the Cliffs Notes series, originally published in 1971 by Cliffs Notes, Inc., Lincoln, Nebraska. Dr. Mansfield, then in the Department of English at Boston State College, understood the book's intention and context in a way that went beyond most readings—especially her insight into the use of irony (page 60).

Escape from Hell: P. D. East's autobiography, *The Magnolia Jungle*, was published by Simon and Schuster of New York in 1960. Gary Huey's biography of East, *Rebel with a Cause* (Scholarly Resources Inc., Wilmington, Delaware, 1985) provides a first-rate account of East's life and extensive coverage on his friendship with Griffin.

Verbal Pornography: Griffin's passages—beginning with "Take the logic out of civilization . . ." and continuing throughout that paragraph and the next—are from *JHG Reader*.

Caritas: Lillian Smith's first novel, *Strange Fruit*, originally published in 1944 and banned the same year, became a bestseller; a Harvest trade book edition, published in 1992 by Harcourt Brace Jovanovich, New York and London, remains in print. The title of the controversial novel—which ends in a lynching—was taken from the song about lynching in the South composed by Lewis Allan in 1940 and made famous by Billie Holiday. The "strange fruit" refers to the bodies of black people.

Between Two Worlds: Jacques Maritain's *Scholasticism and Politics* was a book Griffin knew well; he speaks of going through a marked-up copy of the book in his *Journal* entry of October 31, 1959 (quoted in *Becoming the Other*), but gives the impression in *Black Like Me* (pp 134–35) that Maritain's insights into racism are new to him.

THE AFTERMATH

Return: Among those who influenced Griffin's critique of racism was the eighteenth-century political thinker Edmund Burke, whom he quoted often in his articles and *Journal*. In "The Intrinsic *Other*" he included his favorite insight of Burke's. Griffin wrote: "Racist attitudes begin benignly enough from this basic concept of the other as intrinsically *Other*. Once one views others as 'different,' the stereotype develops. Implicit in this process is a consent to racism. Edmund Burke gave us the touchstone of this error when he said: '*I know of no way of drawing up an indictment against a whole people.*' Racism begins when we draw up an indictment against a whole people merely by considering them *as a whole* underdeveloped versions of ourselves, by perpetuating the blindness of the stereotype."

A New Decade: Dr. Decherd Turner, who was Griffin's first literary executor and a reviewer for *The Dallas Times-Herald*, which published his reviews of *Nuni* and the *JHG Reader,* is a renowned expert on rare manuscripts.

Controversies: Penn Jones is the author of the *Forgive My Grief* series that critiqued The Warren Commission and exposed the strange deaths of witnesses after Dallas. Griffin wrote a Preface to his first volume and *Ramparts* brought national attention to Jones's controversial work in 1967. The Gillespie sisters were entrusted with the original manuscript of *Black Like Me* (211 double-spaced pages of typescript, with corrections).

Exile: The *Paléographie Musicale* are volumes of scores of the Gregorian Chant.

AT THE CROSSROADS

The Public Life: Griffin mentioned Dick Gregory in several published pieces, but the famous comedian and civil-rights activist figures most prominently in "The Tip-Off"—about his trip to Mississippi after the brutal murders of James Chaney, Andrew Goodman and Michael Schwerner in 1964. The essay was published in a special issue of *Ramparts*, "Mississippi Eyewitness," in 1964. Concerning the film of *Black Like Me*, it should be pointed out that several videocassettes of the movie have been produced and distributed by small companies—but without permission from the original producer or the Griffin Estate.

Racist Sins of Christians: Griffin's essay in *Sign* was reprinted as a monograph by the Passsionist Missions, Union City, New Jersey, in 1963. The "Dialogue with Father August Thompson" was reprinted in *Black, White and Gray*, edited by Bradford Daniel and published by Sheed and Ward of New York in 1964. *The Church and the Black Man* included contributions from Father James Groppi and Reverend Albert B. Cleage (a disk recording of their fiery speeches); and two epilogues to the text—an essay by Mathew Ahmann and a manifesto by members of the Black Priests Caucus. The book was published in 1969 by the Pflaum Press of Dayton, Ohio (132 pages); a French edition was issued by Desclee de Brouwer of Paris in 1970.

Legacies: Griffin's photographic books were published during the 1970s, and his portraits of Merton and Maritain continue to be printed as cover art on books by and about the Trappist monk and the French philosopher. *A Hidden Wholeness: The Visual World of Thomas Merton* was published by Houghton Mifflin in 1970, and a reprint was issued by the Norman S. Berg Company in 1977. The large-format book contains photographs by Merton and Griffin, paintings by the monk and text by Griffin (146 pages). *Jacques Maritain: Homage in Words and Pictures* was published by Magi Books of Albany, New York, in 1974. The large-format book contains Griffin's photographs and journal entries, plus an essay on Maritain by Yves R. Simon and a Preface by Anthony O. Simon (64 pages). An Italian edition was issued in 1981 by Editrice Massimo of Milan, with text by Roberto Papini (95 pages). Unicorn Press also published a folio of his black-and-white images, *Twelve Photographic Portraits*, in 1973; as well as *The Thomas Merton Studies Center* monograph, with Griffin text, in 1971. *The Hermitage Journals: A Diary Kept While Working on the Biography of Thomas Merton* was published posthumously, in 1981 by Andrews & McMeel of Kansas City (231 pages); a Doubleday Image paperback was issued in 1983.

A Very Long Dying: The new official biographer of Merton was Michael Mott, author of *The Seven Mountains of Thomas Merton*, Houghton Mifflin, Boston, 1984 (690 pages). Griffin's text about Merton's last years was published posthumously in 1983 by Latitudes Press and the Griffin Estate's JHG Editions. A revised edition of *Follow the Ecstasy: The Hermitage Years of Thomas Merton* was issued by Orbis Books in 1993. This edition features a folio of Griffin prints and includes Griffin's Prologue about his friendship with the famous monk. The story of Griffin's decade of working on the biography and the circumstances surrounding his letting go of the project are the subject of Robert Bonazzi's Foreword. *Follow the Ecstasy* was also published in England by Burns & Oates in 1993; and a German translation is due in 1997.

CRITICAL PERSPECTIVES

Text and Context: The Rutledge prints, which accompany this book, represent a small portion of the series. Many were published in the 1960s—with *Journey into Shame*, as cover art for several editions of *Black Like Me*, and in the international press. Two of Rutledge's prints appeared in 1966—one in Life magazine and another on the cover of the thirty-fifth anniversary edition of the classic.

A Bridge of Dialogue: Stokely Carmichael is known today as Kwame Ture. With Charles V. Hamilton, he wrote the standard text on black liberation in 1967: *Black Power: The Politics of Liberation in America*, published by Alfred A. Knopf.

The Spiritual Dimension: Thomas P. McDonnell (*Ramparts* interviewer) was the editor of *The Thomas Merton Reader* and, while working with the monk, gave him a copy of *Black Like Me*. Reviewing the book in *Commonweal*, McDonnell wrote that it was "more than a sociological experiment. . . . *Black Like Me* is an act of Christian commitment that few, if any, of us would willingly make." *Soul Sister* was published in 1969 by The World Publishing Company (223 pages) and issued as a Fawcett Crest paperback the next year. On the back cover: "A magnificent book by a woman of great courage. To read it is to understand what it means to 'live black' in a white man's world."— John Howard Griffin, author of *Black Like Me*. Lillian Smith's *Killers of the Dream* was published in 1950 and reissued in 1962 by W. W. Norton. Griffin's review was published in *Southwest Review* in 1962. The article about Dr. King, simply called "Martin Luther King," was a chapter in the anthology *Thirteen for Christ*, edited by Melville Harcourt and published by Sheed and Ward in 1963; reprinted in the *JHG Reader*.

EPILOGUE

Thurston Smith's Griffin interview was poignantly entitled "Dying Like Me." "The Terrain of Physical Pain" was included in the anthology *Creative Suffering*, edited by James F. Andrews and published by Pilgrim Press of Philadelphia in 1970. Griffin's final public recognition was The Kenneth David Kaunda Award for Humanism, presented by the PanAmerican/PanAfrican Association in 1980. The chapter's epigraph by Father Gerald Vann is quoted from *The Divine Pity*, Sheed and Ward, 1946.